LEGLESS IN POLPERRO

The Astonishing Adventures and Private Correspondence of Edward Lancing-Lancing and his Bulldog Albion

John Swinfield

PEACH PUBLISHING

By the Same Author

Knock Down Ginger

ISBN 978-1-78036-331-8

Published by
Peach Publishing

Dedication

Bridgit was only humouring me but without her encouragement drowning would have been certain.

Author's Note

As the author of this work, my association with Admiral Lancing-Lancing began when I was researching Diseases of the Royal Navy, the first such work to identify the Poop Deck Poultice as a remedial device for the little understood Gangrene pox Galactose. While staying at his Cornish cottage, The Nest, he gave me free rein to examine his letters and correspondence stored higgledy-piggledy in his summer house. In looking for medical notes, and fending off his dog who thought I was an intruder, and on reading the more general material, I realised I had stumbled on what the French academic and naval scholar, Dr. Marcel Dupont, calls the 'jackpot-historique'. Professor Chuck Stines, of the Centre for Old Wrecks, in Washington, commented: 'The letters represent a post-modernist fusillade; if one played cricket this would be second-base.'

Acknowledgement

My particular thanks go to Sheil Land Associates. With Sonia Land's guidance and support I can see why she and her compatriots are foremost literary agents.

Personae Dramatis

Admiral Edward Lancing-Lancing.
Distinguished naval career. Retired. Married Charlotte, now deceased. Two grown-up children, Jack and Elizabeth. Amateur yachtsman, likes jazz and plays the trombone. Lives in The Nest, a cottage on Dead Man's cliff, near Polperro, Cornwall, with Albion, his bulldog. Has a prosthetic leg he calls his bad 'un, operated on by the impetuous naval surgeon, Dickie 'Butcher' Thrupp.

Captain George Steel.
Former master in the merchant navy. Sailing journalist. Married to Catharine. They live in a flat in a converted gasometer on the Isle of Dogs, in London's Dockland. Steel calls it Gone to the Dogs. Wrote two history books and a slasher-novel which won the Diamond Strangler Award, and an earlier novel he rarely talks about, Emma does it Bareback, which paid the bills during a lean spell and won the coveted San Francisco Platinum Nipple.

Prologue

In the opening letters, mention is made of Dickie 'Butcher' Thrupp, a pioneering surgeon in the Royal Navy. His patients are easily identified, Thrupp being one of the few surgeons prepared to operate when his ship was in violent seas. Persuasive and charming, Thrupp, now deceased, never took no for an answer, believing that a radical response was better than hanging around for pills and potions to work. Married four times, with seven children, he met his last wife, Yvonne, in the Blue Lamp in Soho, after several pink gins in the Naval Surgeons Club off Pall Mall. Twenty-seven years his junior, Yvonne said she only saw him on shore leave, but he remained active to the end.

William 'Two Fingers' Maltby, who lost a thumb and two fingers after being operated on by Thrupp, is also mentioned. Blazered, rakish, Two Fingers is a familiar figure at dockside watering holes. Once a competitive yachtsman, a ravenous appetite for blondes and gin blighted his training routine. Jennifer d'Lisle, the model to whom he was once engaged, said Two Fingers had the most dangerous smile in sailing.

In the testing Fastnet yacht Race, he decked the Australian porn baron, Rupe Glover, fracturing his jaw, while skippering Glover's yacht, Big 'n Creamy, named after one of Glover's magazines. In the subsequent court case, Two Fingers claimed that Glover had stumbled into a swinging boom after over-dosing on Foster's lager. It was never explained how a naked and semi-conscious Glover was found adrift in a rubber boat, with 'Aussie Filth King Go Home', tattooed across his lower abdomen. The bad 'un mentioned in the letter refers to Lancing-Lancing's gammy leg, another consequence of Butcher Thrupp's rare talent.

337b, The Gasometer, Isle of Dogs, London

Dear Admiral

Hope the 'bad 'un' isn't playing up. Do you still use pliers and WD 40? Butcher Thrupp left quite a legacy. I had a Jameson with Two-Fingers Maltby the other day. He took forever bashing out a thousand words in the press tent at the Amsterdam Boat show. He does a bit of public relations these days. He said there should be a Thrupp survivors club and that you could meet up to discuss missing body parts. Two Fingers said his troubles started with nothing more than a torn nail on his little finger. But he got carried away by Butcher's enthusiasm. If Two Fingers waves at anybody they think he's giving them a Churchill. It's made him squadrons of enemies down the years.

George
-

The Nest,

Dead Man's Cliff, Cornwall

Dear George

Good of you to inquire about the 'bad 'un'. I find a nob of Lurpak works better than WD 40, but it draws the flies. Butcher was always keen. I remember a rating, Billy somebody or other. He went into the ship's sick-bay with a headache and came out looking as if Butcher Thrupp had given him a head transplant. I miss the leg. Who wouldn't? The problem was that Thrupp was such a nice chap it was difficult to say no. Two Fingers Maltby waved at me once, and I never forgave him. So you've cleared up a misunderstanding. Poor chap's disability must have caused a lot of bad-feeling down the years.

Lancing-Lancing

The next letter mentions Stag Hake, who spent twenty years in the navy. A prolific author of maritime books, they are so dense and technical that even professional sailors have difficulty in understanding them. A world authority on ropes and knots, he introduced his wife to them. They are now estranged. His last three books on knots are without illustrations, Hake having fallen out with the artist. A dearth of pictures makes them even more difficult to comprehend.

Small, pugnacious, wiry and hirsute, he has a short fuse and is prone to the occasional burst of violence. He writes for a diversity of periodicals, including Boat Planet, known in the trade as Boat Puffery, largely because of its penchant for running flattering profiles of its advertisers, known in the business, as puff pieces.

Gone to the Dogs

Dear Admiral

Ran into Stag Hake the other day. He was in his cups in a bar in Chicago, knocking back the Morgan's and angrily trying to undo an impossibly complicated knot he'd fashioned out of a napkin, much to the bar tender's irritation. Before I had a chance to congratulate him on a piece he'd scribbled for *Puffery* he barked at me, in that challenging way of his: 'Went to sea fifty years ago next week. Professional seaman first and foremost'. Well, of course, anybody who's ever tried to read one of his pieces, knows the truth of that.

I inquired if he was going to have a celebration to mark his half-century at sea. He said not bloody likely. On the day in question he'd be under the sea in *Silver Chipolata*, a submarine powered rather unusually by methane gas, and owned by the San Francisco sausage maker, Bertha 'the beast' Rubenberg, the one with the lips who's suing her plastic surgeon. *Silver Chipolata* is chartered out for corporate parties. Wall Street bankers from de Glut Fled have hired it for a cruise under Antarctica. Stag says it's cramped and stinks to high heaven, due to the fertilizer which powers it. Rubenberg the Beast has to keep a herd of Friesians near her moorings at the Santa Monica yacht club, where she has stationed a flunky with a shovel to gather up the fuel. It's a fly-blown business. There are always drawbacks with any new type of propulsion.

George

-

Nest

George, old chap

Hope it's a non-smoking sub. Methane is awfully volatile. Difficult to imagine oneself being under the briny up to ones gunnels in dung. Beryl Caulthropp, my helper, can't manage the pliers on the bad 'un and she's got one hell of an appetite. I had some Ackerman mints in the pantry, but they've gone walkabout, and I'm also light on a bumper-pack of Mars Bars. She looks as if she's got an ice-belt round her hull.

Aye

Lancing-Lancing

**

Lancing–Lancing has always been inventive. His automatic fly-opener, the Zip Ahoy, was at one time very popular. He offered it to the Admiralty who adopted it for use by the higher ranks, but the Admiralty forbade him from taking out patents, and offered nothing in compensation, which rankled with him.

It was an ingenious device. He had witnessed that at ceremonial occasions, on board ship, senior officers were obliged to use the Heads (lavatory) with their hands full, a balloon of brandy in one, a cigar in the other. Lancing-Lancing's Zip Ahoy was activated by elastic running down the inside leg of an officer's trousers. If the user sharply kicked out a leg, the elastic was jerked and the zipper unzipped. There were, however, a number of incidents in which senior officers unwittingly kicked one another in the Heads, and elsewhere.

4

On one memorable occasion, at a drinks-do in the ward room of the warship HMS Rigid, moored off Great Yarmouth on a goodwill visit, to which an assortment of civic leaders and worthies had been invited, Melissa de Courtney-Jones, the bubbly wife of Rear-Admiral Johnstone de Courtney-Jones, and immensely popular in the mess for her affectionate ways with the younger officers, pinched Admiral Hornby-Piper-Piper on the bottom. It caused him to shriek with delight and to kick out his leg, thus exposing himself to the Lady Mayoress of Great Yarmouth, causing her to spill her cocktail.

Lancing-Lancing was responsible for other inventions. One of the more novel was his solution to victualling. Feeding several hundred men at sea has for generations been a thorny naval problem. Lancing-Lancing came up with a straight-forward solution: drop a large net over the stern and catch ones' own fish. This he did while in command of HMS Bold, and on the first evening of his experiment the entire ships company ate handsomely on freshly caught cod. It became a much-loved ritual, and every Friday the net was dropped over the stern and a large sign put up in the galley which promised: 'Frying Tonight.'

The Admiralty was delighted. The procedure cut down on costs, the men looked forward to it and fish is supposed to promote brains, though there was little evidence of it on board. Unfortunately, and as it transpired, rather calamitously, on one occasion the net became entangled with the propellers and the rudder as HMS Bold was about to enter Whitby Harbour, on another goodwill visit. The wind was in the ascendency and there was a fast-running tide. HMS Bold drifted helplessly into the harbour, destroying en route several small pleasure craft, before coming to rest with her bows poking through the wall of the library of the Captain Cook museum.

Nobody died, but several people were shaken up, especially the curator, who had his head down studying for a degree in maritime history. Lancing-Lancing felt that the Whitby Experience, as it came to be called, blemished his career, though he could never prove it. On the question of compensation for Zip Ahoy, he remained intransigent, with the Admiralty, for its part, equally implacable.

The Admiralty, Board of Patents and Inventions

Dear Lancing-Lancing

The Board have decided there is nothing more that can be done about rewarding you for your automatic fly-opener. Had there not been the unfortunate incident in Great Yarmouth, with the Lady Mayoress and Admiral Hornby-Piper-Piper, it might have looked more favourably upon your invention. As it is, several Board members felt the Admiralty should sue you, rather than pay you any money.

Yours sincerely

Capt. Everard Blower-Knight, Secretary, Adm. BoPI.

-

Nest

Dear Blower-Knight

As is well known, the Mayoress of Great Yarmouth was undergoing psychiatric help at the time of the alleged incident. At the tribunal she claimed to have been flashed several hundred times during her life, and eleven times that week, although every member of the Gorleston Bird's Eye fish processing football team denied the charge.

She even claimed that she had been flashed twice on the way from the Mayor's Parlour to the ship, a short journey undertaken in the secure confines of a taxi. Her condition was doubtless exacerbated by the presence of so many sailors and perhaps the name of the ship further enhanced her excitement.

For this to be a reason for the Admiralty to act in such a churlish and parsimonious manner is disgraceful. The Zip Ahoy has been used widely and with considerable success. At one time, the Admiralty even talked of extending its use to other ranks. This was rejected on the grounds that while the lower decks might have a Woodbine in one hand, and a bottle of stout in the other, they would not be in full ceremonial regalia, so their dry-cleaning bill would be less onerous.

I look forward to hearing from you, once the panel has further considered my protestations.

Lancing-Lancing

**

Lancing-Lancing's fondness for music, especially jazz – for many years he has wrestled with the trombone – has long been recognised, some say tolerated, by his friends and family.

Dogs

Dear Admiral

Only a quick note. Went to see Courtney Pine, the saxophonist. I know you tend to the earlier stuff, and that the trombone is your first love, but you'd have enjoyed it. It's a great pity you're so far away. You could have joined Catharine and I and offered your expert opinion. Cathy sends big kisses.

George

-

In his reply, Lancing-Lancing mentions his late wife Charlotte, and Albion, his elderly and mildly wayward bulldog.

Nest

My dear George

Thank you for your letter. I'm delighted you and Cathy had a good time. Courtney Pine is *so* talented. I was listening to the trombonist, Kid Ory, the other day. The way he holds a certain note on *Muskrat Ramble* is a wondrous thing. I try to copy him, but I'm getting as wheezy as Albion. Charlotte used to like it when I attempted Glen Miller's *Moonlight Serenade*, though Beryl

Caulthrop, my live-in helper, says it reminds her of the war, when she appears to have swapped her innocence for GI nylons and a packet of three (bubble-gum, in case you were wondering).

The GIs taught her to smoke cigars, which make the Nest smell like a bordello in Havana. She and I have come to the end of our collective tether, so to speak, and Mrs. Caulthrop is now working out her notice.

I ran an advertisement in *The Officer* and a very charming nurse came bubbling to the surface: Sophie, an ex-Wren, a quite lovely girl.

I'm off to a Schubert concert tonight. It will make a change from listening to Jelly Roll Morton and the Red Hot Peppers. I'm taking Albion. He gets so bored when he's left on his own that he's nearly gnawed through a leg of the dining table. He's a lovely boy, though I'm praying he won't start his moaning noise in the middle of the concert.

He's prefers Beethoven to Schubert (goes mad with the cannons in the *1812*) but early jazz is his favourite, especially New Orleans funeral dirges. Charlotte used to say he was crying at the moon when he tilts his head back and starts his awful yowling.

Lancing-Lancing

**

Being a high-ranking former naval commander, Lancing-Lancing is frequently invited to give talks and speeches to a diversity of parties and special interest groups. Professor Roly Woolf and his partner Beatrice – Binky to her intimates, of which there are many, she being a believer in free love and an open-marriage – met Lancing-Lancing when they invited him to give a lecture at the Crouch End Peace Collective.

At one point, when booing broke out in the hall, the Admiral's humour being sometimes misunderstood, Albion launched himself off the stage and bit a member of the audience called Rainbow. Rainbow was dressed from head to foot in black and had spent the season living in a tree, trying to stop a motorway being built while safeguarding the last-known preserve of the lesser-bearded tit.

When members of the audience stopped heckling, and unclamped Albion's jaws from Rainbow's testicles, Lancing-Lancing explained that the dog had undergone a personality change after an undertaker, in his frock-coat, accidentally kicked him at a funeral for a naval big-wig in Gosport, since when Albion has had a problem with men in black.

Chico Mendes Drive, Islington, London

Dear Admiral Lancing-Lancing

My partner Binky and I wanted to thank you for your stimulating talk at the Peace Collective. It was good of you to make the lengthy slog from Cornwall. We thought with being ex-naval you'd enjoy bivouacking in the peace hut on the allotment. Rainbow is a sweetie. Now that he's recovering, and his voice is getting back to normal after the *incident*, he's going to visit Iceland to save the whale.

Mission Moby involves capturing a whale and bottling its semen for future generations. This necessitates exciting the whale by playing it underwater graphic videos.

It's a technique pioneered by Professor Edwin Askew at the Alabama and Tashkent Marine Life Centre. He showed similar videos to cows in the Texas Panhandle and was so surprised by their reaction that he thought it could work on whales. Rainbow has always been interested in semen and swims quite well himself.

Binky will be writing soon. She is anxious to talk to you about alleviating unemployment and widespread despair in the West Country.

Peace, brother!

Roly

Nest

George, old chap

Some madman called Roly, who has a thing about sperm and whales, has sent me a note. He's harping on about showing pornographic movies to cows and whales. I was silly enough to accept an invite to speak to a peace movement about Western security. I'd no sooner suggested that we bomb North Korea (being jocular) than I was howled down by a baying mob in balaclavas. At which point Albion went into Polaris mode and grabbed one of the rascals by the goolies.

That night they accommodated me in a potting shed, in which I spent a restless night tossing and turning in a hammock. They said having been in the navy it would bring back memories. At breakfast, a coven of peace people with staring eyes and an eager manner, sang sea shanties, while feeding me almond nuts and soya milk.

There are some very odd people around.

Lancing-Lancing

-

Dogs

Dear Admiral

I would give sperm, whales and anybody called Roly an exceedingly wide berth. Peace people are always at war with one another. All tribes go mad in the end. It matters not if it's politicians, twitchers, keep-fit types, ping-pong players or golfers in Rupert Bear trousers. Eventually they all turn on one another. It's like Lord of the Flies, but more so.

George.

Nest

George

Keep-fitters seem particularly tribal. I went to a gym (only once) where everybody walked around in the nude blow-drying themselves with hair-driers. One had a herbaceous border tattooed on his bottom.

I met somebody the other day entirely devoid of a sense of humour (a cardinal affliction) who said she was studying to be a playwright (*please* God). Her wife and her don't live together, but in adjacent houses. I gather it's quite the done thing these days.

She had spent some years living with pigmies and now, being in the early stages of something dreadful, shoots poisonous darts from a blow-pipe at her neighbours. You might think she doesn't sound an especially convincing witness, but she's adamant (though, in truth, she is about absolutely *everything*) that the tattoo plague is because developed man has a deep-longing to be tribal and to live in a cave.

As for gyms, you can pick up all sorts of diseases. Think of the Somme: foot-rot, trench-foot, machine-gun elbow.

Aye

Lancing-Lancing
-

Dogs

Dear Admiral

Tattoos seem *very* tribal. We had a couple of vegetarian tribalists the other night. Catharine cooked lentils or some such. Very pleasant, but it's all so one-way. They wouldn't consider cooking a fillet steak if we visited their place. Open-toed sandals, meditation, weekend retreats to *find themselves*, long list of hates led by The Daily Mail and everything American. Takes all sorts.

George

Nest

George

Two-thirds of the world starving and still people are picky.

Lancing-Lancing

**

Lancing-Lancing is an accomplished historian and author, spending lengthy periods in libraries and museums, researching his different books.

The Imperial War Museum

Dear Lancing-Lancing

The attack you made on my staff in the Navy section was disgraceful. Lucinda and Sebastian were doing their best.

Brig. Piers Scrote-Barking, Dep. Director IWM (Nav.)
-

Nest

Dear Scrote-Barking

I had no dispute with Lucinda, but with her manager, he of the diamond ear-studs, the curtain ring through his nose and the FCUK tee-shirt. After I said he did not know much about ships – he insisted a Corvette was a car – he screamed at me about being qualified in psycho-therapy from a college in Luton. He then ran blubbing out of the foyer shouting 'I'll tell on you.'

Lancing-Lancing

IWM

Lancing-Lancing

Sebastian was being harassed by your bulldog who tried to nip him. There was no need for you to leap on the Howitzer in the foyer and threaten to blow him to kingdom come.

Scrote-Barking

-

Nest

Scrote-Barking

His tee-shirt was offensive with white letters on a black background. Albion hates bad language and has a thing about black.

Lancing-Lancing

-

The Hollies, Chalfont St. Peter

Dear Admiral Lancing-Lancing

It was sweet of you to send the roses. There was no need.

You said in your note that you were worried you had upset me and that your 'beef' was not with me but Sebastian.

Between ourselves (you will notice I am writing confidentially from my parent's rather than the museum) Sebastian can be a bit *funny*. On the morning of the spat he had had a row with his husband, so he was already weepy by the time you were astride the cannon. When he ran away, pursued by Albion, he looked a frightful snowflake.

Daddy says there are too many army types running things at the museum, not that Sebs was ever in the army. Among other problems, he has flat feet. Daddy is a Rear-Admiral and has huge respect for you.

Lucy Wallington

Nest

My Dear Miss Wallington

I am delighted you liked the flowers. Your father is renowned for his exemplary courage in the Falklands. As for Scrote-Barking, he too has been brave in his time. But as I am sure your father will confirm, sometimes army chaps can be awfully silly (think Charge of the Light Brigade).

I am most charmed by your letter.

Lancing-Lancing

＊＊

Most of the invitations Lancing-Lancing has received over the years, to join this or that institution, he has turned down, saying he is too busy. In truth, he doesn't see himself as 'the clubby type,' though, contrarily, he is a member of The Reform, one of London's premier clubs. The majority of invites have a naval or military connection, but he is also approached by charitable and sporting associations. Since his encounter with Butcher Thrupp, his sporting prowess has been somewhat curtailed, but he still sails and enjoys the occasional round of golf.

Dove Valley Golf Club, Sheffield.

Dear Admiral

We were delighted that you have accepted our invitation to become an honorary member. As one of the leading golf clubs catering for what was once 'Steel City' we are proud that the former commander of HMS *Blade* is to be a part of us. Your speech about personal mettle and the need for steely leadership was extraordinarily well received by all the members.

Humphrey Joice, Secretary

Nest

Dear Mr. Joice

I am proud to have been invited to join such a fine club. In my talk I forgot to mention that I once had a hole-in-one on a course in Atlanta. Pure fluke of course, as these things are. I was with a party of US Navy people and they wanted to celebrate back at the 19th. As is the way of such things, drinks were on me, and they flowed until the small hours. Charlotte, my wife, found me the next morning lying in a dahlia bed outside the bedroom window of our motel. Fortunately, it was summer, which in Atlanta is very warm.

Another chum of mine, not a golfer – but a gifted yachtsman – won a prestigious sailing race in the Gulf of Mexico.

The following day, after the customary celebrations, he appeared in court accused of stealing a police car and crashing it into a 'nodding donkey,' one of those little contraptions which pump oil in Texas. The car was written off, there was a sizeable oil spill, and he spent a month in the clink.

Lancing-Lancing

**

Lancing-Lancing has travelled the world. His wide circle includes Guiseppe Falconetti, a sloe-eyed Italian about Monaco. His father made a fortune from a Milanese lime quarry, which Falconetti is not reticent about spending. He achieved notoriety after an incident in Port Hercule, Monaco, where he lives. The headless corpse of a diver was found floating in the port. The head was later discovered on the back seat of Falconetti's power boat by an Italian policemen who spotted a nose poking from beneath a copy of 'Hallo Monaco!'

In court, the policeman said of his find: 'Big Roman nose dead giveaway'. Witnesses alleged that Falconetti made a full-throttle turn which decapitated the diver. Charges were dropped after two of Falconetti's friends swore they were in bed with him at the time of the accident.

Club de Hercule

Monaco

Hillo Admiral Lunging-Lunging

I know you is good sailor boy like Engleesh Nelson, you with funny leg and Nelson with one eye and bad arm, but I don't want you messing up Monaco tax fiddlo as you as been saying in papers. This business not yours. You welcome at my home when you here. You stay at my big house in harbour Hercule. We met with Two Fingers at hotel Carlton in Cannes. You remember maybe, yes? With two nice girls, no? Two Fingers good boy, bit norty. He know good girls in hot sun Riviera.

Good luck yes, but stay out of way on money and tax man. This our habit.

Luck you, and nice things

Guiseppe Falconetti

-

Nest

Dear Mr. Falconetti

Thank you for your letter. I am pleased the legal difficulties with your power boat in Port Hercule have been resolved. I think you must be referring to my recent comments in which I bemoaned the UK's defence cuts. I said that if tax dodging could be thwarted Britain might have enough money to buy planes for its aircraft carriers. I also mentioned that tax havens like Monaco should not be tolerated, and I still hold to that view.

Thank you for inviting me to stay at your house, which sounds delightful. I recall Two-Fingers Maltby telling me it was regularly raided by the Inland Revenue, Customs & Excise and, every now and again, the drug squad. Two-Fingers said apart from that, your home was very peaceful, its tranquillity broken only by your fondness for bunga-bunga parties, with nubile young masseuses from Bangkok and Monaco's crème de la crème in attendance.

Yes, I can recall our evening in The Carlton in Cannes. I have sometimes wondered what happened to the two young ladies from Manilla. I last saw you and Two Fingers staggering along the Croisette in Cannes, with Two-Fingers becoming trapped in a French urinal with automatic doors, while you vanished into the night, trying to recall where you had parked your Lamborghini.

Lancing-Lancing

**

The editor of Boat Planet, aka Boat Puffery, is Nicola 'Buttocks' McButtley. The king of knots, Stag Hake, says she's as 'beamy as a tug-boat,' which to the non-maritime suggests a certain width at the hip. She was also described by Hake as 'diminutive, lumpen, roars a lot and kicks up a wash'. McButtocks is fond of telling anybody who will listen that she is proud of being a non-writing editor, as writing would be an impediment to her primary role of focusing on profits, and securing advertising by having freelance hacks pen flattering portraits of her advertisers.

Ruddy-faced, with suspiciously black-hair severely cut, she is fond of hacking jackets, cavalry twills and Gloria, Puffery's circulation manager, who was formerly a stoker on a Mersey ferry where they met, and who over the years has consistently refused to marry her.

Boat Planet

Dear Admiral Lancing-Lancing

As the editor of a foremost sailing title, I would like you to contribute to our series: 'What makes a *real* sailor.' The fee is modest, but negotiable, and the article should be about 2000 words. I see it being the story of your life as a distinguished member of the Navy.

Ms N. McButtley.

Nest

Dear Ms. McButtley

Thank you for your kind suggestion, which is most generous given our previous contretemps in your organ about navy cuts. I am afraid I am too stretched at the moment. I would like to offer an alternative, however, in a desire to be helpful: Stag Hake, the knot maestro. Hake had an extensive career in the navy, long before he began to tie everything up. Could he not do an entertaining piece for you?

Lancing-Lancing
-

Nest

George

Ms. McButtocks of *Puffery* wants me to do something for it. I said I couldn't but suggested Stag Hake, knowing how *well* McButtocks and the rope-man get on.

Lancing-Lancing
-

Dogs

Dear Admiral

Delighted your sense of mischief remains intact.

George.

**

Lancing-Lancing has always been a great family man. He was devastated by the loss of his wife, Charlotte, as were his two children. Though separated by geography and distance, the Lancing-Lancing family is close-knit, and his two children, and grandchildren by his daughter, are regular visitors at the Nest. Jack, his son, turns up with a different girl-friend every time, the latest one being Alice.

Camden

Dear Dad

Thought I'd pop down at the weekend to give support at the Mousehole jazz festival. Can't wait to see you. I'll bring Alice. She's very nice and it's getting serious. Mum always said she liked a good wedding.

Jack xx

-

Nest

Dear Jack

Wonderful! Yes, your mother would have been over the moon. I am attempting a solo with the Mousehole Strollers. Bring ear-protectors. There's another chap on clarinet who's also doing a solo. He's not Jimmy Noone or Johnny Dodds and I'm certainly not Kid Ory. So you will have to be forgiving.

Dad xx

-

Camden

Dear Dad

We had a marvellous time. Thank you. You outdid Tommy Dorsey on *Song of India*. It always makes me sad when I see the piano in the cottage. I have this picture of Mum playing Chopin. Anyway, mustn't get too maudlin. Maybe we could have Elizabeth playing Jelly Roll's *Naked Dance*, with you on the trombone? I envy my sister's musical skills. You'll be the first to know if Alice and I decide anything.

Jack xx

Nest

Dear Jack

It was a lovely weekend, and Alice is a stunner. Jelly Roll's *The Naked Dance* is very difficult. Legend has it that more than one pianist was at the keyboard when Jelly made the recording. I know what you mean about your mother. Years ago we went to a club to see Blossom Dearie, and later that evening Charlotte played *Quiet Night of Quiet Stars*, performed by Blossom and, famously, recorded by Stan Getz with Astrud Gilberto. You were still a baby, but during my posting to Brazil, Getz's Bossa Nova rhythms, and Gilberto's beguiling whisper, were everywhere. Wonderful to see you, son. Let's do it again soon.

Dad xx

**

Clube de Hercule

Monaco

Dear Admiral Lunging-Lunging

I see you on TV and all over papers still going ten to the onions about taxi avens. Some of my friends don't like what you is saying. They bad people who know more bad people. They live Antibes, just down road, and know Italian nasty men. They no pay taxis. These Italians I control not. I ring Three Fingers with this taxi compliant but he said fuck off.

I think it better you not keep taxi talking on TV and have good bunga bunga, yes. Nice time we have. Where is Polperry, pleese. It looks in sea on map. I bring girls to Polperry in Cornish, no. Nice Malteser has long black hair and jewel up button-belly. You like her below deck.

Please halt, achtung, taxi talking. Italian men in Cap d'Antibes turn nasty, yes. These come Polperry and do bad stuff. I want be

20

friend not enemy on taxi dodger men.

I love you

Guiseppe Falconetti

-

Nest

Dear Mr. Falconetti

I am not sure what the implication of your letter is, though it appears rather threatening.

As a consequence, I have increased the security at my home. Albion, my bulldog, has gone into training and is on a high-protein diet. I have renewed the licence for my Smith & Wesson rifle and have handed your note to the police.

Be assured, sir, that you and your Italian friends will be in for a very warm reception should you turn up in Cornwall. Don't think for a moment that the English have forgotten Mussolini.

Lancing-Lancing

-

Flat 21

Forte de la donkey, Lagos, Algarve

Dear bad leg Lancey

You see, I now have move to new hideout, much is quiet yes. No police or Italian knives out, thank you. No bunga bunga. This makes Guiseppe wet sad in eye, especially no having bunga.

I want you change mind on taxi bad business. I promise you like Malteser very mucho. Two-Finger say she non-stop go go. Nice girl, sparkle diamond in button belly.

No police, yes. I am on run. Antibes gringos say I not stop you on taxis talking so they now stop me yes and want break my head.

All love, no

Guiseppe

PS I send you nice photo, yes.

-

*The photograph was a close up of a diamond in a belly-button.
Beneath it was tattooed a small heart inscribed: 'GF like sucking nice
Malteser, yes.'*

**

Gone to the Dogs

Dear Admiral

Did you read about the solar-powered yacht *'Sun's Up?'* She
ran into trouble when she hit a cold spot. Her owner, Guiseppe
Falconetti (he of the head on the back seat of his speed boat in
Monaco) said the weather had been scorchio when he left Genoa,
but that a nimbus cumulus suddenly rendered him powerless.

Pity it had to happen off Dover, and it was very bad luck that
his boat got chopped in half by one of those weekend booze cruise
ferries. All the passengers were squiffy and thought that they
were hallucinating when they looked down and saw Falconetti
thrashing around in the wreckage.

Still, from what I gather, he's making good progress, under all
that stubble, and well done Dover Infirmary for putting him back
together again. Customs and Excise were much taken with the
large quantity of white powder stowed in his life-jacket.

George

-

Nest

George, dear boy

As a matter of fact, I've been having a spot of bother with Guiseppe

Falconetti. He recently sent me a bizarre note about the big tax debate, fiddlers hiding accounts in Switzerland and Monaco and so on. I'd rather rashly sent a note to *The Times* and done a bit on the telly and suddenly Falconetti pops up and starts making dark threats about Mafia types. He mentioned Two-Fingers and offered me bunga-bunga tuition.

Lancing-Lancing

**

Another acquaintance of George Steel and Lancing-Lancing is Herman Grindlevald, the elderly boss of Fobbi, the Italian super yacht company.

Known in sailing circles as Herman the German, he's red-faced, bristling and porky. He likes leather shorts, braces, playing the flugelhorn and marching music, the more rousing the better. Being the recipient of ambitious cosmetic surgery makes it difficult to be precise about his age, but he is said to be unrecognisable from when he disappeared into South America, shortly before the fall of Berlin.

In the following letter, Steel makes mention of the Green Room, in which guests who are putative boat buyers, or journalists with whom a proprietor wishes to curry favour, are wined and dined. It's also called hospitality, or sometimes hostility, should guests over indulge.

Gone to the Dogs

Dear Admiral

There's a good run ashore coming up. I'm off to Palma for the press launch of the *Fobbi 250*, the latest model to come out of Herman the German's boat-building empire.

Herman's never too meagre in the Green Room, especially when he's been on the tequila and starts on about the old days, all that goose-stepping.

The *Fobbi 250s* got a golf course on board. An electric tee rises up from the poop deck. The owner and his guests whack balls out to sea at floating Greens and flags. The crew don frogman-suits to retrieve the balls. They must wonder why they got their Royal Yachting Association certificates if all they have to do is keep leaping overboard and swimming around picking up Russian oligarchs' balls. Imagine the dung-driven *Silver Chipolata* sub coming to the surface only to be blitzed by stray Dunlop 75s.

Incidentally, Catharine was mulling over one of your earlier missives and says you must keep the flies off your bad 'un. You mentioned that Lurpak butter tends to attract them. If they drew blood it would drive you mad, and Albion barking.

George

-

Nest

George

Herman the German comes from dicky stock. I was on patrol on HMS *Brave* off Rio when we found one of his relatives at the wheel of a tug boat. It turned out to be brimful with Leica cameras, worth a fortune and of a doubtful provenance.

On closer inspection we found a false floor in the Heads (lavatory) in which were hiding a couple of Loony Tunes off to start a new life in sunny Argentina. Fascinating, is it not, to speculate on the way Herman escaped the ruins of Berlin. One would have thought a face which grew younger with every passing year, on an increasingly decrepit torso, would have been something of a giveaway.

Your golfing yarn reminds me of a chap on HMS *Defiant*. The bounder had a putting machine in the wardroom. If you sank the ball a little bell went ting-a-ling and shot the ball back to your club head: tap-ting, tap-ting, an infernal bloody racket which drove everybody mental.

One evening Rear-Admiral Fyffe-Herbert-Herbert was paying a visit. Always slightly deranged, and a bit of a stickler for doing things properly, he skidded on a ball and went A over T taking with him a decanter of Tio Pepe. As you can imagine, all Hell broke loose.

I've got to take Albion in again. The poor chap has bad gnashers, probably because he keeps trying to file them down on the table leg. What with his poorly teeth, and his breathing, he's getting terribly geriatric. The vet's even talking about fitting him with false teeth, though I'm not convinced about a bulldog with dentures. He's getting more expensive to run than the Jag. My affectionate regards to Cathy.

Keep the bottom scraped

Lancing-Lancing.

**

As well as Lancing-Lancing's son, Jack, making the trek from London to Cornwall – his daughter Elizabeth (known as Beth) tries to make the long journey as often as she can. Elizabeth is married to Harry. They have two children, Fred and Rosie, who are doted on by their grandfather.

Shoreditch, London

Dear Daddy

We'll all be coming down on Thursday. Make a long weekend of it. Harry is taking the day off and Fred and Rosie are doing cartwheels with excitement. Do you think we can sail?

Beth xxxx

-

Nest

Dear Beth

Marvellous news. Yes, of course, we can. I'm airing the lifejackets.

Dad xx

Nest

Dear Beth

It was wonderful seeing you. I hope Harry has forgiven me. I tend to forget he's not a sailor, and I must admit there was a bit of a breeze out there. I think the ferocity of the waves and my generous ladling of baked beans rather did for him.

Dad xx
-

Shoreditch

Darling daddy,

I had to drive all the way back as Harry wasn't up to it. We were obliged to make four emergency stops at service stations, but he seems to be getting over it now. He says he thinks he'll stick to golf, though the children loved it. Fred couldn't stop talking about the way we got so close to the rocks. Rosie was disappointed that we didn't have to call the helicopter.

Lots of love,

Beth xxx

PS. I thought our duet was rather good. You were much better on the trombone than I was on Mum's piano. The Jelly Roll piece was just *impossible*. You always said he was a genius.

**

Lancing-Lancing's cottage is 'looked after' by Gordon Trumble, an ex-naval rating, the accident prone odd-job man at The Nest. Variously known as Grumble or Bumble, Lancing-Lancing is loyal to him because of his affection for the works of Charles Dickens and, also, because of Trumble's doughty naval past.

Of a growing importance in Lancing-Lancing's life is his new live-

in nurse, Sophie Cornwallis. From eminent naval stock, she's charming, spirited, long limbed with an engaging smile. She has had numerous flings, none serious, beyond a married naval officer, an ultimately sad affair from which she eventually managed to extricate herself, knowing in her heart that it could only end in catastrophe.

A trained nurse, Sophie had followed her mother into the Wrens. Her father had been a decorated naval commander. As the beneficiary of her late parent's estate, and having left the Wrens, she quickly tired of doing little and changed her life by answering an advertisement in The Officer, which led to her appointment at The Nest.

Note pinned on the fridge at the Nest

Sophie,

I've just nipped out. Bumble says he's going to drop by. I've left a note on the downstairs loo door to say it's temporarily out of bounds. Bumble managed to unblock it but some bossy woman down the hill has complained that bucket-loads of unmentionable has coursed down the slope and swept through her lounge. Be a sweetie and tell him to go easy with the rods.

Edward
-

Reply on fridge

Edward

Grumble Bumble is getting impossible. I told him to take it easy but he started rodding as if he was possessed. He then gave me a stern lecture about the onward march of women. It centred on Wrens – aimed at me – and turned into a full-scale rant about women bishops, car-drivers, lady submariners and the woman down the hill and her free-flowing incursor. Just popped out for some Gordon's. We're getting low.

Sophie

Note on Trumble's potting shed door

Dear Trumble

Sophie was rather upset about your strident views on sex equality. Do try and be a little more circumspect in airing your opinions, there's a good chap. These things can so easily turn incendiary. Incidentally, there's a broken tile on the summer-house roof and I'd be grateful if we could replace it. A little water's beginning to seep in.

Lancing-Lancing

**

Boat Planet

Dear Admiral

I am sorry that you will not be writing a piece for my magazine, Thanks you for your suggestion, but Stag Hake is better at knots than writing. It's not just the readers who say so, it's also endorsed by his wife, poor woman. He is prone to blethering and lacks the credibility of a full-blown Admiral.

Ms. N. McButtley, editor *Boat Planet*.
-

Nest

Dear Ms McButtley

I've put on a little weight but I'm hardly full-blown.

Lancing-Lancing
-

Octopus House, Wormald Jetty, Gosport

Dear Lancing-Lancing

I'm told that McButtocks, the outsize witch who runs *Puffery*, has asked you to write for it. Allow me to raise the storm-cones.

I once wrote her a piece about the triple-sliding-shank, a long-time favourite knot of Peruvian alpaca herders. She used it in a *Puffery* consumer test and refused to pay me on the grounds that firemen had to cut the subject free before he could be airlifted to A&E. When I said I'd take her to court, she said she had photographs of burn marks on the subject's throat. Unlike the triple-sliding-shank, McButtocks is a slippery piece of work.

It's a while since you and I met up. Perhaps we might splice the proverbial? Do hope you've had a look at my latest tome: *'Fifty things you never thought you could do with Rope.'* It's not a big seller, though there's always a niche market. Hope all is well. How's your 'bad 'un'?

Stag Hake

**

Always abreast of current affairs, when the banking crisis struck and helped to drag the world into recession, Lancing-Lancing wrote to The Times, something he rarely did, believing that most people who write to newspapers are usually in need of psychiatric help. The fact that he did so indicates the seriousness with which he viewed situation.

Nest

Sir

I walked by a Nubile Bank the other day. Customers lolled in easy chairs reading newspapers and drinking coffee. Its décor included a pile of logs (in a smokeless zone). Was this to give it a Hansel and Gretel appeal? Bankers should ditch the cosmetics and repent, for they and their sort have helped wreak destruction.

Lancing-Lancing

Nubile Bank, Friedrichshafen, Germany

To the editor of *The Times*

Sir

The design of a Nubile bank makes clients feel at home. Our rates are competitive, the atmosphere friendly, Nubile Colleagues serve loose tea and decaffeinated coffee while dispensing wisdom on the sometimes bewildering world of money. The logs are from sustainable trees grown in Nubile Valley forests in Indonesia, where indigenous peoples are paid more than the local rate. We are on *your* side, that of the customer. We want to be on *your* side too, Admiral.

Klaus Bimmershaven,

Nubile Communications.

-

Nest

To the editor of *The Times:*

Sir

Sphericals.

Lancing-Lancing

-

To the editor of *The Times*

Sir

My Nubile colleagues and I are pleased that the Admiral recognises we offer a rounded service. He is welcome to visit any branch for free decaffeinated coffee and newspapers (recyclable paper) in Nubile's 'wood-cabin' ambience.

Klaus Bimmershaven

The editor of The Times declined to print Lancing-Lancing's response saying it was actionable.

**

Nest

Dear Trumble

I am sorry you are in hospital. To be encased in plaster must be very uncomfortable. Albion had a lucky escape when you crashed through the roof. But for him to nip you while you were lying in the debris wasn't cricket. The summer house appears to have been hit by a bomb. The important thing is to get you up and about. I'll call in at the hospital when you're allowed visitors.

Lancing-Lancing

**

Being in public relations, Two-Fingers Maltby spends lengthy periods trying to widen his social and professional circle, or what George Steel calls, with the vitriol many journalists reserve for PRs, 'greasing and licking.' Though his yacht racing days are behind him, Two Fingers still cuts a dash.

The King's Road model agency, Crotch, to which he is signed, says that he is ideal in promoting clothes for the older man, especially those who see themselves as younger than they are.

Clube de Croisette

Cannes,

France

Hi Admiral

I'm Two Fingers Maltby. We've met a few times, boat shows and the like. I used to be an ocean racer and I recall that you fired the cannon at the start of the Round the Island race at Cowes. That's where I first met you and your delightful nurse, Sophie. I've been asked to do some modelling – yes, I know, it sounds rather *peculiar* – but I wondered if you would care to join me for a shoot at the Pavilion in Brighton?

My agency, Crotch, want me in white flannels and a rather well-cut striped blazer that they're trying to promote. Other props include palm trees and a couple of lovelies with a Saluki. The advertising boys would like you to be in the montage wearing your full Admiral's regalia, funny hat and medals, accompanied by Albion (quite a star after he left his mark on the peace protester; it read well in the *Daily Mail*).

Everybody thinks you would give the campaign authority, they call it *bottom*. Your fee would be considerable, certainly enough to replace your Jaguar; as you know, these advertising boys are financial madmen.

May I ask one small favour? I wonder if you would be good enough to bring your nurse, as I have an urgent condition I'd like to share with her? Forgive me for writing unannounced. I always think that straightforwardness is best.

Two Fingers

-

The Nest

Dear Mr. Two-Fingers,

As do I. No thank you.

Lancing-Lancing

PS. My Jaguar improves with age.

**

32

Note on fridge

Trumble

I'm so pleased you're out of plaster. Just a small thing: the plug for the TV has become a little wonky and has started fizzing and crackling every now and again. It looks as if Albion has been chewing at the lead. He's also had a go at the standard lamp and I'm a little concerned about the sparking. When you have a moment, be a good chap and take a look.

Good to see you up and about again after the summer-house debacle.

Lancing-Lancing

**

While life ticks along at The Nest, with Lancing-Lancing writing a new book – a biography of the Norfolk lifeboat legend, Jude 'Flint Boy' Flagg – and the relationship with his live-in companion, Sophie, continues to flourish – his friend and confidante, George Steel, maintains a regular stream of letters about his adventures as a peripatetic sailing journalist.

Gone to the Dogs

Dear Admiral

In Italy recently for the launch of the new *Rip Avenger* at the Rip yard on the Med north of Viareggio. It sprawls over three miles of once unspoiled coastline. Partly financed by 'family' money: wink, wink,'nuff said, mind your Vermicelli.

The usual intimate supper for the worlds press: 1400 hacks and hangers-on in sheds eleven to eighteen. Fish, fish and more fish. A concentrated Crustacean assault.

All the usual suspects in attendance. Old Stag Hake looking morose, and Two-fingers with a leonine creature from Naples clinging to his blazer. Hake's been made to walk the plank by

McButtocks who seems to grow larger by the minute. She's oceanic. Hake had been hitting the Morgan's and loudly compared her to a Newcastle collier. Between mouthfuls of chocolate mousse she swore she'd never let him write for *Puffery* again.

Halfway through the braised turbot, the Blue Danube struck up, the cutlery danced around and Hake cupped his hands over his ears. There was a big bang, a cloud of smoke, and a curtain fell away to reveal the *Avenger*, bathed in spotlights, a gamine lovely sprawled across its foredeck.

Everybody sprang to their feet, whistling and cheering, except for Hake. He stayed sitting, arms folded, saying it would compromise his journalistic integrity if he were to clap before he had inspected the goods. He can be such a curmudgeonly old tart when the mood takes him, which these days is most of the time.

Paolo Artelli, the managing director (three-day's growth and Italy's gold reserves round his neck) said *Rip* had retained its character since being taken over by Lambretta, the scooter lot. 'They give us plenty lira but not stick fingers up tender', all the usual PR guff, but I'm not persuaded. His 'n her scooters, in blue and pink, rose up from the stern garage on a butler's pantry.

Rip knows its buyers are knocking on a bit, so geriatrics can now be lowered into the jacuzzi on a crane. And there's an operating theatre so they can have heart surgery on board.

The master cabin had been done up by the French designer Brigitte 'potty' Pottier. Nicely understated in Potty's trademark luminescent purple silk, lots of mirrors and orange suede with a tiger motif. Potty had a rumpus with Jade O'Connor, the American designer. O'Connor's always up for a fracas. After the crab truffle, Potty said something about Syria and O'Connor's Chassagne Montrachet '99 quickly vanished down Potty's cleavage.

Suddenly, it was mayhem. We got out before the Carabinieri arrived in a fleet of Alfa Romeos. All very enjoyable, but I paid for it later, when the monkfish and escargot in garlic butter kicked in.

George

Nest

George, old man

Excellent to hear from you. It's always good to catch up with your globe-trotting. If boats like the *Rip Avenger* are aimed at monied old codgers why aren't they called *Twilight*? or *Embalming Fluid*? Hake will have to watch his goolies if he gets caught up in McButtock's wash. I'm afraid I've given up on *Puffery*, it's so full of advertorial squit.

I wish the Fourth Estate would take a peep at the red tape pouring out of Brussels. Radar regulations, pollution laws, pages about the galley saying you're not allowed to cook a lamb chop if you're out in a blow. Some jobsworth in Brussels thinks the cooker door could spring open and burn the cook in the galley, or somewhere worse.

The very time you need some hot broth is when there's a nasty one kicking up and you're donning waterproofs and reaching for the sick bag. What are you supposed to live on? Salad? I've never been able to see the point of Belgium? Poirot? Chocolate? Or the Swiss? Heidi, cuckoo clocks, vaults full of stolen money.

Anyway, getting back to that which you mentioned ... crustacean assaults. I know what you mean if things start getting too fishy. I often used to get into quite a state after all those Admiralty binges. They always served fish, it was the nearest most of those buggers ever got to the sea.

After one gargantuan fish supper, Butcher Thrupp had to sort me out. He wanted to operate, but I managed to resist, even though I was in a weakened state. Not sure which bit he'd have chopped off.

Instead of brandishing his knife he gave me a dreadful potion which had me in the Heads for a week, though it eventually did the trick. It's usually crab that does me in. I always end up like HMS *Hood*: head over the pan, bows down, stern up.

Lancing-Lancing

Note on fridge

Dear Trumble

The village has been in darkness for a week now. The unspeakable woman down the hill who said she couldn't clean the glass in her conservatory, after you unblocked our lavatory, now says that she's going to take me to court over the melted contents of her deep-freeze.

One couldn't have imagined that rewiring a plug would lead to such chaos.

I'm afraid I'm going to have to relieve you of your electrical duties. I know this will be disappointing, but from now on I feel it would be prudent for you to concentrate on cultivating the vegetable garden, in which you have always excelled. This will give Sophie and I a little more peace of mind, and should also help ensure your personal safety. I do not want you to be electrocuted.

Lancing-Lancing

**

Lancing-Lancing served in strategic roles in America. He corresponded with Admiral Chester 'Kenny' Pepper. Both men enjoyed eminent careers with Pepper seeing out his later years at his home on Newport Rhode Island.
-

Nest

Dear Pepper

It amazes me how a country as rich and clever as yours can still be arguing about a national health service. One has an obligation to look after the lower-decks. This is not Victorian patronage. It's

trying to lead one's life in a half-decent manner. As for your gun-laws, *please*, what's wrong with you people?
Lancing-Lancing
-

Newport US

Dear Lancing-Lancing

It must be your bad 'un that's playing up? One has long suspected that the royal navy has its share of pinkos, but to find its senior commanders are Reds comes as something of a shock. With regards to firearms, I was a given a Glock as a Christening present. It was kept under my pillow in the cot. I'll put your comments down to bizarre English humour, always beyond me.

Pepper
-

Nest

Dear Pepper

When you're old and frail and confronting the Maker you won't have a medical system to look after you, that's assuming you aren't shot before your time.

Ted
-

Newport US

Dear Lancing-Lancing

As you're pondering on my demise, I thought you'd like to know I'm to be buried at sea. US Health & Safety tell me I have to fill in forms because they're worried about pollution. I know I'm ancient but I didn't realise I was contaminated. I had a word with Old Banger (Admiral William Banger, ex-USS *Scythe*; you met him in the Pentagon at that cocktail do with the Mormons). Banger says he'll pick up my corpse on his yacht and drop me into Newport Sound, wrapped in plastic and weighed down with bricks. It'll be OK as long as that dung-driven submarine doesn't surface. I don't want to be a stiff impaled on its conning-tower.

Pepper

-

Nest

Dear Pepper

I remember the Mormon do. Several lunatics were scratching themselves to bits. They blamed it on their underwear. There was a chap with numerous wives and somebody who told me he had vertigo and was down in the dumps because he couldn't go up a tall tower in Salt Lake City to be closer to the Messiah. Were they breakdown cases?

Lancing-Lancing

**

Clube de Croisette

Cannes, Cote d'Azur

Dear George

I recently asked your pal Lancing-Lancing if he'd do a little modelling with me. He sent me a lengthy and detailed response, carefully outlining his reservations. I was looking forward to having him in the shoot and renewing my acquaintance with Sophie, his nurse. I pointed out that there would be a hefty fee. Would you mind using a little gentle persuasion? You can usually find me at the above watering-hole.

Cheers

Two-Fingers.

Dogs

Dear Two Fingers

No.

George.

**

Note on potting shed door

Dear Trumble

I'm pleased you are now out of the wheel-chair and that your foot is getting better. Garden forks can be *so* dangerous. The vegetable patch has become a little overgrown in your absence. Living off frozen stuff is OK, but it's not as tasty as your freshly grown stuff. Don't worry about a thing.

As soon as you're back on your feet, so to speak, you can crack on as usual.

Lancing-Lancing

**

The Maxim Gorky Collective, Crouch End

Dear Admiral

I am Roly's soul mate. We met briefly when you gave your stimulating talk about peace-keeping and came up with your novel suggestion of bombing North Korea (people didn't realize you were joking, which is why so many walked out; Albion chewing on Rainbow's assets scared others away).

You'll be pleased to know that Rainbow's still immersed in sperm whales and has had success in exciting them with a range of videos and unusual toys which worked well underwater.

This is really by way of a begging letter. Roly and I are coming with little Leon and Che and 'doing' Cornwall in our old (sorry, that's so rude! I meant, *elderly*) VW camper-van, Vanessa. We love her so much. She's called Vanessa after Ms. Bell of the Bloomsbury Group.

We've been all over in Vanessa. From Albania to Transylvania and we went to an anti-Nuke-camp in Georgia, where Vanessa had several breakdowns (as did her namesake) and where fighting broke out between freedom fighters and the fascist pig police.

We would like to stay a few nights with you. Roly and I believe property is theft and what's ours is yours. So if you ever want to borrow Vanessa for a night or two, as a sort of swapsie, we'll let you have her for a touring holiday of your own.

She's got little bunks (which as a sailor you're familiar with), a small sink (cold water, but it's nice getting back to nature), a paraffin stove for making apricot tea and keeping warm, and a Green toilet of reeds in a pan which you must empty, otherwise it slops over on bends (we bag it up for our friends Orville and Cosmo to use later on their allotment; we recycle *everything*). You've probably got a veggie patch of your own, so whatever you *do* on that front, would always come in handy. Once you're inside Vanessa, you'll have a lovely time, she gets nice and warm and somehow draws you in.

I wonder if you have a goat? Little Leon loves goats milk and takes it straight from the teat. We weaned him off cows milk because of what the exploitative supermarket chains are doing to dairy farmers. We'll be coming in two weeks and staying a night or two, but it could be longer.

Roly and I have started naturist classes, so if the weather's not too unkind we will be able to indulge ourselves in your garden. It sounds so romantic. We can't wait! We'd love to see you and Albion, as long as he stays away from the children (and Roly, especially if Roly's wandering around in the altogether; he wouldn't want to end up like Rainbow).

We'll all have a lovely time and be able to see in the summer solstice. I'll bring some rose hip wine, it's yummy, though Roly says it gives him irritated bowels. The last time he had it, the doctor gave him pills, but they were non-herbal and made in America, so he didn't take them.

What sort of music are you into? We love Planet Earth and Sod and most things folkie. Little Che and Leon love doing moon & stars dancing. I can't wait for your reply. We're very excited about seeing you again. The children think you are *so* funny.

Love, forever and ever

Binky (not forgetting Roly and the little ones).
-

Nest

Dear Binky

Thank you for your letter.

I'm afraid I'm sailing in the Baltic for the next three years, departing first light tomorrow. You have no idea how I feel about missing you and your family.

The fascinating way in which you fertilise allotments is, sadly, entirely beyond my ken. I know about poop decks, though they have nothing to do with fertilizer.

Thank you for offering me Vanessa's services which, unfortunately, I will have to decline.

Do have a splendid holiday. In 'doing' Cornwall it might be prudent to give Polperro a wide berth as it is currently under several feet of floodwater, and though you will not have read about the atomic leak (the authorities worry about tourism and keep a lid on such things) it has been rather alarming. One wouldn't wish you, Roly, Leon and little Che, to be drowned or radiated.

Yours

Lancing-Lancing.

Note on fridge

Sophie

Over the next week or two we must watch out for some crack-pots
in an old van who have threatened to drop in and do unspeakable
things in our garden. The driver could be in the nude. If you spot
anybody you must tell them I'm on a long voyage and won't be
back for years. They believe that what's yours is theirs so they
might try and move in, or squat in their van in the garden.

I want you to shout out at your first sighting of them, which
will give me a chance to disguise myself as a pin-cushion. If they
give you any trouble I will abandon my subterfuge and break cover,
and you will have to stop me from shooting them or unleashing
Albion.

I've told a fib about there being a nuclear leak in the vicinity, so
hopefully they'll take a hint and stay away.

Ted

-

Nest

Dear George

I've had more difficulties with nudist peace people obsessed with
sperm, whales and dirty videos. They want to come to Cornwall
and do awful things in my vegetable patch.

I told them I was going to be sailing round the world and that
the village was a no-go area having had a nuclear leak which has
been hushed up by the authorities. What a mistake that was!

As a consequence of my white lie, the other day Polperro was
suddenly invaded by an army of naked protesters wearing only
tattoos and gas masks and ranting about a government cover-up.
Nobody, of course, had a clue what they were shouting about.
They were in a convoy of ancient VW camper vans and have now,
mercifully, gone off to a peace and love festival in Glastonbury.

It was a bitterly cold day so their parts were turning blue. One banner-waver was treated for frost-bite on the end of his manhood by the local GP. The doctor found teeth marks as well as frost-bite. The chap in question went by the name of Rainbow and lives in a tree. Albion had nipped him when I first came across this group at the Crouch End Peace Collective.

Lancing-Lancing

–

Dogs

Admiral

They could have worn radiation suits.

George

–

Nest

George

Perverts.

Lancing-Lancing

–

Dogs

Dear Admiral

Enough of the unclothed with their well-gnawed protuberances. Your new nurse, Sophie, sounds a cracker. Have you tried her on your bad 'un with the pliers and Lurpak?

On another tack, a word of warning: I heard a whisper that these surfboard brats are heading your way. You've probably read about them in the papers? Freddie Ffrench-Browne's nipper, Jonty, has got caught up in it. Freddie nabbed him stuffing glue up in his nose in the conservatory. He had to be rushed off to the local A&E with a Gloy bottle stuck to his hooter. He goes surfing with a band of young toffs. Let's hope they don't invade your corner.

George

-

Nest

Dear George

Young Jonty was always a pain. He was never the same after he won the Penge poetry bowl. For a long time afterwards he told everybody that he was Shelley and they had to call him Percy Bysshe. I'll keep a weather-eye out for surfers on glue.

Lancing-Lancing

**

George Steel was born in Norfolk. When he and Catharine find life on the Isle of Dogs, in London's East End, too claustrophobic, they escape to their small yacht, Puck, which they keep on the Norfolk Broads.

Dogs

Dear Admiral

We've had some choice airs so Catharine and I managed to sneak up to Norfolk for a few days sailing on *Puck*.

Do you remember our mishap under Potter Heigham bridge? Running nicely with the wind (and the Jameson). It's still hard to credit that the bridge was lower than the mast.

On this trip the Broads were swarming with twitchers in search of a triple-breasted Bittern or some such. We were happily floating down Meadow Dyke on *Puck*, sailing out of Horsey Mere down to Heigham Sound, thinking we'd meander up to Somerton, when suddenly, an electric punt shot out of a reed bed and damn nearly stoved in *Puck's* bows.

It was weighed down with twitchers. Some are nice enough, but others can be a very smug, self-righteous lot: hunched up, bush hats and binoculars, Yashicas at the ready.

They come from all over the country, but the way they yawp on about Norfolk you'd be forgiven for thinking they actually *know* the place. Lawyers, PRs, advertising types, hedge-fund managers, *baristas* (save me, please!).

Why can't these people twitch overseas? There must be tits craving to be stared at in Croatia. Down river they disappeared back into the reeds and I stood in the cockpit and shouted: '*Puck! Puck! Puck it!*'

On the north Norfolk coast there's now a dwarf Wembley where rows of twitchers can sit and stare at the marshes: the ultimate spectator sport. It stands out like a sore thumb with a sizeable car-park for the tit-chaser's vehicles: squadrons of four-wheel drives ensure each twitcher has their own personalised hole in the ozone layer; *very* Green.

Twitchers used to be content to loll around in the long grass disguised as commandos. But not anymore. Today's birds must feel they're sharing their lives with the Stasi.

Women and children first

George

-

Nest

Dear George

Norfolk has always been sublimely beautiful and it's especially well blessed with having the sea on two sides. It's always been a bit birdy, of course. The whole place was for generations dominated by Brenda and a handful of barking aristos.

Real Norfolkmen are a delight, but they're thin on the ground these days, displaced by rather brash incomers. Too many little towns and villages are now a sea of twee, with bijou shops selling glittery stuff; it's magpie country. Silly prices are paid for damp tenements only lived in at weekends when hordes of Hooray's descend, all yellow wellies, shiny Barbours and red trousers. Everywhere is now a *'destination'* location.

Wiggin-Henry has a place on the green at Appleby Mare. Did you ever meet him? He did time on HMS *Sword* and that old tub HMS *Resolute*. I spent a weekend with him and Marje. Everybody round there now called Jolyon and Octavia up from the Smoke for the weekend. Brayin' triumphalists, the post-Thatcher lot.

I wanted to get some victuals, thought I'd help Marje stock up and do a bit of cooking. Peas, potatoes, lamb chops, the usual stuff. All I could find was a deli selling kalamata pitted olives and Cajun chicken.

It's Nelson country, he was born just down the lane from Marje's place. He wasn't buggered about by twitchers. Lost an eye and an arm, and for what? So Hooray's could run around on his home turf munching guacamole and sushi?

There's a big influx of Russians and Chinese. Awful lot of Ivan's crawling around in the rushes, or jogging up and down St. Hilda's Bay. Everybody's in usury or big in retail (we used to call them shopkeepers). They're much taken with a neighbourhood stately, the one that looks like a Gothic asylum. There's not a barn or a pig sty that hasn't been converted into a des res.

Most of the Hooray's seem to have been fired from their corporations and given dollops of loot for failing.

It used to be that if you put your ship on the rocks that was it: curtains, a courts martial, out on your ear. And it was cardinal you looked after your men. This lot don't seem to give a damn about the lower decks. Snaffle your bonus and to hell with everybody else. Flee to a bolt-hole in Norfolk, or run off to your yacht in Frejus. Good broadside across their four-wheel drives, that'd sort 'em out.

To happier matters.

I took nurse Sophie for a gin the other night. Lovely girl. Name like Cornwallis, it's what you'd expect. You can't get prouder maritime lineage than that. Teach these Hoorays a thing or two about breeding. On the way back she asked me to slow down. The

Jag's still got a lot of go in her. Starry night, she was worried I'd lose control. It's the pink gin, the blind bends and the gammy leg that scares 'em.

Hold her steady

Lancing-Lancing

-

Dogs

Dear Admiral

Of the geographic, Catharine and I went up to Holywold some weeks ago. Hell is the A12. Hadn't been to the Suffolk coast for an age.

Holywold has been subsumed by second-homers. The permanent population has shrunk and the whole place seems to be up for rent.

Terraced hovels ('artisan cottages') command grotesque prices, as do beach huts. Given half a chance, they'd be flogging sandcastles. It was out of season but the place was alive with plumbers, roofers and interior designers (faux architects, *help*) taking instructions on mobiles from faraway owners.

There were pictures of the writer Eric Blyth everywhere, with quotes from his famous *1954, The Bovine Revolution* and, of course, *Down and Out in Bradford and Bingley*. His parents lived in Holywold, in a house now near a fish 'n chip shop and a Balti takeaway. His sister, April, once said in an interview that he hated the place, no mention of that anywhere. Ironic that Blyth – of *all* people – should be censored by the Ministry of Holywold Speak.

From there we went up to north Norfolk, close to where you were. But Blakenham was as bad as Holywold. Teams of builders tarting up rows of second-homes, holiday cottages and buy-to-lets. Everybody in red trousers talking hovel money. Butchers and bakers *curate* their wares. It's getting as bad as Surrey.

We were going to have a drink. But Catharine was cast into despair when she saw that bossy woman off a TV property show, the braying, loudly dressed one. So we upped anchor.

George

PS: You ask why Catharine is spelt so. Her father was at the Cambridge college of the same spelling, though he maintained that he was dyslexic and cocked up the birth certificate.
-

Nest

Dear George

Eric Blyth's *Down and Out in Bradford and Bingley* should be compulsory for the types you mention.

In the old days local nobs used to hop aboard when we flew the flag in different ports on goodwill visits. The Royals were relatively rational, but the squirts in their circle were insane. Most should have been in an institution. I always pretended that I had to rush back to the Bridge to attend to an emergency.

Must stop, old chap. I don't want my irritability to bring on palpitations, though it's *very* enjoyable when Sophie has to give me an emergency medicinal massage.

Lancing-Lancing
-

Dogs

Admiral

Is this chicken and egg? Could Sophie cause the palpitations?

George
-

Nest

George.

Perhaps.

Lancing-Lancing

**

Herman the German, the cosmetically enhanced boss of the Fobbi superyacht company, is passionately engaged in politics and in awe of Lancing-Lancing's distinguished naval career. He sees him as the perfect type to be recruited into a secret military grouping which wishes to re-order the world in Herman's likeness. Out of the blue, Lancing-Lancing received the following missive:

Block 18, Berlinastrasse,

Asuncion

Paraguay

Admiral Lancing-Lancing yes

Many years back since you halt who goes there my family tug boat off coast Brazil, and found good boy General and Panzer Tank man hiding under lavatory. I forgive. You only do duty. General and tank man do prison and later live happy compound, but unhappy to miss old friends, all hanged.

Time we make stand. We organ fit young men, good working-parts and cojones. Drilled in training wood Paraguay. We well-rich. Swiss Gnome back us. Swedes give steel. Swedes make money in war. Like Swiss. We have good German boy leader. He *thinks* right way and will lead to victory, yes. We not name him now. Keep him wrap under blanket, as English say. Later, he pop out of blanket. Like Jack in blanket, you say in English.

We like you fly Paraguay, we pay, you stay in safe lodge in wood. You meet members brigade and shoot boar. You make sea bend your will. You be Doenitz, yes. Nelson, bad eye, yes.
I am, sir,
Herman C. von Grindlevald. Managing director *Fobbi* craft
PS. You think Engleesh gud, yes. I tell secret. This ritten by gud riter of Engleesh. He spy prisoner in compound and does wot we say. He now starved and much tired, maybe we shoot, yes.

49

Nest

Dear George

I've had a peculiar note from Herman the German. He's hinting at world domination via a secret army being got up in the forests of Paraguay, where it appears a captive letter-writer is being held. He wants me to go on a boar shoot and sees me as the next Grand Admiral Karl Doenitz of the Kriegsmarine (Adolf's top submariner).

Lancing-Lancing

-

Dogs

Dear Admiral

Word is that Herman now lives on bananas and monkey meat in a jungle clearing. The heat must have got to him. I don't see you as a Perisher.

George

**

Lancing–Lancing and George Steel became friends when Lancing-Lancing, in command of HMS Razorback, gave assistance to Steel's merchant vessel, the Rotherham, off Peru.

Steel had been making slow headway in mountainous seas when the Rotherham suffered engine failure. Lancing-Lancing picked up Steel's distress calls and went to his aid, taking him under tow to Lima, thus avoiding what could have been a catastrophic incident.

That evening Lancing-Lancing and his officers hosted a dinner on HMS Razorback for Steel and Catharine, who always travelled with her husband.

After the merchant marine, Steel turned to journalism. Some of his liveliest correspondence was with commissioning editors, and he could be as forthright as Lancing-Lancing.

Dogs

Dear Mr. Halpern

I am afraid I am not prepared to write a thousand flattering words, as you request, on Mr. Randy Bellow's superyacht *Loadsawash*. I understand Mr. Bellow has taken a double-page advertisement in your magazine for his advanced washing machine, the Mighty Whoosh. Let me be plain: I do not write puff-pieces.

Secondly, a friend had a mishap with his Mighty Whoosh while trying to wash a pair of Y Fronts. When the machine finished its cycle he opened the door but could not see his pants. So he stuck his head in to see if they were caught in the drum. With that he was dragged head first into the contraption, the door clicked shut and the Mighty Whoosh went into super-spin.

By the time the police, ambulance and firemen got him out he was unrecognizable, and he's never regained his balance, saying that his head is always in a spin. He is suing Mr. Bellow, who, I understand, is also on multiple-fraud charges in Washington DC over the collapse of his bond and gilts corporation. The last I heard was that he had barricaded himself in his penthouse in Belize.

Yours etc

George Steel

**

Lancing–Lancing was forever having difficulties with his boatyard in Cornwall, where he moored his sailing yacht, The Lily and George, named after his late parents.
The yard was run by the curmudgeonly Grimbles. Herbert Grimble,

the third generation of Grimbles at the yard, was no administrator or letter writer, leaving such duties to Doreen, his wife. Why he did is a mystery, she being as literate as Herbert.

Doreen was broad-hipped and swarthy, with bushy eyebrows, a birds nest of coal black hair, giant hoop-earrings and lashings of eye shadow. Some insisted Herbert had found her on a website, and that she hailed from a long line of Romanian gypsies.

The main complaint about the yard was that it did little for its money. If covers blew off dinghies, as an example, it was in the yard's interest never to reinstate them, allowing craft to fill with water, and varnish to crack in the sun.

It was whispered that Herbert, or his three sons, the Grimble Gremlins, all being small and chubby with great tangles of black hair, deliberately pulled covers aside to ensure that Herbert could run up repair bills.

Herbert was a man of few words, trudging around the yard, his shoulders bent, head down, always muttering about 'rich bloody boaters and second-homers think I'm their bloody lackey.'

Birch Boatyard

Dear Mr. Lansing

Herbert and me have decided to get rid of all boats like yors and have one big one insted. It is owned by a Russhan. We are having the dike dug deep so we can get the big Russhan in. We want yor boat out quick. You owe us £185 for stitching yor sales. Send the money quick so we can dig up the dike.

Mrs. Grimble

-

Nest

Dear Mrs. Grimble

Thank you for your letter. As you know, the boat yard is in a conservation area and I think you will have to get permission before you can start altering the dyke.

As for owing you money, I think the reverse is the case. My sails were torn when one of your delightful young sons, Brian, I believe, was trying out his new Swiss Army knife and took a lunge at me. I dodged and he stabbed the foresail, inflicting a sizeable gash. He said he had seen something familiar in a film called Pirates of the Caribbean, and that he had only been joking. Fortunately, my bulldog Albion was able to take the young man in hand, or should I say ankle.

Honours being about equal, your husband and I subsequently agreed to say no more about the matter. Thank you so much for writing to me in such courteous and generous terms.

Lancing-Lancing

-

Birch Boatyard

Mr. Losing Losing

I don't know nothing about Brian and his knife. His dad took it off him and threw the bugger in the dike. You owe us £185. Pay up quic and get your boat out to let the Russhan in.

Mrs. Grimble

-

Nest

Dear Mrs. Grimble

If you do not stop being silly, I shall write to the police reporting Brian as a knife-wielding psychotic. I shall tell them I was only saved from your infant retard by the quick-witted reactions of Albion. Brian will then be birched regularly, locked up in a home for the criminally insane, which is probably where you should be, and if he ever gets out he will be deported to a mosquito infested swamp full of crocodiles and tribes of people who eat children.

Lancing-Lancing

Lancing-Lancing heard no more and the boat yard resorted to its old habits of using one coat of watered-down varnish, while charging for four, loosening covers and removing drain bungs.

Brian Grimble is now held in a halfway house near Bolton after he and his parents were interviewed by psychiatrists following what the police called a 'disturbance.'

Brian told a jury that he had been seeking to assist an elderly arthritic by offering to carry her shopping. She had just picked up her pension, and Brian said she started screaming after he'd tried to befriend her, and that he had only offered to clip her finger-nails with his knife.

**

A curious interlude in Lancing-Lancing's career concerned his unwitting involvement with illegal substances. Careful sifting of the Lancing-Lancing and Steel correspondence revealed letters which give an insight into the astonishing story of the Percy incident, which newspapers later dubbed 'The Trilski Affair'.

Dogs

Dear Admiral

Had a few days in Amsterdam at the Hugo van de Crump yard. A pair of New Russians – husband and wife team, Boris and Tsarina – have set up a boating rag and kindly asked me to write a thousand words about Hugo's yard.

When it came to recompense it was the usual story with the Russians: cash crisis, a run on the rouble, economy subject to sanctions, so they had to pay me in vodka, some iffy caviar (not Beluga) and a large quantity of budgerigar seed (don't ask) which now occupies much of the garage.

They operate from a fortified villa in the hills overlooking Monte Carlo. It's got all the usual refinements. Forests of aerials, Jodrell Bank dishes on the roof, armed guards, coach-loads of leggy-blondes coming and going day and night. Neighbours have dubbed the delightful Boris and Tsarina, Bortsch 'n Tears.

The unspeakable Buttocks of *Puffery* reckons Bortsch 'n Tears' Russian magazine is a front for money-laundering. Buttocks has been anti-Russian since the Black Sea boat show when she took Sergei Lipski (a Kremlin public relations man attached to intelligence) back to the Hotel Novotski for what she called an in-depth profile.

Sergei must have read more into this than Buttocks intended. He clearly didn't know she batted for the other side (her partner, if you recall, is Gloria, the ex-Mersey ferry stoker). Guests complained to the concierge about Sergei's shrieks of horror in the early hours – the imagination boggles at what he tried to do to her, or she to him – but the top 'n tail of it was that Buttocks ended up doing two nights on black bean soup in a Moscow nick.

The Dutch do a lot of business with the Russians. Hugo Crump is Dutch down to his clogs, but he's now known as Count Crumpski. He's taken to wearing furs and a Cossack hat.

The next *Crump Rapier* that he's building is for Igor Molotov, the Georgian ice-skating obsessive. Molotov obliges his captain and crew to wear hockey strip, awfully chilly in the Baltic regions. Molotov fancies himself as a media mogul as well, and he's also very big in pilchards.

Some equally doubtful Czechs have asked me to write for another new magazine that they're setting up. Once I've scribbled a piece for them, doubtless they'll suffer the usual cash flow crises. Still, I suppose we might get a weekend in Prague out of it, though Catharine says she'd prefer a Bohemian chandelier. Is this *really* what it's come to? Living in a flat in a converted gasometer in London's East End, writing articles for dodgy publications and being paid in chandeliers, pilchards and Trilski budgie seed?

George

Nest

George, dear boy

I mentioned your letter to a chap who once gave me some sound advice about Albion and his continuing travails with his teeth. He runs Percy's Pets of Polperro. He says if it's genuine Russian Trilski budgie seed there's a good chance that it's Grade A stuff and he'd be pleased take it off your hands.

Percy tells me that there's been a budgie explosion in the West Country, which sounds painful, but which, as you know, is full to the brim with the elderly. If they lose a loved one they tend to buy a budgie or a goldfish. Can you imagine what my darling Charlotte would have said if she knew I'd replaced her with a goldfish?

Nurse Sophie, who these days looks really quite lovely in her uniform, has observed that Cornwall is stuffed to the gunnels with what she calls CDs. Coffin Dodgers.

Your budgie seed has, it seems, hidden qualities. Percy the Pisky tells me that smoking Trilski roll-ups is popular with thrill-seekers, especially the surf-boarding Johnnies who have invaded this once peaceful idyll.

Their number, as you predicted a while ago, includes Charlie Ffrench-Browne's nipper, the awful Jonty, who over the years has led his Ma and Pa a terrible polka. He runs up and down the beach saying he's Bysshe Shelley and telling anybody who'll listen that if he drowns on his surfboard, as Shelley did on his sailboat, he wants to be cremated here on Dead Man's beach, as was Shelley at Viareggio.

One of the surfing king-pins is known as Pretty Boy. He's got all the usual piercings and tattoos but also sports a small mirror and a bell through his nostrils. Locals reckon this is because he's a Trilski chain-smoker on about sixty a day. Heavy users of Trilski, like Pretty Boy, are prone to springing the odd feather and given to whistling.

Percy says he'll bring a van and clear out your garage. But he told me that he would have to be discreet as top grade A budgie seed is classed as an illegal substance.

Changing tack, as I mentioned, nurse Sophie's shaping up very nicely. She's become a dab hand on the tiller and the other night, in the Jag, I gave her an initial lesson in celestial navigation. We had enjoyed a pink gin or three in the Joan of the Wad, and later on she showed me how nifty she had become with a pair of pliers and a nob of Lurpak.

As I have mentioned in the past, Lurpak is as good as WD 40 on the moving parts of the bad 'un but, as you may recall, I pointed out that butter attracts flies and even the odd hornet (which your Catharine had rightly warned me about).

The other evening,, in a deck chair in the garden, watching the sun go down over the sea, I could well have ended up with a nasty sting in the nether regions had it not been for a prompt intervention by Albion.

He always sleeps with one eye open and he suddenly sprang to life, swallowing in a mighty gulp a formidably combative hornet.

By the way, Sophie says that should you be doing any more writing for Eastern bloc publishers, she'd very much like a sable coat, a case of Smirnoff, a barrel of Beluga and a cut-glass Bohemian chandelier. So if you'd kindly have a word with your Czech and Russian pals..

Aye

Lancing-Lancing

-

Dogs

Dear Admiral

Well, it's been quite a week. Percy the Pisky called in and spent a couple of hours clearing out the garage. He rolled a Trilski saying he had to sample it before he could make me an offer. Within a minute or two his eyes had glazed over and he was whistling like a kettle.

When he'd recovered, to my amazement he gave me £5000 in

well-thumbed fivers and declared it the finest Grade A Trilski he'd ever come across.

I'm sending you half the money which should keep you nicely stocked up on pink gin and Lurpak. I had a word with Bortsch 'n Tears about writing more stuff for their dreadful magazine, and said that now I was more familiar with their local customs, I'd be delighted to be paid in seed money.

I also inquired about Sophie's sable. Sadly, they could only offer me coney, which I felt was a bit lower deck for Sophie, who sounds an absolute bobby-dazzler. Doubtless you'll be instructing her in more sophisticated manoeuvres once she knows which way your bad 'un is buttered.

Mind your wash

George

-

Nest

George

I am afraid I have some shocking news. Customs & Excise raided Percy's Pets and closed it down. Pisky the Percy has done a bunk and a mountain of Trilski has been impounded.

Apparently, Percy was part of an international smuggling gang. He and his compatriots shot out of Mevagissey harbour in a high-powered *Sunseeker* in the early hours, believed to be heading for a Costa Lotta hideaway in Spain.

Mad-eyed hamsters have been running all over Polperro. They'd somehow escaped and nibbled through Percy's huge sacks of Trilski that he'd hidden near the gerbils at the back of the store.

Thank you for the cheque. Given the news, I think I'll refrain from cashing it until things have quietened down. At least Sophie's not strutting around in sable and knocking back the Smirnoff, which might have looked a tad suspicious.

Percy was seriously hooked on Trilski and Sophie says he had begun to sprout the odd feather. Albion had taken to giving him the odd nip, thinking he was quail. It might be wise to hose down your garage and button down the hatches

Lancing-Lancing
-

Dogs

Dear Admiral

I'm hoisting the storm cones and keeping a watch out for Customs & Excise. They might have my garage under surveillance and I'm trying not to panic.

To other matters. I accepted an Italian invite to see the restoration of a wooden 1926 gentleman's motor yacht built by Gilbert and McGill, the distinguished Glaswegian constructors.

She had fallen on hard times and had been towed into a Ligurian yard near San Remo for new planking and myriad other repairs. There were insufficient numbers of people who knew about working in wood, everything being glass fibre these days, so the yard had to import a small army of Corsican fishermen.

It should have been pretty obvious that such a move would result in labour problems, given the preference Corsicans have always shown for keeping things in the family.

Almost inevitably, one of the Corsicans stabbed his landlady, for carrying on with his brother's son, who's engaged to his daughter. The husband of the landlady blew a bulkhead, and led a raiding party. Six Corsicans and three Italians were hospitalised.

As you can imagine, progress on the refurbishment of the yacht was somewhat hampered. To cap it all, a huge lead keel which was being swung across the yard, detached itself from a crane and fell on Sheikh Abu Khaled's Bentley.

Mercifully, Khaled was out cruising at the time with his many wives on *Black Gold*, his new *Rip*. Had he not been so engaged, there could have been another oil war. As it was, he merely threw a wobbly when he returned to find that his Bentley had been transformed into a rough approximation of a spent Coca Cola can.

Marco Umberto, who runs the yard, locked himself in the lavatory and hit the Barolo, with the Sheikh and his minders hammering on the door, threatening to cut off his hands and have what was left of him flogged.

As the likelihood of afternoon tea and scones seemed pretty distant, I felt it prudent to beat a rather hasty exit.

Keep the kite filled

George

**

Two close friends of Lancing-Lancing are Lord and Lady Claremont. Elderly and impoverished, with little left but great courtesy and good manners, they are the charming possessors of a kindly air and the 48-room Tin Hall, a crumbling stately with leaking roof, doubtful plumbing and situated worryingly close to the edge of Dead Man's cliff, near to where Lancing-Lancing lives.

Edward Claremont is a former paratroop officer, while Wilhelmina, known as Minnie, chairs countless charities and is an indefatigable defender of the poor. They have three children, and through giving them a first class education, very little money.

Nest

George, my old friend

Thank you for your letter. Corsicans can be far worse than Mexicans, and you're quite right, it's all to do with this rather exaggerated sense of family with which they all seem hampered.

Sophie has thrown the bad 'un into the Jag and taken it into town for, ahem, running repairs, which means I'm trapped.

If anybody sees a leg on the back seat, they'll think she's a killer. Aldous Huxley wrote *Eyeless in Gaza*, so I'm now *Legless in Polperro*.

When Sophie returns, we'll sail the *George and Lily* up the creek and call in for a quick one at the Bosun's Locker. We might take Albion. He's a good sailor, though he can get rather sea-sick and tends to dribble. His teeth have become wonky with age, so at least he now refrains from gnawing through the sails and the sheets (boat ropes; he's not allowed in the bedroom).

We've had a bit of bother with these young retards partying on the beach until the small hours. They're part of the hooligan surf board set.

The other morning I found a spent plonker hanging from the Nellie Moser. The council said that before the cut-backs they'd have offered me counselling. Good job Albion didn't find it. I don't want that sort of thing being dragged across the Axminster.

Lord and Lady Claremont, from Rose Hall, just up the coast, are going bananas. Some young tearaway broke into their place. Eddie Claremont let him have it both barrels. He missed, but winged the chap who looks after what's left of the Friesians. Eddie was always a lousy shot. He bagged a beater some years ago, nothing terminal, just a few pellets in the posterior.

I must fly. I hear the Jag on the gravel. It'll be Sophie back with my leg, and not the Trilski Cop Squad, thank Providence. I have heard neither peep nor whistle of the absentee Percy Gang.

There seem to be a surfeit of Percy's in my life at the moment. What with Pet shop Percy, and the surfing Jonty who thinks he's Percy Bysshe Shelley, I'm beginning to get Percyitis, a rare condition for which there's no known cure,

Yours aye,

Lancing-Lancing
-

Dogs

Dear Admiral

I have been pondering on your vandal problem. If the sky were to rain stale Cornish pasties it could have a startling effect. Why not rig up a catapult and bombard the invaders on the beach below with pasties fired from your eyrie on the cliffs? Such missiles could be deadly. Stale pasties would have a brick-like velocity. Nobody would wish to be hit from a great height by a Cornish pasty, fresh or stale.

Some gossip for you: Stag Hake, the knot man, is not his real name. He changed it from Humphrey Bottom. And who could blame him?

The truth was revealed when Hake/Bottom fell into the drink at the London Boat Show at Excel a couple of weeks ago after imbibing a Morgan's or five. He was rushed to the Royal London for stomach pumping and a tetanus jab. Two Fingers Maltby accompanied him and spotted the name difference on the admission form.

You can imagine the jokes about Hake/Bottom getting himself tied up in knots over his name. O'Connor, the American designer from New York, said she had always thought that Hake/Bottom was a bum. Buttocks is threatening to expose him as Humphrey Bottom in Boat Puffery. It would be entertaining, if a little, shall we say, below the belt.

I ran into Buttocks the other day. She'd been on the chocolate creams and quite winded me. Hake/Bottom, for his part, is threatening to tell the world that Buttocks fills her *Puffery* magazine with advertorial, and, on a more personal note, that she needs to go on the Atkins diet or have surgery. He insists that he met more personable guards at his Yokohama prison camp after HMS *Valour* went down in '43.

Incidentally, I saw that an abandoned *Sunseeker* power boat had been found off Benidorm. The coastguards wondered if the Percy gang had swum ashore.

I have not discounted Spanish reports of feathered persons living in a forest near Alicante. Doubtless, in some sun-drenched corner, Pet shop Percy is whistling happily and learning to fly.

Check all stop cocks

George

Nest
George, old chap

Life has become a little grim in these parts. One used to nod off listening to the seagulls and the ocean. How different it is now. I have not had a wink because of the infernal din from these young surfers down on the beach.

An Old Bill raiding party turned up the other evening. But the Black Maria became stuck in the sand. The Council said they couldn't afford counselling for me but they're offering it to the young lunatics. Teams of hirsute shrinks in sandals want to know if the youngsters have had a deprived background. I wonder what was so terrible that they now feel compelled to hurl used plonkers into my rose garden? I don't know where they find the energy. One would have thought that after sniffing bottles of Gloy and smoking Trilski's they'd lie sated on the sand, arms round each other, watching the stars and swearing undying love.

Some local bigwigs have asked me to chair a so-called regeneration committee. Eddie Claremont said bugger regeneration, let's machine-gun the retards from the cliffs.

He said he'd done something similar during the North Africa campaign. There is a rum-looking chap whose joined the committee (he has a Mercedes franchise in Bromley and a million pound beach hut down here). He said he had heard rumours that a developer plans to build a marina for super-yachts and reckons the local powers that be have already had their palms greased.

You know the game: 'We'll give you a village hall so oldies can play ping-pong, more roundabouts than Milton Keynes, and a freebie cruise in the Bahamas for you and yours which nobody need know about. All we want is to dredge the harbour and build houses for foreign potentates. We'll call it Venice Springs, so it sounds like Miami'. It's similar to that which supermarkets have been doing for years.

I found my antennae bristling when a certain name was being bandied around, a chappie by the name of David McDougal. He's supposed to be the mystery developer. I think it wise to keep one's powder dry at this stage, discretion being everything. But I'd be grateful for anything you might glean on your radar.

Lancing-Lancing

PS: I like the JK Galbraith joke: 'Who the hell is Milton Keynes?'
-

Dogs

Dear Admiral

There'll be more bedrooms than berths if it's a David 'Call me Dave' McDougal development.

Flats, golf courses, pop-up brothels. Sales brochures in sepia tints, yachts and sunsets and blondes with long legs. It'll be bon voyage to the unspoiled Cornish coastline. McDougal bribes councils by giving them what think they can't live without: self-cleaning lavatories, pet crematoriums, free bus rides to supermarkets for the infirm.

He's also religious convert. Anglican turned Catholic, and they're always extreme. Big on committees and charity balls and aching for a Gong. Bursting with endless guff about corporate responsibility, team players, brand integrity, the bottom line (lap dancing).

His selling line is that it'll bring employment. Any impoverished council is always a sucker for that. In reality, a few poor souls will build the development and then be shooed away, leaving the odd shelf-stacker and cleaner earning a pittance.

McDougal doesn't pay any tax. The business is registered in his wife's name. She used to be called Tina, but changed it to India and now lives in the Cayman Isles.

He's big in double-glazing, but his latest venture is that fancifully known as a craft brewery, which, naturally, he'll flog when the time is ripe, as he has does with all his businesses. Did you see his donation to the government, just before they licensed round-the-clock drinking?

His main brand is a luminous orange drink called Gasket, much favoured by surfers.

'The police tried to control a baying mob but it had been on the Gasket,' was how Dr. Henry Limpswell, of the Royal Institute of Condensed Milk, described anti-social behaviour, in his evidence to the Home Affairs select committee, when it was looking into the Frinton riots.

Even small quantities of Gasket can induce frenzy. It's not just youngsters. An old codger threw herself off the roof of her care home shouting 'I'm a Super Gran, I can fly.' Another drove her handicapped car without due care in the frozen food aisle in Sainsbury's (in fairness to her, she told the magistrates she was teetotal and hadn't been herself since she ate poisonous chops).

If McDougall the Kilt is behind your marina, he can only be stopped by a sizeable hole beneath his water-line.

Arm the torpedoes

George

-

Nest

George, old friend

Heartening to know that one can count on stout shipmates when storm clouds gather. I haven't come across a pop-up brothel. It's a new one on me. What is that pops up?

'Call Me Dave 'McDougal's poison has already polluted the Beach Regeneration Committee from which I am now thinking of resigning.

It's my belief that some members have already taken McDougal's shilling and are now in his pocket. It beggars belief that Polperro has become a hot-bed of graft and corruption. After all, we're not talking Greece or Italy, but it's getting as bent as Botswana.

I know what you mean about religious converts. They can be alarming. We had one on HMS *Resolute*. On a misty night on the Bridge he was at the wheel when he suddenly keeled over.

65

He fell to the deck and started rolling around speaking in tongues, foaming at the gills, eyeballs everywhere. He said he'd witnessed a miracle. It was very difficult. You can't have somebody like that on the helm, you don't know where you might end up.

We thought at first he'd been hitting the altar wine. Turned out that in his time he'd tried a bit of everything: Jew, Muslim, Catholic, Greek Orthodox, a smidgeon of Buddhism.

He used to wander around the aft deck in a saffron robe ringing a bell. When he fell to the deck in the wheel-house he'd apparently become a Charismatic, with a bit of Zen thrown in. His cabin was all incense and candles and sitar music.

We had to have the poor chap helicoptered off, jabbering and salivating ten to the dozen. Last I heard he was working as a signal-man on a mountain railway in Kashmir, as one does.
Knowing that McDougall is on some sort of religious helter-skelter makes matters far worse.

Aye

Lancing-Lancing

-

Nest

Dear George

With McDougal and his plans – and the surfers in nightly swing on the sands – we feel besieged. Eddie Claremont wants a full scale assault and a landing on the beach. He talks of Arnhem and paratroopers and has erected a watch tower in his garden on the cliff.

From his clifftop garden he shines a huge spotlight on the revellers below. But instead of deterring the rascals the beam further excites them. When it's switched on cheering erupts and they cavort like dervishes caught in its glare, catapulting pebbles up at the lamp and driving Claremont to near insanity. The whole place looks like Camp on Blood Island.

Half the locality wants the youngsters exterminated. Others

like the cash they bring. The landlord of the Joan of the Wad says he's making so much money selling McDougall's Gasket that he's bought a timeshare on the Algarve.

Trilski Grade A budgie seed is changing hands for huge amounts. Everybody has little mirrors and bells hanging off their nose. I haven't seen anybody sprouting feathers but there's an awful lot of whistling.

Here at the Nest, once a peaceful little haven, hails of used Johnnies continue to be thrown into the garden. When one opens the curtains in the morning they're hanging limp and forlorn on the rose bushes.

Sophie collects them in her yellow washing-up gloves (and looks *very* trim in them). She's a lovely girl, but this rubber bombardment is getting her down. They're all colours and in the early morning dew they look like a Damien Hirst creation.

The other day, some jobsworth from the council complained that Sophie had put them in the wrong bin. It's come to something when you have to sort out and recycle used plonkers.

Lancing-Lancing

-

Nest

George, dear boy

I have already mentioned that I was thinking of giving the Cornish Regeneration Committee the heave-ho. Well, I've done so. I didn't care for the cut of their collective jibs, so I decided to jump ship.

Things came to a head when I was approached about heading up a new and more radical cell which called itself the *Real* Cornish Regeneration Committee. They wore black hoods and lured me into the church vestry, trying to disguise their voices.

Lord Claremont was their leader. He didn't fool me for a moment. You could tell Eddie's bark at fifty paces. He further betrayed himself when he began talking about stocking up on sticky bombs. At first, I thought he said sticky bums, as it was so difficult to tell what he was saying.

He was quite beside himself, and foaming at the mouth (not that I could see his mouth, his face being hidden in a balaclava) to such a degree that he couldn't get his words out. It's all become too much for him. He's now several knots short of a sheet.

Aye

Lancing-Lancing

-

Dogs

Dear Admiral

It might be wise to put clear water between yourself and Lord Claremont. If he's going off his rocker one would not wish to be caught in the bang.

I have been adding to the 'Call me Dave' file. One discovery I've made is that he's a legendary drinker, but he's as tight as a sporran's clasp, though he likes a dram or four if somebody else is paying.

I had forgotten about the City saga which involved the ancient Mission for Distressed Mariners (MDM). It had been around since the Plimsoll Line and McDougal thought he could make money out of it.

He took it over and launched it on the stock market. But there was the usual jiggery-pokery which attaches to all his dealings. Sailors pension pots were raided, weeping widows of deceased mariners threw themselves under passing tramp steamers and there was rampant insider trading.

Dimitri Costos, who 'Call me Dave' appointed as the chief executive, claimed that he had been an officer in the Greek navy. It turned out he'd run a pub in Palmer's Green.

'Call Me Dave' emerged unblemished, as always, smelling of gorse and heather. When the scandal subsided he started another charity called Alcoholic All Stars which dealt, in the main, with Gasket addicts. He ended up with an OBE (Other Buggers Efforts). It's not a knighthood, but he's on his way. Not bad, eh? He gets an OBE for setting up a charity which helps those whose brains he's addled by flogging them Gasket. It has a certain symmetry, don't you think?

As you have probably seen in the newspapers, he recently laid claim to a defunct Highland clan, and now calls himself David Hamish McDougal OBE of that Ilk.

He's so lucky that if he fell down a lavatory he'd come up with a gold watch and chain.

Mind the shallows

George

-

Nest

George

I'm beginning to think that Mc or Mac is a handle for any nasty piece of work. McButtocks, McDougal, the world seems full to bursting with McBuggers.

Do you remember Admiral Byng? He was far from being a McByng. Sensibly, he wouldn't engage the French because he was outnumbered, a judicious decision to save his men. But the Admiralty still hanged him. Voltaire said it was what the English did to their admirals to encourage the others.

One thing's for sure, if 'Call me Dave' McDougal showed up here, he'd be strung up from the pub sign at the Joan of the Wad.

Our golden sands look like Omaha beach in Normandy. Claremont's watch tower looms over the cliffs. There's barbed wire and searchlights and everybody's high on Trilski, shaking the little bells and mirrors on the end of their noses, plastered out of their minds on Gasket.

Lancing-Lancing

Dogs

Admiral

I implore you to be careful. You have a responsibility to Sophie as well as yourself. These things can get out of hand (counter-measures, not Sophie). Might be worth boarding up The Nest and evacuating: you, Sophie and Albion. After all, it's only what so many people had to do in the Blitz.

George

-

Nest

Dear George

You're a valiant friend. But retreat is not in my nature. Admittedly, though, everybody's jumpy. There was a hell of a bang last night. I quite thought we were being shelled and headed for the cubby hole under the stairs, dragging Sophie and the dog with me.

People were running around saying the Real Regeneration Committee had let a bomb off, that Claremont and his pals had gone too far, that they'd really done it this time.

Turned out it was the vet's potting shed that had gone up. He says the nightly racket from the beach had shaken up his elderflower wine. Blew the roof fifty-feet in the air. Destroyed the lot. Rhubarb, cabbage, even his filthy beetroot plonk, a sort of faux Burgundy.

Last year Chez Beetroot had me in the Heads for a week. At least now we won't have to endure the nightmare of his annual tasting ceremony. Not a bad chap, the vet. He's been good to Albion, sorting out his wheezing and his molars. Ever tried flossing a bulldog? Not easy, I can tell you. But his wine .. well, dear oh dear, that *really* is quite a different matter.

We now have a row of vending-machines selling spearmint Johnnies, installed by the lifeboat station. There are Aids and Skunk posters everywhere. It's all rather reminiscent of Jakarta. I was there when that frightful chap and his unspeakable wife – the one had a shoe fetish – were in control. A very rum lot, they were. I have to say, Indonesia was never one of my favourite postings.

A luminous orange barrage balloon floats overhead advertising Gasket. Lady Claremont – dear old Minnie – says Eddie is trying to buy an anti-aircraft gun to bag it. Half-starved Rottweilers are running loose in Eddie's garden. There was a nasty do the other day with some poor devil who had simply dropped by to read the electricity meter at the Hall.

Some cheeky little blighters on the beach asked Lady Claremont to judge a culinary contest. In these parts, her hare and rabbit pie is legendary and she was totally charmed by the invite. She thought that peace was beginning to break out, at long last. But she was mortified to find that it was a wet tee-shirt contest, and that jugs and hair had nothing to do with an Aga.

Yours aye

Lancing-Lancing

-

Dogs

Dear Admiral

I'm sorry to hear of your continuing problems. I have more intelligence on McDougall of that Ilk.

I met Tim Luckell at his sail loft in Great Yarmouth. The loft was nearly scuttled when McDougall read in *Puffery* that it needed capital. McDougall arrived as its saviour and raised money by exaggerating the accounts. The loft could not meet expectations and McDougall sailed off with the cash which he laundered through one of his dodgy old folks' homes (did you see his Heavenly Rest centre at Frinton had been raided by the boys in blue, investigating unexplained screams?).

Luckell was left to clear up the mess. McDougal left no finger-prints and nothing could be proved. But Luckell had come to the attention of the authorities and he's been trying to cope with a

Force Ten ever since. 'Elf and Safety dropped in and insisted that his sail stitchers wore goggles, crash helmets and wicket keepers' gloves. Consequently, a new suit of sails for a yawl looked like a pair of badly-sewn Long Johns.

Luckell's now got Common Market inspectors from Brussels poring all over him. I mentioned how you loved Belgians, and he said you ought to pop over to the loft for coffee and patisserie and some of those bitter chocolates from Bruges. I said you'd be delighted!

Swill the Orlop

George

-

The Nest

Dear George

Thank you for your thoughtful suggestion but I'll give the raiding party from Belgium a wide berth. Good to know you've made Luckell's number. He's a nice fellow.

This is going to be a very short note, for which I apologise. Nurse Sophie's just come flying through – and goodness, she looks *so* fetching in her crisp white uniform and her rakish little cap – to tell me that we're due for tea and sympathy at Grimbles boat yard, as was.

The yard's been taken over and the Grimbles have disappeared back to Transylvania or some such. A new woman called Posie Billing is now in charge. I'd never heard of her, but apparently she came ninth in some type of international paddle-board (what is it?) contest in Galicia.

First dispatches are hardly encouraging. She's establishing a reputation as a harridan of the first order and is selling burgees printed with a skull and crossbones and peaked caps bearing the motif 'I'm the Skipper'. Please God! Sophie has taken to calling her Posie Unwilling and had to restrain Albion from giving her a welcoming nibble.

I had failed to log 'Posie's Welcome Aboard Party', as she bills it, and about which I am already having doubts, knowing that the 'deliciously wide range of free wines' are being supplied by the vet, who's been hard at work in his replacement potting shed, the previous one having blown up, if you recall.

The vet has an exciting new hobby: as well as persisting with his poisonous vino, he now also cultivates mushrooms in the dank and dark of the basement at his home. There was a vile rumour doing the rounds that his wines will be accompanied by a warm version of his unique Dead Man Mushrooms served on home-baked olive bread, lovingly made by Penelope, his equally talented and enthusiastic wife. As you can imagine, I can't wait. I must now cut and run (always something of a trial with my bad 'un).

Lancing-Lancing
-

When Patricia Windthrush moved into the redundant 16th century cliff-top church of St Ignatius and the Properly Righteous, with its stunning sea views, and not far from Lancing-Lancing's home, she and her husband, the modernist garden designer, Chuck 'Buddy' Holden, from Chicago, had not anticipated the nightly mayhem which now engulfed the area.

'Peculiar Patricia', as she was known, largely because of her early morning habit of running up and down Dead Mans Beach naked apart but for a bobble hat, was the sister of William 'Windy' Windrush, a high-ranking civil servant in the Ministry of Rivers, Ecological and Rural Affairs.

Some months after Peculiar and Buddy had completed the conversion of their steeple into a glass-topped tower, where they could lie in bed staring at the galaxy and practising astronomy, and renamed the church, Telescope House, there came an astonishing turn of events.

The authorities, armed with a range of protective notices, suddenly moved in on the corner of Cornwall which had been plagued by raucous revellers.

George Steel and the Admiral were delighted, though both were of the view that perhaps the well-connected Peculiar had had a quiet word with Windy, her brother. Windy's garden, in Church Street, Chelsea, had recently been given a radical makeover by the shiniest star in the horticultural firmament, Buddy Bolden. Buddy had created a Japanese garden, with a small forest of even smaller Bonsai trees, a bubbling stream, fountains that changed colour, a little known species of giant koi carp and the odd pink Flamingo strutting about. Neither Buddy nor Windy were sure that Pink Flamingoes were entirely 'authentic', in a Japanese garden, but they looked so striking, nobody cared.

Buddy would normally have charged tens of thousands for his services, especially as he now had his own TV show, Don't Be A Clod, but he created, and even 'curated' its planting, all for free, as a special favour to his influential brother-in-law.

Dogs

Dear Admiral

I am so pleased with the leader in *The Times*. There's no doubt that to have the area given Super Coast status (rarely deployed and immeasurably more powerful than such instruments as ordinary National Trust protection) would solve so many problems. It would force out the glue-sniffing surfers and stop this rather nasty outbreak of Johnny-flinging. Between you and I, three cheers for Peculiar! Long may she enjoy her bobble hat and her naked scampering on Dead Mans beach.

Now that Brussels has joined the fray – and of course I am sensitive to your reservations about chocolate and statues that wee – you will have an opportunity to make a persuasive case about noise, pollution, vandalism, Trilski and Gasket.

It is most promising that the 'granting of any new planning permissions will be subject to the most intense scrutiny.'

This is precisely the approach needed if one is to put a spoke in Call me Dave's wheel. The bureaucrats who are heading your way to see for themselves the severity of the problem, would be unimpressed by the incident of Albion and the peace protester's tackle. Had Albion's molars been in better shape, he could have been facing the Chair.

My advice is this: Albion, lovable though he is, should be muzzled and caged for the duration of their inspection. This should also apply to Lord Claremont's Rottweillers. It would be unwise to risk savaging a member of the delegation. Claremont's watch-tower should be dismantled, the barbed wire rolled up and the Belgian bureaucrats wined and dined on anything but pasties and what's left of your vet's exploding elderflower.

As one who has to cut daily through forests of PR balderdash, as I go about my ordinary journalistic duties, I know the importance of spin and presentation.

It is paramount that the more radical members of your Home Guard look and act as if they are as docile as sheep. They must come across as confused innocents, bewildered old geezers, caught in the eye teeth of unfettered free enterprise.

You and your embattled cohorts must appear as frightened, benign, silver-haired victims of unbridled capitalism.

It would be worth claiming that your collective health has deteriorated, and that if something isn't done soon, you'll end up as yet another costly burden on the NHS. It's always worth dragging in the NHS.

Lord Eddie Claremont is a loose cannon. He should be gagged and spirited away for the duration of the Brussels inspection. Any talk of machine-guns, mortars and paratroopers on beaches would scupper your campaign.

As ever

George

-

The Nest

Dear George

Thank you for your advice. Eddie Claremont means well but remains a bit of a problem. The Hall's a big place so we're going to keep him under lock and key in the loft until the bureaucrats have done their stuff.

Nobody's been up in the roof at the Hall for years. But as long as we keep him fed and watered, and the vet says he's got plenty of morphine if he gets obstreperous, he should be fine.

We're not expecting the Brussels lot to hang around forever, so we won't keep him incarcerated longer than is necessary.

Eddie means well and he can be the most charming of men – especially when he's not ranting and pelting all and sundry with stale pasties. He's taken to dunking the pasties in vinegar and baking them in a hot Aga to make them bullet-like. He says it's a technique which brought him success as a boy when he won the Eton conker champ medal.

Incidentally, will Sophie and I be seeing you and Catharine at Cowes this year? I do hope so.

Top-ho!

Lancing-Lancing

-

Dogs

Dear Admiral

Sadly, we'll be unable to make Cowes. I'll be in New Zealand gauging the health of the Kiwi boat industry. If one thinks how many super yachts are in the world today, and how the market has been collared by Italy, France, Germany, Holland, America, Uncle Tom Cobley et al, it makes you want to head to Tahiti, like Gauguin.

Question: where is Britain in this bonanza? Answer: with one or two honourable exceptions, almost nowhere.

Were we not the world's greatest maritime country? Are we not an island nation? Did we not have the world's greatest navy? The finest shipbuilding skills? Did the world not queue at our door for us to build their navies and cruise ships?

The cruise industry has grown like topsy. Vast numbers of

cruise ships have been built. But by whom? Super yachts, owned by potentates and tax dodgers, have been another boom business. And how do they thank Britain for giving them such a cosy tax climate? By having their craft built in anywhere but Britain.

You can't move in the Solent for half-submerged bankers and high-tech billionaires who seem better at feathering their nests than being competent sailors. And the majority fall off continental-built boats. Britain's economy seems to hinge now on call centres, charity shops, hairdressers and Albanians who wash cars.

God bless all who sail in her

George

-

Nest

George, dear boy

You make good points. Cornwallis, Boscowan, Keppel, all sublime sailors. They must be spinning in their graves.

Steering a different course, you're right, I will definitely keep Albion incarcerated for the visit by the Brussels bureaucrats. He can be a naughty boy when he chooses to show off his new molars which the vet's fitted.

Albion gets on well with Sophie, but like me he has a thing about uniforms. He backed her into the larder the other day and the poor child became hysterical. It took a while to convince her that he was only being his playful self. Thankfully, she was in her nursing whites (guaranteed to get one's flag up). Imagine if she'd be done up as a nun. You know how he feels about black.

Lancing-Lancing

-

Nest

Dear George

So sorry you couldn't make Cowes. Sheikh Khaled was moored

offshore with his several wives on *Black Gold*, all cheetah-skin wallpaper and mirrors over the bed. He's more horsey than yottie. I read that he'd had one of his jockeys thrashed for bringing up the rear at Newmarket, a habit commonplace in desert countries.

Cowes is now sponsored by the milk marketing outfit with yachts called '*Skim Off,*' and '*Gold Top for Regularity*.'

One craft proved especially competitive: the firm of 'Cramp 'we do it digitally' Undertakers, sponsored *Six feet Under,* with black sails and hull and crewed by Germans dressed all in black. Albion came close to a breakdown.

The Australians got in a fracas at a party thrown by Vulture Derivatives, which sounds an alarming company. Some fellow who was a hedge fund manager, whatever that is, received a nasty right-hook from Buttocks, after he dared to be mildly critical of *Puffery*. She's quite scary, and so muscular she must be working overtime with Gloria and the chocolate creams.

I tried to make conversation with some hedge fund type. When I said mine needing trimming, and had been festooned with flying Johnnies, he gave me a mind-numbing lecture about bonds, base rates and two-year trackers, of which I didn't have the foggiest, and still don't.

When I asked about yachting, he said he had always liked sailors and was keen to promote Gay mortgages. He wore pink trousers and a blazer with gold buttons dress a la mode Two Fingers.

The usual insults flew around about Aussies and sheep, and the Swiss having to cheat at sailing as they are landlocked and noted only for Heidi, cow bells and as McButtocks was quick to point out, Toblerone.

Stag Hake/Bottom demonstrated his knots on dear old Hubert Skidmore (now well north of 90 and Commodore of the Royal Island Club; totally gaga, of course).

I'm afraid his advancing years couldn't save him. Hake/Bottom showed him no mercy and soon had him done up like a kipper, bound hand and foot.

He left the poor old bugger writhing under a table in a corner of the marquee. I tried to free him, but it would have needed shears. Hake/Bottom was the only one who might have helped, but by then he'd hit the Morgan's and couldn't tell a reef knot from a bow line.

I also met an unhinged American called Bugsy who said he ran some crackpot company called Dead Serious TV, of which I've never heard.

He's making what he calls a reality show which goes by the name of *Big Sailor*. Ten nobodies are cast adrift on a raft in the Atlantic with limited victuals. Viewers vote on who should be given provisions. The programme returns each week to see who's died.

Bugsy said he was coming to Polperro to make a series called *Surf 'n Sex*. Sophie was in earshot, so I told him to keep his voice down. I'll heed your advice about diplomacy and the EU lot. But if Bugsy and his film crew appear I might be tempted to let Albion demonstrate his rebuilt gnashers.

Yours aye,

Lancing-Lancing

-

Dogs

Dear Admiral

I'm sorry we missed Cowes. It sounds fun. A pal in Brussels says there's intense interest in the Cornish project. You might get compensation. The money would help Lord and Lady Claremont buy a new roof and you could afford a further makeover for Albion (hair transplant? Teeth whitening?). McDougal would be driven back to the Cayman Isles, where he could shove his bagpipes up his Ilk. I tipped off Harry Bent of FAT (Fogeys against Tax) about McDougal's residential homes and the unexplained screaming. Mr. Bent, who can be extreme, said he'll picket them with, *er*, squads of flying pensioners.

I've never seen *Big Sailor*, but most TV these days seems to be made by the deranged for the abnormal.

Did you see on the news that three people had been spotted flying over the Bay of Cadiz? With no sign of a plane. Where *is* the Whistling Percy Gang? There's now an international manhunt underway for the Pimpernel Piskies.

George

**

One of Lancing-Lancing's most renowned adventures was an ambitious balloon trip. He and Albion, in the wicker-basket of the balloon Joan of the Wad, negotiated lift-off from the vegetable plot at Seagulls Nest. It was a momentous scene witnessed by a large contingency of newspaper and television reporters. Lancing-Lancing was to fly across the Atlantic to the United States. The flight was sponsored by Radio Pisky, the commercial station which serves Cornwall. The balloon had a transmitter by which the Admiral could send live reports back to the station and to its star disc-jockey, Frank the Lemon.

Broadcast 1

'Calling, calling Radio Pisky .. this is Lancing-Lancing in the balloon *Joan of the Wad* broadcasting about three miles off Cornwall .. I hope you can hear me, my bulldog Albion seems to have become a little hysterical, he's barking like a mad 'un and trying bite his way out of the basket .. for God's sake, Albion, will you please, please be quiet! .. so sorry about that .. he's obviously trying to come to terms with being a ballooning bulldog .. everything is proceeding satisfactorily .. gentle airs and we're floating nicely through the heavens .. I think I'll just turn up the burner (a loud whooshing noise as Lancing-Lancing adjusts the burner which gives the balloon more height) .. it's a lovely sunny day .. colder than on the ground .. but all in all perfect weather for playing around with + my dirigible. Over and out."

Broadcast 2

'*Joan of the Wad* calling Radio Pisky .. hallo Pisky .. can you hear me? This is one of my night-time broadcasts. I'm cruising along quite nicely through the clouds. It's a bit of a murky night, not much of a moon. Albion has got over his air-sickness. He's now slumped in a corner of the basket, snuggled up amid the tins of baked beans which will soon provide my supper. I'm looking forward to cooking them over my little stove, though the weight of the tins has undoubtedly hampered the flying qualities of the balloon. If the balloon should need to be lightened, I might be forced into throwing some of them overboard and into the drink. I hope there aren't any fishing boats down there .. it's too dark to see .. but it would be dreadful if some poor chap was hit by a tin of baked beans when he was just out and about doing a spot of fishing and generally minding his own business. I like to think he'd have taken cover as I've got my trombone and he might have heard us coming. If there is a such a fellow down there .. he'd be staring up into the dark heavens and probably couldn't see the balloon hidden in the nimbus cumulus or whatever these banks of cloud are called .. but he'd have heard the strains of Muskrat Ramble coming out of the sky, just before being zonked by a can of Heinz 57. Albion seems to have adopted a rather sulky, resigned demeanour. He's pretending to be asleep, in his usual way, but I know him too well, he has one eye open and it's fixed on me and he's giving me a fierce and unblinking stare. The evening seems to have closed in very quickly .. the clouds are beginning to clear .. there's the odd star .. it's getting colder .. and I'm now wearing two layers of jumpers beneath my duffel-coat. Below me I can hear the ocean .. and just about make out the white crests of the waves. .. all in all .. we're making steady progress. This is *Joan of the Wad* for Radio Pisky .. signing off for now .. over and out ..'

Broadcast 3

'This is the balloon *Joan of the Wad* calling Radio Pisky .. come in Pisky .. Are you receiving me?' (at this juncture there is loud hissing and interference and a distant voice saying: "Yes, yes Admiral .. it's Lemon here..").'Some ruddy maniac in a jet fighter just went over at rooftop level and nearly shook us to pieces .. I s'pose it was on one of those low-level training flights from Truro (wild barking and growling can be heard in the background) Albion be quiet! .. poor chap was a little disturbed by the roar of the jet (more growling) .. I just hope that they know we're out here. Over and out ..'

Broadcast 4

'*Joan of the Wad* calling .. hallo Radio Pisky .. are you receiving me?' The station DJ Frank the Lemon replies: "Clear as a bell sailor boy .. Frank the Lemon here of good old Radio Pisky, or Radio Pesky as its sometimes known .. and we're all ears." .. 'Well, how do you do Mr. Lemon. There's a bit of a wind suddenly kicked up .. and we're being blown about all over the place. The compass seems to have gone slightly haywire .. hang on a moment while I turn up the burner, get a bit of height (whooshing noise) .. yes, that's better, getting a touch too close to the sea .. whoops! Now we're shooting up again .. like a bloody rocket .. Albion's dribbling like mad .. and I'm holding on to the basket like grim death .. I'd better be off Mr. Lemon .. things are getting a little bit tricky .. over and out for now..'

Frank the Lemon tells his audience: "It sounds as if things are getting slightly awkward .. that's our fave Admiral live from his balloon, *The Joan of the Wad*, somewhere high up above the angry, boiling, freezing waters of the mighty Atlantic ocean .. rather him than me folks, sounds as if the old boy is having a bit of time of it. Kiss me Hardy, that's what I say! Yes indeedy .. anyway, I was going to play you '*Up, Up and Away*', but we felt that was a bit too ice-cream corny Cornetto, not that that's ever stopped us before, no indeedy not! not on Radio Pisky, no indeedy! So here's that lovely little lady from Kangaroo land, it's kooky wooky Kylie with *Lucky, Lucky, Lucky*' .. and let's hope that's exactly what our Admiral is .."

Broadcast 5

'*Joan of the Wad* calling Radio Pisky .. the compass is shot and so is the altitude thingie which tells me how high we are .. it's registering that we're lower than I thought .. it can't be right ...' (there follows a mighty crash, the splashing of water, a great deal of yapping, barking and cursing, and another, unknown voice shouts: 'What the Hell's happening ..?' Then total silence.

Mr. Lemon said: "Well the old boy seems to be in real trouble now .. we'll get back to him as soon as we can .. and here are the Strolling Bones with *No Satisfaction* .. and it sounds as if that's the case with our fave ballooning admiral .. We're prayin' for you sailor boy .. heavens above, we're really prayin .."

It transpired that Lancing-Lancing had gone down in the drink and the basket had been dragged across the waves before becoming entangled on a fishing boat out of Falmouth. But a howling gale helped the dirigible to tear itself free and after an alarming moment or two it was once again airborne, but only just. Once he was up in the clouds, it took the Admiral a long time to sort out the chaos that had ensued in the basket. Some vital supplies, including a dozen cans of dog food, had been lost in the incident.

Broadcast 6

'This is *Joan of the Wad* calling Mr. Lemon and Radio Pisky .. come in please .. well, Albion and I had a little altercation for minute or two .. but I got the burner back on, filled up the balloon, and we're sailing along very nicely now .. though Albion does look a little mad-eyed about the whole thing and he's slobbering a lot. There's another slight problem, it's very much windier than it was and I've got a feeling that we've rather changed direction .. although it's so ruddy black up here in this night sky that it's difficult to make out exactly what's happening or where we are .. if only I had a rudder .. we're also in thick cloud which doesn't really help things. Anyway, we're fine at the moment, I'm just going to light the little camping stove and see if I can get a few basic victuals on the go .. it's always a slightly precarious operation .. especially when one is bouncing around as we are .. but I think a few hot beans will help keep out the cold. If you hear an enormous bang you'll know we've blown up – although it's more likely to be something along the lines of a slow crackle and a pop if I manage to set the basket alight. Only joking, of course! I wouldn't want to upset the listeners. On another question, Mr. Lemon, you very kindly asked me to choose a favourite piece of music .. well, there have been one or two distractions as you've probably gathered .. so I haven't given it the degree of attention that I ought .. but I think I would like to hear the clarinetist Mr. Jimmy Noone playing *Indian Love Call*. It's a most haunting and rather soothing piece. I think it would help to calm Albion down. He's taken to grinding his teeth again. It's probably anxiety. Noone has a very lovely, rather watery tone, which I s'pose is appropriate .. if you can't find anything by Noone then look for something by Johnny Dodds – another fine clarinetist .. and failing that you could, of course, come up with anything by the quite wonderful trombonist, Kid Ory. Before I sign off, I'd be very grateful, Mr. Lemon, if you could contact the fishing boat. I think it was called something like *Happy Days*, but I wasn't sure, as I only saw it momentarily as I was being dragged across the wheelhouse,, before we got rather tangled up in his mast and radar aerials. Please give my huge apologies to the skipper .. I've an idea the basket did a bit of damage to his cabin. Over and out ..'

Broadcast 7

'Calling Pisky Radio .. this is the balloon *Joan of the Wad* .. dawn has come up, the clouds are clearing, and something quite amazing has occurred. We have changed course completely, the winds must have shifted in the night .. and we now appear to be back overland .. down below I think it's Truro, yes, it's definitely Truro, not the United States, sadly .. we seem to be dropping rather rapidly .. I can see people quite clearly now .. they're waving their arms .. Oh dearie, dearie me! We seem to be heading for a spot of bother .. must fly, as they say .. over and out ..'

There followed a loud screaming noise, fabric being ripped to shreds, the distinctive roar and whoosh of the gas burner, and a sudden, piercing cry from Lancing-Lancing.

Broadcast 8
'Come in Radio Pisky .. well, I'm afraid this looks like curtains .. but what an adventure it's been! .. we've had a little bit of a mishap with the top of Truro Cathedral .. the *Joan of the Wad* has draped herself around the spire, the weather-cock is poking me in a most unfortunate place which I don't want to mention on the radio .. and I'm hanging upside down, clinging on to Albion, who has an unhappy air about him. The basket broke away, but before it fell to the ground I managed to grab the transmitter. I don't mind telling you, Mr. Lemon, that with having to hold both Albion and the transmitter, my hands are rather full. From what I can see the basket appears to have fallen through the conservatory of the Dean and Chapter's house. I fear it's caused some damage. From up here it looks as if the conservatory has been bombed. I can see an awful lot of vicars rushing around, cassocks flying in the wind. There's a large bird of prey, only a foot or two away from me, and he's watching me with a very beady eye – I think it's a falcon. It seems to be flexing its talons in a slightly worrying way. Probably thinks I'm up here trying to steal its eggs. I can see the nest quite clearly. There's a small camera looking at me. I think this must be the Westward Ho! TV people who have been giving their viewers live coverage of the bird on its nest. Now that I appear to be on camera they'll have something more interesting to look at than a bird's nest. I'm sorry to be such a frightful nuisance, but here come the doughty chaps from the fire brigade .. with their extending ladders .. they're out to try and untangle me. I think the time has come for Albion and myself to sign off ..so, from the balloon *Joan of the Wad*, what's left of it, I'd like to thank all my supporters .. and particularly you, Mr. Lemon, and Radio Pisky. For the very last time .. this really is goodbye, au revoir if you like, though I don't think I'll be trying the trip again, over and out.'

The adventure saw Truro Cathedral become an immediate magnet for tourists. In the weeks that followed thousands of trippers arrived by car and coach to climb the hundreds of steps which led to the top of the spire, all the visitors seeking selfies with the badly bent weather-cock, determined to witness at close quarters the exact spot where Lancing-Lancing impaled himself.

The surprise fillip to church funds paid for a new organ and covered the cost of rebuilding the conservatory at the Deanery. Fridge magnets, and lapel badges, in the shape of a balloon bearing Lancing-Lancing's likeness, and that of Albion, with his fangs bared, became a best-seller.

The Kennel Club

Paddington

Dear Admiral Lancing-Lancing

Given the publicity generated by your balloon exploits, and the fact that Albion has become – as have you, an international celebrity – we would like both of you to be our special guests of honour at Crufts, the world's most prestigious dog show. I would be most grateful if you could let me know if this idea appeals to you, and I enclose the relevant timetable and details

Many congratulations to you and Albion. Though, personally, I have always been head over heels in love with Tibetan Mastiffs, which is probably why I never married, there has always been a special place in my heart for the great British bulldog.

Yours in anticipation

Monica Howling (Gen. Sec & vice-pres. Tibetan Mastiff section).
-

The Nest

Dear Ms. Howling

Albion and I are most flattered by your kind invitation and have great pleasure in accepting. Albion, however, can sometimes be a little unsociable (I think his bouts of grumpiness are to do with his teeth and his age as much as anything) and I have some minor concerns about how he will react to being in the company of so many other dogs. Perhaps it might be possible for you to give me a little reassurance about such questions, after all I imagine it is a far from unique worry on the part of all the other dog owners at the show.

As you probably know, or have read about, he was a very naughty boy when we were invited to take part in the BBC TV *One Man and his Dog* programme. The shepherd said he hardly recognised several of his flock. It was my own fault for allowing Albion his freedom.

Yours aye

Lancing-Lancing

-

Kennel Club

Dear Admiral

First of all, let me say that I am delighted that you and Albion will be able to attend Crufts. Some owners keep their animals caged or gently sedated (though they're not supposed to, of course). Others rely on stout leads to keep their dogs in check. I am sure Albion will be well-behaved, but if he proves wayward, well, it won't be the first time, and it won't be the last, that doggies can be troublesome. At Crufts we have become adroit at coping with such difficulties. Please do not become too exercised about canine frailties; we are used to them, and know how to handle such problems.

From what I read, the mauling of both the sheep and the shepherd was not your fault.

As I understand it, you slipped over in the mud, with Albion pulling you along, until finally – after you had put up the bravest of fights to hang on to him – he at last managed to break free and set off after the sheep. When it was all over, he looked such a scoundrel covered in all that wool.

There was surprise at the Kennel Club that a bulldog could move so quickly, as fast as an athlete. One or two people wondered, quite unfairly, if he was on drugs. Some of our members said Bolt would be as good a name as Albion.

It was extraordinary how the sheep scattered and fled, while the shepherd, poor man, was left to confront Albion. He shouldn't have tried to beat him off with his crook. It was that which put Albion in a huff. Had that not been the case, I don't think the shepherd would have ended up in A&E. The BBC said they had never had such record ratings.

The world adores Albion, even when he is being naughty and at his most – *tenacious*. As his balloon exploits have shown, he is, like Tom Cruise, made of special stuff. I am thrilled to hear that the Bishop of Truro is going to give Albion a special doggie blessing at the Cathedral. We will all be praying that he behaves himself.

We're so looking forward to seeing the two of you.

Very best wishes

Monica

–

The Nest

Dear Monica

You have, to a degree, put my mind at rest. I am still worried, however, about the Cathedral blessing, given that Albion has a well-known thing about men in black, and there will be a lot of churchmen and choristers attired thus. If he does manage to behave himself, and if I can control him – he is capable of extraordinary pulling power, which I know is a misused phrases these days – it will be, given that it's an ecclesiastical fixture in Albion's increasingly busy diary, a *miracle*.

Lancing-Lancing

The Nest

Dear Monica

A week or two has elapsed since we last communicated. You will have read about Albion's disgraceful behaviour.

The trigger point came when I was holding him at the font and the Bishop sprinkled him with Holy water. Once he had the Bishop's sacred ring between his teeth there was no stopping him, even though the Bish was screaming in agony. Finally, Albion wrenched the ring off and swallowed it. Fortunately, the Bishop's finger didn't look too bad, all things considered. But the heavy ring was encrusted with emeralds and centuries old, so Sophie, my companion, had to keep an eye out when she took him for a walk (not pleasant, looking for a Bishop's ring while poring over a pooper-scooper).

Eventually, it passed, but only after the local vet gave him a laxative comprising his notorious beetroot wine containing bits of broken Bonios, which to my mind looked rather like tomato soup with croutons.

In Albion's defence, as with the shepherd and his crook, the Bishop might have got off more lightly had he refrained from setting about him with his staff. For a man of God, he certainly had a temper on him, rolling around wrestling with Albion in front of the altar, while most of the parishioners legged it, with those who remained baying like savages for either the dog or the Bish to win.

Given this latest outrage, you might wish to rescind our invite to Crufts. I would rather you spoke candidly, and I shall not be in the least offended if you have had second thoughts.

Yours

Lancing-Lancing

The Kennel Club

Dear Admiral

In no way can Albion be blamed for the fracas at the Cathedral. Nor would my colleagues and I wish to withdraw our invitation to the show.

At the kennel Club and Crufts we are not the sort of people who would abandon a doggy in his time of need. The suggestion by the Neighbourhood Watch committee, no member of which was even in the church at the time of the affray, that Albion be put down, is both wicked and preposterous.

As *The Times* asked, in its magnificent leader column: ' Latratu demens', when is a Cyclops not a Cyclops? Albion is a noble creature with the jutted-jaw, steely-eyed determination of a canine Churchill. He personifies the indomitable spirit of England, what's left of it.

With all those jewels on the Bishop's ring, Albion's must have been the most precious poop in history. Well done to him. What a mighty effort it must have taken.

In the Kennel Club we have a tame lawyer (known in the office as Fang). He is on stand-by and fully primed, ready to spring into action like a Finnish Spitz, if any busy-body dog-hating psychotic in Neighbourhood Watch should try to pursue their murderous vendetta.

If poor Albion could defend himself he would be a Rumpole, a Bulldog of the Bailey.

One has to ask, as does Fang: can a Bishop's ring ever be worth the life of a bulldog? That, I think, puts everything into perspective. Here at the Kennel Club we wait with bright eyes, nostrils twitching and ears pricked, for your arrival at Crufts in a few weeks time.

Yours ever

Monica.

The Nest

Dear Monica,

Hopefully, you will not have to release Fang. I am emboldened by your confident response and trust none of this will mean court action or, even, Albion having to hang around on Death Row. I gather the Church has the rather shadowy and little-known Consistory Court, but it's only usually used for unfrocking vicars. It dealt with the poor vicar of Stiffkey, whose wife and tots were turned out into the snow when he was accused of bringing the church into disrepute, but one suspects he was merely befriending fallen angels. He ended up in a barrel proclaiming his innocence from the top of a pole, before being eaten by a lion in a circus cage. When I mentioned all this to Sophie, a tear came to her eye, and Albion, who seems to understand every word, took on a sad-eyed, hang-dog look, fretting about his future.

All being well, we shall be at Crufts as promised.

Lancing-Lancing
-

After the Crufts show Lancing-Lancing wrote again to Monica Howling.

The Nest

Dear Monica

Well, I did try and warn you. Also, I heeded your subsequent advice about booking Albion in for an intensive session with the dog therapist, Prof. Julian Clover (one was tempted to call him Rover).

First, let me apologise for Albion's behaviour at the show. Secondly, and rather dispiritingly, Clover said that in his decades of dealing with canine behavioural problems he had never come across a dog with such pronounced psychotic tendencies.

We got off to a bad start at the Hospital for Small Animals, just outside Cambridge. It had been a long haul in the car from

Polperro, several hundred miles, so Albion was in something of a huff by the time we reached our destination.

Before going to the hospital, Sophie and I let him have a run in a nearby wood, thinking that after being cooped up for so long he would enjoy a little exercise and some fresh air. We had failed to realise that the copse bordered the American Memorial Cemetery for World War 11 fliers, on the Madingley Road, into which Albion casually sauntered, cocking his leg up on one of the headstones, much to the understandable consternation of the Superintendent.

This led, inevitably, to something of a contretemps, but the chap calmed down when he recognised Albion as the intrepid, and now famous, bulldog-aviator. He then insisted on having my autograph, and took a selfie with Albion, Sophie and myself. Albion was overcome with excitement – he seems to relish stardom – and by this juncture was trying to slobber heartily over the lens.

When we got in to see Prof. Clover, Albion appeared docile and rather tired. He is, after all, getting on a bit, something one tends to overlook, given his remarkable bouts of sudden and frenetic energy. He had been subject to a long and arduous journey from Polperro, and the excitement at his fame in the American Cemetery seemed to have further exhausted him.

Clover was, however, sporting a turtle neck black sweater, which quickly brought Albion out of his reveries. He started to growl. His customary guttural, throaty croak. We know it as an early-warning sign. His lower lip was thrust forward, he had a slight tremble and was dribbling more than usual. He had taken on his serious, frowning face, and had assumed that squat, bullish stance, that we have come to know so well, as if he's looking for trouble.

There could be no mistake: this was Albion in a strop. I tried to warn Clover of the impending tsunami, but he said he had seen it all before. He would regret those words.

The breaking point came when he tried to stick a thermometer up Albion's bottom. Albion whirled round with an astonishing lick of speed and in one ferocious move, with the thermometer still poking out of his rear, sprang at Clover's throat. Within moments he had him on the floor, trapped in a corner, writhing this way and that, desperately trying to reach the alarm button.

His colleagues came running, bursting into the room, and eventually Albion began to simmer down. Some brave soul managed to extricate the thermometer, which had become wedged. All in all it was a lucky escape for everybody involved, though Clover's cashmere sweater was, by this time, in shreds.

So, in short, it was not a particularly successful therapeutic session.

That evening we stayed at what used to be called The Garden House Hotel, on the River Cam in Cambridge, and Albion was as good as gold, lying on the end of the bed, snoring and dribbling. The next day we even took him punting on the Backs of the colleges, which he seemed to enjoy, apart from one minor incident when he tried to bite the head off a passing duck.

Professor Clover had noted that Albion suffers from what he called 'occasional relationship difficulties,' so we put it down to that, even though I thought it was a rather mild diagnosis.

I rather feel that the ballooning, and the Blessing, and what he clearly thought was some sort of pervert trying to abuse him, probably upset his nervous system. We'll keep a careful watch on him, but he seems to have gone back to being his usual lovable, playful self. He's always been a bit of a scamp, and as a dog-person, I'm sure you will understand this better than most.

As ever

Lancing-Lancing
-

Whittlebottom & Smike, Solicitors

Temple Inn

Dear Admiral Lancing-Lancing,

Our client, Humphrey Pendleton-Mater, the proprietor of the Gorse and Heather Kennels, East Cheam, breeders of the world renowned miniature species, the Bulgarian Bald Terrier, are seeking compensation for the incident at Crufts, in which your dog, Albion, ate the bitch, Michaela Pogal Hamblin-Oasis the Third, better known, and for the purposes of this letter, as Pog.

Pog was a champion Bulgarian Bald Terrier, weighing less than six ounces, which had won the Starred 1st Prize in the Dubai Bitch-in-a-Bag contest. Pog had also received a coveted rosette at the Austin, Texas, all-breed show, and won a silver medal at the Pint Pot Best in Breed Festival in Hampton Wick.

Mr. Humphrey Pendleton-Masterton is seeking substantial damages for the loss of this valuable creature. We wait to hear what settlement fee you are prepared to offer, as my client has no wish to see this matter go to court.

Incidentally, noting your address, I have a little second-home hideaway quite near to your place; perhaps I could pop in for a Bristol Cream? What say you? I'd like to get to know some of the locals.

I remain Sir

Yours Most Sincerely

Jeremy Smike, partner

-

The Nest

Dear Mr. Smike

Thank you for your letter. Albion obviously thought the little bitch was a rat, which he knows to kill. I cannot be held responsible for the fact that he saw Pog as a rodent. He was doing that which any dog worthy of the name would do.

Perhaps it was unwise of Mr. Pendleton to allow the pint-sized Pog to be skipping around so close to Albion's jaws. I would like to stress that Pog didn't suffer. It was over in a trice. One moment Pog was there, skipping around on the end of her diamante string, her hair tied up with a pink ribbon, doing little cartwheels on her tiny legs. And in the next second she was gone, with Albion spitting out the bones and the pink ribbon.

It is conceivable that Pog thought Albion was asleep. In reality, he would have had one eye half-open, as is his way. I deeply regret that I cannot be more helpful over this matter, and I am dreadfully sorry for Mr. Pendleton's loss. However, I am not prepared to offer compensation, and if Mr. Pendleton should wish to pursue this business through the courts, then, without wishing to appear intransigent, so be it.

Lancing-Lancing.

-

No further letters about this matter could be found in the Lancing-Lancing files, though there was a scribbled note, which Lancing-Lancing had left for Sophie on the fridge at The Nest: 'There's some two-bit, glint-eyed lawyer on the make, called Black Bottom or Spite or some such, who says he might call in here about compensation for the shindig at Crufts when Albion forgot his table manners. If I'm not here, set Albion on him (he's a ghastly second-homer with a place near the quay; doubtless he'll be in red trousers and yellow blazer, like that awful ex-politico who makes TV programmes while riding on trains)'.

**

The Lancing-Lancing International Waterborne Scholarship at Hereward College, part of Oxford University, was established to encourage especially bright youngsters into joining the Royal Navy. Young men and women, aged between the ages of 17 and 25 are eligible. Several distinguished naval commanders began their careers at Hereward as recipients of the scholarship.

The Nest

Dear Professor Toddington

With the other members of the Foundation we are now in a position to recommend the most suitable candidate for the

Lancing-Lancing Scholarship. After much deliberation we have decided to recommend Ivan Gudinuv, the applicant from Russia. He struck me as a first-class young fellow and I have strong memories of his homeland, having served, in my early years, as the naval attache in the British Embassy in Moscow. He has the requisite academic qualifications as well as the necessary degree of presence, authority and charm, the essential characteristics one would hope to see in a young naval officer.

As ever

Lancing-Lancing
-

Hereward College

Oxford

Dear Lancing-Lancing

A while has passed since we last communicated. I thought I would drop a line about the progress of young Ivan. He has made remarkable strides and, as you know, achieved a brilliant First in Maritime Studies. His post-graduate research is highly original and he should, as one might say, sail through his doctorate.

There have, however, been one or two worrying developments. As you know, from your membership of the Joint Security Council (and thank goodness we have managed to keep this from the Press) his room was swept by Spooks at the time of the great Polonium scare.

Again, you will be aware, that a certain Oscar Teeming-Browne of MI5, and Florence Portas-Fiddler of MI6 (false monikers, of course) interviewed Ivan about traces of the stuff being found not in College, but at the Hereward Boathouse on the river Isis, where Ivan is a regular visitor being, among his numerous other talents, a phenomenally good rower. Nothing has come from any of this, but there is a lingering suspicion that he is not entirely the full Moscow Sandwich, as we originally believed. I am keeping an eye on the situation. It could be worth eating this note, after you have digested its contents, as we might be entering seriously murky waters.

Toddington

-

The Nest

Dear Toddington

I think eating ones correspondence might be a smidgeon over the top, but I am monitoring the situation through the Joint Security Council. I was surprised to learn that he was taking Mythalagnium, which indicates why he was such a formidable oarsman and, also, accounts for his rapid and astonishing upper-body muscularity. The rather sophisticated gadgetry found in his locker at the boat house was, I gather, some sort of communication device. As for the Polonium, my understanding is that it remains a mystery, although it was found at The Bear, in Woodstock, and also at The Trout, where Ivan was well known for knocking back the Smirnoff. We must keep a close watch on developments.
Lancing-Lancing

-

Hereward College

Lancing-Lancing

Again, several weeks have slipped by, but you will obviously be aware of the truly shocking revelations concerning Ivan, or as *The Sun* headlined its story this morning: 'As if Things weren't Badinuv already.' When Gudinov joined the Royal Navy, after finishing at Hereward, he was subject to the usual stringent vetting procedures and, apart from the blips that we have already discussed, he was given the all-clear.

One could see why the Examining Board let him slip through the net. Given his extraordinary abilities, its members could not resist the lure of such a tempting catch. He had excelled in all subjects, and his later dissertation on the conflict in the South China Seas won accolades. Indeed, his thesis was of such insight, I confess to wondering at the time if he had 'inside' knowledge, which we now know to be the case.

In fairness to the Ministry of Defence Employment Executive, the previous inquiries into the Polonium business drew a blank, and the communications equipment, though dismembered and scrutinised by those clever chaps at GCHQ, was thought to be little more than a glorified crystal-set, which tied in with Ivan's robust assertion that he was merely an over-enthusiastic enthusiastic radio-ham.

With hindsight, of course, the plethora of antennae and aerials which had sprouted on the College roof should have given the game away. Instead, they were discussed at High Table in college only in terms of their aesthetics, their unsightliness, and whether or not Hereward should have a wind-turbine installed in the quad, a conversation guaranteed to stir the passions over the port, especially when Professor Marcus Grebe of the Environmental Faculty, joined in to voice his usual strident opinions.

The most shocking aspect, without doubt, is the slur on the good reputation of Hereward. The Vice-Chancellor said this morning that in the 700 years since its foundation, this unfortunate business has inflicted the most damage on the College that it has ever had to withstand. I will keep in touch with you as developments occur.

Toddington

-

Nest

Toddington

I am afraid I don't agree. I think the most shocking aspect is the damage done to national security. It is not that Gudinuv was a sole bad apple, but that he was allowed to establish a nest of vipers.

The barmaid at The Trout, now exposed as Ludmilla, but who

was known for years to all and sundry as Marge, should have been exposed much earlier. How she managed to get into the country seems quite extraordinary, given that her grandfather, it now transpires, had been one of Uncle Joe's most trusted henchmen.

This distressing tale has only come to light because Marge/Ludmilla was sleeping with Hereward's Professor Abel. Abel's long-suffering wife made a surprise visit to The Trout and caught him and Marge/Ludmilla going at it hammer and tong, under a tarpaulin in a punt, moored near the pub. Professor Abel's protestations, that as head of the Slavic Languages Faculty, he was simply testing her Albanian conjugated verbs, sounded thin, especially as he had no trousers on at the time.

We all bear a terrible responsibility and I do not, in any way, absolve myself and the Foundation for picking Gudinuv in the first place. The College, the security services, even the chap called Barry from Sky TV, who said the forest of aerials on the college roof were a bit odd .. all of us, I'm afraid, are to blame. There were plenty of warning signs and they should have been recognised and acted upon. As you suggest, perhaps we were all overly dazzled by Ivan's astonishing abilities.

To give Gudinuv command, shortly after he left Hereward, of Britain's newest aircraft carrier was, without dispute, a tragic mistake. Mercifully, the vessel was pretty toothless, as Britain couldn't afford to arm it with aircraft. Beyond that small spat in the South China Seas, all in all the United Kingdom has got off pretty lightly.

Gudinuv, as you know, is now back in the Kremlin and tipped to be the next head of the Russian Navy. It was good of Putin to give us our ship back, but of course he would not have budged an inch had we not agreed to swap it for Marge/Ludmilla, and Abel, her erstwhile lover.

Lancing-Lancing

The Moscow Naval Institution

Gorky Park Zone 7

Dear Admiral Lancing-Lancing

I wanted to write and thank you for the magnificent opportunity you and your colleagues gave me. At Hereward College I was taught all the courtesies which are expected from officers in the Royal Navy, as well as those disciplines of a more academic and practical nature. So it is only right for me to acknowledge, formally, the great debt I feel I owe to you, your colleagues and the college.

The recent revelations must have come as a bit of a shock. As we say in Moscow, the beaver is out of its pen, which in English is the same as you saying the cat is now getting out of its bag. I do not intend, and nor would you expect me, to apologise for serving my country. Nevertheless, I can entirely sympathise with the frustration you must feel. My actions were not in any sense a betrayal of the high regard in which I hold you, and the college. As you have demonstrated throughout your long and illustrious career, I am simply a naval officer serving my nation, doing my duty to the best of my ability.

Perhaps, one day, we might meet again. The Russian Fleet is intending to conduct exercises off the Cornish coast – in the same way that our Russian Bear aircraft carry out regular sorties up and down the British coastline. Who knows, it may be possible for me to one day sneak ashore and enjoy a vodka with you in the Joan of the Wad. After all, our submariners during WW2 (as well as German U-boat commanders) managed such covert forays now and again.

If ever you happen to be passing through Russia you would be most welcome to stay with my wife, Ludmilla (Marge), and our two lovely children, Natasha and Nikita, in our splendid dacha near the recently liberated Kiev. Ludmilla is now a Commando First Rank serving with the Ministry of the Interior on anti-drugs control.

She faces the usual problems of any working wife and mother, being often away on drug busts when she should be tucking our kiddies up in bed. If you do decide to come across (only joking) it would be nice if you could also bring Sophie and Albion. My knowledge of your more personal affairs may surprise you. Forgive me for this, but before I 'came out', as an officer in the Russian Navy, I was expected to be something of a spy, so taking the occasional personal peep into your private life was all part of the job.

Professor Abel sends his warmest regards. He is now Colonel Abel in the Ministry of Foreign Talk, and is busy teaching Lithuanian, Estonian, Albanian and Latvian to new conscripts, the different languages which our Supreme Commander thinks will be of enormous utility in the coming years.

When we returned to Mother Russia, unfortunately Professor Abel still entertained what he foolishly imagined to be affectionate yearnings for Ludmilla, not realizing that she had been merely play-acting, carrying out intensive surveillance duties in the punt. However, after an extensive programme of re-education at a remote and special institution which corrects such thinking, he now fully understands that it was a passing infatuation, and one which was not in his best interests, or Ludmilla's, or those of his adopted nation; such bourgeois feelings have now been erased.

I remain, Admiral, a most loyal friend and admirer.

With very best wishes

Na zdorovie (Cheers, as we say in the homeland)

Vice-Admiral Ivan Gudenuv

**

Since a young man, Lancing–Lancing has always been what his friends and colleagues call a car-buff, that which a younger generation would today term 'a petrol-head.' Over the years he has had many makes and models but the Jaguar has long been his favourite marque.

The Jaguar Owners Club

Knightsbridge, London

Dear Admiral Lancing-Lancing

As a Jaguar driver of long-standing we would like to invite you to take part in the Portuguese Algarve Rally due to take place in May. It is estimated that the rally will take something in the order of two weeks as the cars move from one location to another, with overnight stops en route at different hotels. This is not a race, but an opportunity for the manufacturer to promote and display its cars. We invite you to drive one of the newest Jaguars. You may also bring a partner. All costs, flights, hotels, meals and petrol, are covered by the company. This will be a most enjoyable and memorable event and we hope you are able to join us.

Yours faithfully

Monty de Lambo (Secretary).
-

The Nest

Dear Mr. de Lambo

Thank you so much. I have great pleasure in accepting your kind invitation. I shall be bringing my companion, Miss Sophie Cornwallis. I am sorry I have not replied more quickly, but I was delayed by having to find somebody who would look after Albion, my bulldog. I met with a surprising reluctance in this regard, so making the necessary arrangements took somewhat longer than I had anticipated. He is now, I am delighted to be able to tell you, going to be 'kenneled' with my handyman, Mr. Trumble, for the ten days or so that you think the rally will last.

Yours sincerely

Lancing-Lancing

The rally began on the eastern Algarve in the small town of Tavira, close to the Spanish border. It was intended that it would conclude at the Algarve's western extreme, on the rocky headland that is Cape St. Vincent.

Villa Mimosa

Quinta de Lago

My dear George

Just a quick line to let you know that we are having a first-class jolly on the Jaguar rally. There are twelve cars and drivers and we're staying at the above for just a night or two, which is something of a zillionaire's paradise. I'm enjoying a round of golf or three, which is how people here seem to while away their days. On the road in my gleaming borrowed Jaguar I feel a bit like Mr. Toad. Parp! Parp! I wanted to let you and Catharine know that Sophie and I have not forgotten your kind invitation to dinner at your place in Gone to the Dogs. We would be delighted to accept.

When we get back to England, we'll be staying for a short while in London at my club, The Reform, and thought it would be fun if you and Catharine would join us for a drink before going back to your place for supper. Does that appeal? I'd like to show you The Reform. It reeks of history, is unmatched in its beauty, and has one of the finest cellars and private libraries, in Europe. We are looking forward to seeing you both on our return.

Lancing-Lancing and Sophie
-

The Yacht Albatross

Vilamoura Marina

Algarve

Dear George

I fear we may have to postpone drinks at The Reform and supper

103

at your place for a little longer than anticipated. Instead of being feted with bouquets of bougainvillea, as we swept in convoy along the Algarve, we ran into a spot of bother in the little town of Loule. Some of the locals took exception to our ostentatious parade and started to pelt us with bad peaches and rotten tomatoes. The mayor was apologetic and said it was down to the recession, the dispiritingly foul weather which screwed up the peach harvest, and a lively delegation from the Workers Revolutionary Party. Property prices have collapsed, corruption is rife and unemployment at a record high, so one can appreciate their stridency.

Having cleaned up the cars, and ourselves – getting the peaches out of Catharine's golden locks was tricky – we continued on our way. But we only got as far as the nearby enclave of Almancil and exactly the same thing happened – though on a rather grander scale. It turned into a full-scale riot at a little restaurant at which we had stopped for lunch. Poor Monty de Lambo, head honcho and chief tour guide, was hit over the head with a bottle of Rose Mateus, followed by a steaming vat of came de porco a Alentajana (pork marinated in wine and garnished with clams). If you get a chance, do try porco de Alentajana. It's a tasty, traditional dish. Being the excellent cook that she is, I thought Catharine might be interested, though it would be wise to choose a less-volcanic café than the one in which we ate.

The top and tail of all this is that the entire excursion was turning into a PR fiasco and the organisers decided to cut their losses and abort it there and then. We could have flown home from Faro, but Catharine and I have opted to sail back on a vintage 36-footer, *Albatross,* owned by an old naval friend, who keeps it moored here in Vilamoura. He normally does the run single-handed, but said he'd be glad of some company, and we're always game for a bit of blow out in the Atlantic. So it should be fun. We'll re-arrange things when we get back. Trust this hasn't messed up your plans too much.

All the very best to you and Catharine

Lancing-Lancing and Sophie.

The Yacht Albatross
Albufeira Harbour, Algarve

Dear George

I'm afraid we've had a spot of bother with the roller reefing. The damn thing jammed, so the sail wouldn't open or close properly, and at the very moment the jib was playing up the engine went kaput. As you know, with sailing, it never rains, but only pours. Consequently, we were swept back into Albufeira. One tries to make the best of these things, so, looking on the bright side, it's a very novel and rather unexpected way of seeing different parts of Portugal. With its red cliffs, golden sands and the mighty Atlantic rollers, Portugal has a stunning coastline, although, frankly, we're beginning to feel we've now seen enough of it.

Our return might, unfortunately, be somewhat delayed while we expedite repairs. These frustrations are probably all my own fault; given the name of the yacht, I really should have guessed. I'll keep you posted.

Lancing-Lancing and Sophie
-

The Yacht *Albatross*

Albufeira Harbour

Dear Trumble

Due to unexpected circumstances, I'm sorry that I'll have to ask you to keep an eye on Albion for a little longer than expected. Rest assured, I'll recompense you most handsomely on my return. I am sure Albion is enjoying himself. He must think he's on holiday. It's very good of you and Mrs. Trumble to take him in, especially given his moods.

Lancing-Lancing

The Yacht *Albatross*

Somewhere in the Atlantic

My dear George

I do hope this reaches you. I'm going to give it to a Liverpudlian chap who is a passenger on a passing liner. He has promised to post it to you as soon as the liner reaches England. We've had a spot more bother. Before we set sail I hadn't seen Archie Quick, our skipper of the yacht *Albatross*, for a very long time. I remembered him as a first-class chap back in the day. Sadly, the intervening years have not been kind to him. He's still a good sailor, when he's sober, and his yacht is extraordinarily beautiful, when it's not leaking. I'm sure we'll be fine. We didn't want to abandon him, mid-ocean; that would have been terribly mean, although, I confess, one was rather tempted to hop aboard the cruise ship and leave him to it.

We'd broken down, yet again, when I spotted the liner on the horizon, looking like a giant block of flats swept out to sea by a passing tsunami. So I let off a flare and the liner came across, but by the time it reached us we'd managed to unjam the roller-reefing and got the bailing under control. It was only a small hole, just beneath the water-line, which was causing a bit of a headache. So we stuffed in a few rags and glued them down, the usual thing. We finished it off by sticking a pair of Sophie's knickers on the inside of the hull, which caused Archie to think he was hallucinating, saying they had got him so excited he would have to have another drink, or four.

There are very few tools on board for expediting running repairs. He has a puncture repair kit for a bike (there's no bike; on a bender he rode it into the drink in Lagos harbour on the Algarve) and a dog-eared copy of Newnes Practical Handyman from the 1940's. It tells one how to build an air-raid shelter and a bookshelf but doesn't say much about boats. The other slight problem is that the radio is shot and the navigation aids are a touch unreliable. From what the captain of the cruise ship told me about our position, it seems that we have been going round and round in circles. So I have returned to old celestial skills, navigating by the stars and the sun.

To our consternation, we have found that most of the Volvic water bottles are full of vodka, and because of our circuitous route we were running a little short on provisions. However, things are looking much brighter now. We've stocked up on victuals – the captain of the cruise ship was most generous – and in a minute or two we'll be underway once more. Archie's habits can be wearing. If he's been on the juice we have to lock him in the stern cabin, where he lies on the bunk reciting passages from the world's longest poem, The Ancient Mariner. For all this, it is truly wonderful to be at sea again (if not *all* at sea).

As ever

Lancing-Lancing, Sophie & Archie (who would wish to send his pleasantries, if capable).
-

Eventually, the yacht Albatross and its exhausted crew managed to get back to England. The adventurous voyage was reported extensively on television and in the newspapers, the welter of publicity adding to Admiral Lancing-Lancing's burgeoning fame. On his return Lancing-Lancing sent a thank you letter to Trumble, his handyman.

The Nest

Dear Trumble

This is to thank you and Mrs. Trumble for looking after Albion during our unexpectedly long break. He clearly enjoyed his extended sojourn at your place and, of course, I will reimburse you for the sofa, the standard lamp and the double-bed. He means no harm but can become rather excited.

I am sorry about the incident in the village. It would *have* to be, of course, with the dratted woman who suffered the sewage problem. I still maintain that if she hadn't been wearing black leggings it would never have happened. Anyway, for what it's worth, you'll be pleased to know that the police seem relaxed about it, especially when I pointed out that some of Albion's molars are made of plastic, so it could only have been a playful nip, a far cry from the near amputation that she was wittering on about.

After his 'holiday' with you, Albion's been scampering around all over the place. He looks to have been given a new lease of life thanks to his change of scene. Perhaps we'll have to try and do something similar in the future, if Mrs. Trumble can be persuaded. The new furniture will, I'm sure, help soften her opinion of him. We'll see you up at the cottage soon. We've got to set about that small part of the roof which needs to be re-thatched.

Lancing-Lancing.

**

Conservation of naval relics has taken on a new importance as the heritage movement gathers momentum. Being a naval grandee, Lancing-Lancing has been at the forefront of maritime historical projects.

HMS *Glorious*

Portsmouth

Dear Lancing-Lancing

I'm writing this from Haycock-Cock's quarters on *Glorious*, sitting at that which purports to be his desk (newer than it looks; the base is Ikea, though cleverly worked, and cunningly camouflaged by being beaten with chains to make it look old and *stressed*; goes on all the time in the antiques trade, apparently). As I sit here, imagining myself two centuries ago, as Orville the Cock must have done after Pigeon Stool, I wanted to assure you that as an important member of the steering committee your expert opinions are always carefully heeded.

The refurbishment is coming along nicely, but there was an

awful lot of rot on the dear old *Gloria*. I think we'll have no trouble in accounting for the entire £35 million (including Heritage grants and National Lottery money). The hull, thankfully, was built of stouter stuff than the decks and all the above-water paraphernalia. Roddy Parker, the surveyor, says she's amazingly watertight down below, so, God willing, one day she'll be a stirring sight while sailing in the Solent.

Parker gets black moods, something to do with his wife (I heard a whisper about swingers' parties in The Explosion Museum down this way). But he's an awfully nice chap and we took the right decision in giving him a second chance. He's put in a tremendous amount of work for half what the other surveyors were going to charge. Confidentially, his name has been passed on to you-know-who for a Gong, and it would be well deserved, in my view.

The curator, young Ossie Warboys, has turned out to be a bit odd. Admittedly, I think his decision to boost the fund-raising by holding 'alternative' parties, was correct. It's just that I don't like seeing crowds of Goths and crack addicts dressed up like Nelson, let alone their partners in crinolines and plunging bustles in imitation of the delectable Lady Hamilton. It rather demeans the old man and his consort. Warboys is not a bad fellow, but I wish he'd stop dressing up like a mad old Tar in that white jumper with black horizontal hoops. Every now and again he goes into a peculiar horn-pipe dance on the poop-deck, with some pretty young thing of whom he seems awfully fond, and who is, I gather, a student at the Gosport Academy of Drama and Balinese Dance.

I'd also like Warboys to cease wearing rings through his nose, lips and ears. He looks as if he's in face armour, ready for some sort of medieval jousting match. I s'pose I'm of a different generation, and it's the way money-raising is conducted these days. On the other hand, I was there when a little girl began screaming her head off when she first encountered him. Between you, me and the forestay, consternation swept through the place when it was learned Warboys had been singing sea-shanties and dancing his hornpipe in the Ministry of Defence. As you know, *Gloria* is still, technically, on the Navy List, and Warboys was at the MoD trying beg more cash. Apparently the Minister walked out in a huff when Warboys went into his routine, muttering far that too much public money is falling into the hands of crackpots.

I am very pleased that we are going to refloat the old tub. Like you, if one is spending all this money, I feel the least one can expect at the end of such an ambitious refurbishment – after all, it's taken twenty-five years – is that she damn well floats. I'm not so keen on the *Victory*, parked up in this neck of the woods, and the *Cutty Sark* in Greenwich, tarted up as static exhibits on dry land. Ships are built to sail. When they're beached or dry-docked they can look like, well, fish out of water. I'll keep you posted if anything new crops up. We'll be launching soon (ish).

Kind winds

Barclay-Barclay (Sec. *Glorious* Re-Build Ctte).

-

The Nest

Dear George

Just had a note from Adm. Herbert Barclay-Barclay about the *Gloria* being rebuilt. It's taken forever and consumed crocks of gold. They're going to refloat her soon, and I wondered if you and Catharine would like to join myself and Sophie at the launch ceremony? It should be a fun day out. I'll ring you with the dates et al.

Lancing-Lancing

-

HMS Glorious was the flagship of one of Britain's most renowned sailors, Admiral Orville Haycock-Cock. Haycock-Cock was cut down at the Battle of Pigeon Stool, off The Mumbles, in 1740, when the Royal Navy, outnumbered and outgunned, routed the combined fleets of the French, German, Spanish, Dutch, Haiti, several canoes from the Solomon Isles and an early submersible from the breakaway Russian state of Visigongorsky, the latter being merged into the Prussian empire in 1743, after the famous naval skirmish of Balls Bag, off Beachy Head, in 1742.

One of the finest ships ever built, HMS Glorious, a 150 gunner, with seventeen miles of sail, was scheduled to be refloated at Portsmouth after her twenty-five -year restoration programme. The world's great and good had gathered to attend the ceremony. The Rt. Hon. Cecil Persephone-Plume, represented the Queen, and the French Vice-Admiral, Auguste de Bronsweeney, whose forebear, Admiral Louis de Cornee'ouse, (known to naval historians as Lyons Cornerhouse) who won the Department of French Maritime Affairs Silver Spur, in the Battle of Biarritz, in 1698, represented the San Marino Philately Society. The launch of the refurbished Gloria didn't go entirely to plan. Later, George Steel commiserated with Lancing-Lancing.

Gone to the Dogs

Dear Admiral

Well, I know it was a bit of a shambles, but I don't think you should worry about it too much. After all, she can always be lifted and refloated (though goodness knows what that might cost). The saddest part of the whole affair was, of course, Roddy Parker, subsequently shooting himself. Again, though, I think it was more to do with revelations about his wife's pole-dancing in the Explosion Museum than anything to do with *Gloria* going down.

The sinking will remain in my mind for a long time. She went under quite slowly. It seems that Ossie Warboys didn't realise she was getting lower and lower in the water. I suppose he was too caught up dancing his hornpipe. It reminded me of the last moments of the *Titanic,* with the band continuing to play.

It might have been less ignominious if she had actually got out to sea. But to go under only a yard or two offshore seemed very silly, especially after a 25-year refit. One had to admire the astonishing turn of speed with which the glad-handers suddenly decided to call it a day. It was extraordinary to see so many politicos and bigwigs herded together in the lifeboats. They must have thought that a schooner or two of Tio Pepe in the Mayor's Parlour was never quite like this. None could have been to any sort of civic cocktail party which ended so swiftly and in such total mayhem.

The most entertaining sight was the Minister of Defence (so grey and boring I can't remember his name) trying to swim for it. When it became clear that as the chief of the navy he couldn't swim, his cries for help were drowned out by the cheering.

Don't be too downcast. Nobody was lost, apart from poor Parker. Worse things happen at sea (not that she got that far).

George

PS. Catharine sends her fondest and says to tell you that it was a wonderful day out and one that she will never forget.

-

The Nest

Dear George

Thank you for your kind words. Absolute tragedy about Parker. He'd got it into his head that he'd missed some rotten planking and it was that which was letting in water. But the preliminary investigations indicate that it was nothing of the kind. The various funding bodies had insisted that *Gloria* be made, what they called in that fashionably hideous phrase,' user-friendly' (dumbed-down, in other words). So a row of lavatories and fast-food outlets had been installed in the hull, for the throngs of tourists who were subsequently expected to pore over her.

I maintained throughout the long and extensive refurbishment that having a Harry Ramsden's fish'n chip shop, a Kentucky Fried and a McDonald's outlet built into the hull of an 18th century warship, seemed incongruous. But there were too many worthies in blazers, all desperate for their OBE's, and who craved to be *modern* (most had never been in a McDonald's) who stuck their oar in. Being the lackeys of the funders, their imprecations proved impossible to resist.

112

The restorers used plastic plumbing for the pipes and joints, which is customary today. There was such pressure on the lavatories, from all the Hoorays and free-loaders on board, that something appears to have clogged and then burst. There were numerous signs warning celebrants not to drop inappropriate things down the Heads. But everybody was so sozzled I doubt they read them. The divers who are trying to ascertain what went wrong have so far brought to the surface a plethora of Kentucky Fried boxes, Big Mac wrappers, half a dozen used condoms, a ripped ceremonial robe with gold piping, a mayor's chain – turning rusty – and a sodden tricorn-hat, with a bedraggled feather, as once worn by a town hall Sherriff.

It makes you wonder about the quality of our civic leaders. It amazes me how many of them still exist. I thought most of them had been put out to grass in the Great Recession. Didn't that little fat politico called Pickled-Egg, or some such, say he was going to have a cull? Whatever, the first indications are that some sort of civic orgy took place. It's what happens when you serve lashings of navy rum mixed with champers, and you try and plumb en-suite facilities into a 300-year-old warship.

At least we gave Parker another chance. At the outset, all those years ago, I was a little worried that his quotation for the renovation work was very cut-price compared to all the others. I suppose his tender had to be competitive after the Royal Barge went down in the Thames. He had a big hand in its restoration and took a lot of flak over that particular episode. Thankfully, I'm sure you remember, HRH was a good swimmer. Nothing was ever proved, but Parker's reputation was trashed, though divers did eventually come up with the sceptre.

Thinking about it, just like the *Gloria* going down, HRH's Barge was also up to its gunnels in Hoorays and worthies who were on board celebrating her birthday. The official inquiry suggested that they were all pie-eyed and probably desperate for the WC. Who knows that they too didn't bugger up the plumbing with used Johnnies and Moet corks, and poor old Parker had to take the royal rap? When you've got to go, you've got to go, Royal Barge or not. Toffs they may be, but nobody is self-contained.

All the best

Lancing-Lancing

-

The Sun Turf & Fun Club,

Monaco

Dear Admiral

Thought I'd drop a quick one about the *Glo* going down. As you know, her launch was broadcast live across Europe and we split our breeches here at the club. I have never seen such a circus. We thought it hilarious! I am not sure that the modelling contract I mentioned a while back would still be available as it seems to be the view in France – probably across Europe – that the Royal Navy has rather lost the plot and that its more celebrated craft are no longer up to the job. In days gone by somebody would have been strung up from the yard-arm.

Yours

Maltby (Two-Fingers)

-

The Nest

Maltby

The French reaction is *hardly* a surprise.

Lancing-Lancing

-

Bunker17c

Glow Worm road near Spandau Memorial

Asuncion,

Paraguay

Hi you Admiral Lancing-Flushing

We in Combat Command First Battalion Paraguay Division want offer support over big loss of old boat. Now just firewood, yes. Our offer to run Ocean Division still running and now is time for kwik action. You ready now join us. Your old boat has gone up and you need more ships. We have ship. We have good men ready go as sailors. They are fit with vegetable. We struck deal with grocer Lidl in UK to sell million ton famous Paraguay fruit. Is like peaches but look more American doughnut. Is name Paraguayan. When gone hard Paraguayan can be fired at enemy by cannon. When soft is good eating. Like peach and good woman. Nice juicy, yes. Remind me of jam doughnut eat in New York in secret talks Tea Party.

Our first target is like this: we train sniper battalion take out drug cartel run by scumboy Messiboco family. We look through sites on guns and shoot bad men in back head and back. Bang bang. Kaput. Juan Messiboco greasy pan-scrubber. When we have him we interrogate him clever way before garrot slow. The seas must be all over covered to sink without doubt all ships on drugs or filthy pollute muck like blow-up Mexican dolls and dirty books with pictures showing everything. If they not carry dolls, you sink anyway. It big mistake they make. They should not be there. We back you all way. Mistake in war. Collatterrall damage (spelling ungood when me is exciting).

This will be job of your boat. You can have Messiboco in bag with big torpedo or rocket out sky. You want submarine? OK. We have. We take plenty money in Messiboco house and make world run nice straight lines. Good order. Bad people pay. What you think Admiral, we like you lot, yes. You good baby.

You are old friend in the end

Herman (1st Field Battalion Commander)

The Nest

Dear Herman

Thank you for your kind thoughts and for thinking of me as the chap to run your navy. I am sorry, but I am rather tied up at the moment and feel that this would be too much of a commitment given my busy schedule. I am also a little concerned about malaria and shooting people in the back. We often shop in Lidl and enjoy the occasional Paraguayan. My muse, and expert shopper, Sophie, says they are very good value.

Lancing-Lancing

**

As a high-ranking former naval commander, Lancing-Lancing maintained top-flight contacts in the security services.

If he wished to make contact with the secret services he had to ring a branch of Poundland in Bolton and ask for the customer complaints department. Once he was put through he would then have to ask for Fat Fred and would be told: 'They are all Fat Freds here. Which one do you want?' He had to reply: 'I want Fat Fred who has bad spots.' He would then be told: 'They all have bad spots.' He then had to complete the code by saying: 'He weighs 21-stone and loves chips from Greasy Gob Chippy near Middlesborough Town Hall.'

Within an hour a courier would arrive at The Nest on a motor-cycle, wearing a crash-helmet, green Barbour and wellies, with binoculars and a compass round his neck, saying that he was from the Royal Society for the Protection of Birds, and was just checking on reports that a rare Squat-Legged Cormorant had been spotted in the vicinity.

In real-life, he was a Commando dispatch rider in the Polperro Liberation Army, who did an occasional turn moonlighting for British Intelligence. Lancing-Lancing would then give the courier a letter addressed to Mrs. Dottie Patching, All over the Place Holidays, Caravan 2C, Tree Top Farm, Bognor Regis, West Sussex, which, of course, didn't exist, and of which the following is an example:

The Nest

Dear Dot[1]

Given that you're in the vacation business, I thought you'd be interested to know that a few chaps are setting up activity holidays near Glow Worm road in Asuncion (used to be all pushers and hookers when I knew the place). Usual stuff: everybody called Fritz, adventure breaks, living under canvas, outdoor activities, lots of physical education, rifle-shooting and a spot of underwater sailing. Thought there might be opportunities for you to extend your activities. I do hope that your daughter Avril is well. Please give her my very kindest regards.

LL

-

The Caravan that doesn't exist

And it's nowhere near Bognor

My dear LL

How on earth are you? Long time no hear. Thought you'd probably snuffed it and I'd missed the Obit (one can't rely on The Times these days; full of drug-addled former drummers). I was sorry to hear about Charlotte. It was a while ago now. I'd have dropped a note but I was holidaying in Libya, testing the water for sun-seekers. I miss the old days, up on the Bridge, but I've had an enjoyable time since. I've learned new skills and there are lots of opportunities for seeing the world and all its glories. I've been all over the place: Berlin, Prague, Lisbon (full of *fascinating* people; always was, of course). And for the more cultural traveller, Kabul, Kiev, Aleppo and one or two others. They're all full of history and ruins.

1   *Newly-opened files in Moscow suggest Dottie was the cover-name of Ronnie Haynes, a British Intelligence officer and naval colleague of Lancing-Lancing; Poppy was Hilda, not Haynes' daughter, but his wife.*

Avril's well, thank you. She doesn't travel with me. We spend long periods apart and that's a pest. Sometimes my travels are just too hot for her. Must fly, being a rep keeps me on my toes. Off to Somalia, then the Yemen. Couple of fun breaks. See if we can organize a bit of tourism out there. Nice to hear from you again. The office already knows the cemetery in Asuncion. Interesting bunch out there. Used to be a Fritz who built boats in Italy? Maybe we'll catch up with him, see if there's any development work to be had. In the holiday business we're always looking for hot spots. Wonderful that you're still alive and kicking old chap.

Keep your dander up!

Dottie

-

The Nest

Dear Dot

Good of you to send the Costa Lotta brochures. Trumble, my handyman, saw them and is under the impression that I'm off to Jamaica or somewhere exotic. He's getting himself into a state because he thinks I'll want him to baby sit Albion, my dog, who can be a bit of a handful if the mood takes. Take care. Too much sun can do funny things to people. Delighted we have mutual acquaintances in South America.

Mind your back

LL

**

Over the years a number of publishing houses approached Lancing-Lancing about his life-story. Some were old-established but on their last legs, while those who prospered were more interested in 'contemporary issues', such as the soap-actress Simone Peyton, having her bottom pierced, and the rock God Hubie Mons, becoming a father for the ninth time at the age of 87.

Lancing-Lancing knew that writing his life-story would entail a huge amount of work and research and was irritated by the meagre amount of money being offered by would-be publishers. He was surprised to learn that most writers are on the bread-line, and that many publishers face a bleak future. He mentioned his concerns to the following publisher, but his imprecations fell on stony ground.

Crackerjack Publishing Incorporated (CraP Inc.)

Fetter Lane, EC4

Hi Admiral

We can't increase the advance as autobiographies do not sell well, unless they are about footballers with bulging crotches and even bigger egos, warblers with huge chests, spivs running global corporations (you're a sailor; why not write about moguls on yachts in Monaco who don't pay tax?) politicians who've had their hands in the till, or peers who demand penal reform having served time for perjury or molesting children. In the case of the latter, it helps if there's a 'current' angle: if on release, for instance, they've 'seen the light', or 'found religion' (Lord Granville-Watson is emphatic he never laid a finger on his fellow inmate, but that he was touched by God in the shower in Pentonville; Granville-Watson turned that into a vital passage in his best-selling life-story, *'A Stain on my Ermine'*).

However, Crackerjack Publishing is still keen to progress this project, as yours has been a full and most interesting life. We are confident that there could be a television series based on the book, which might prove lucrative in the longer term. As you appreciate, we are specialists in military history, so the *'life and times of Admiral Lancing'* (a working title which would have to be more commercial) would sit comfortably with our other titles.

One of our most admired volumes is *'Ahoy there me Hearties!'* the brilliant autobiography of the now-ennobled Vice-Admiral

Jackson Ogle-Worth. We had to give it a racy name to make it sell, though it has nothing to do with the content. This is now standard practice in publishing. Gunship Television, an independent production company, is turning Ogle-Worth's *Ahoy* into an animated series for E147 Kapow! the most-watched satellite channel in the Asia-Pacific basin. *Ahoy* is also being considered for production by Wally TV, serving Walsall and the Black Country, one of Britain's thrusting community-based TV channels. However, Wally TV is insistent that Ogle-Worth injects more sex into it, and preferably lots of bondage and flogging, given the success of other titles.

Wally TV made headlines recently, and boosted its ratings, when its star teenage presenter told his pensioner guest that she was a 'rich old cow who should have been put down years ago to save the NHS money.' It was a stunning piece of PR.

We live in a fast-changing world. The future of publishing is now heavily dependent on PR and the success of social media and the visual industries. My colleagues believe that even words will soon be a thing of the past. I appreciate that the advance is modest, but there is an opportunity that you will earn money from royalties, the amount dependent on how many books we estimate will be sold.

Can you think of anyway that we might be able to sex it up?

Yours

Danny Yodell

Executive Editorial Director (CraP Inc.)

-

The Nest

Dear Mr. Yodell

Vice-Admiral Ogle-Worth was a scallywag who should have been drummed out of the Brownies long before he was.

I am afraid there is no way I could consider being published by a company responsible for the astonishing pack of lies and fabrications which comprise the life-story of Bogus-Unearthed, as he was known in the navy, and long before he was elevated to the Peerage, or as most now call it, 'going on the social'.

I am grateful for your interest, and complimented by your desire to turn my life into a book. Sadly, however, I feel I must decline your offer.

Incidentally, when I telephoned your office a confident young lady on reception, who said she should have been on the switchboard but couldn't work it, told me I had mispronounced your name. Could you tell me how it is pronounced please? I had imagined it was yodel, as with Maid of the Mountain toffees, or Frank Ifield. The young lady said she came from Peckham, that she was an unpaid intern, and though she knew the incorrect pronunciation, she didn't know the correct version.

Lancing-Lancing

-

Sometime after this letter the Mevagissey Star, an old-established weekly newspaper, reported that there had been a 'nasty incident' at sea when Lancing-Lancing's yacht was 'cut up by a bounder in another yacht,' as Lancing-Lancing described it to the Star reporter, ccutting@ packolies.com. Lancing-Lancing subsequently sent a note about the incident to his confidante, the master mariner, George Steel.

The Nest

Dear George

I was sailing the *Lily and George* the other day when some damn fool nearly ploughed into the side of me. He was in a bigger craft and would have sunk me (and probably himself) had I not taken swift evasive action. Being a mile or two off-shore, it could have been a very nasty episode. Anyway, the rogue craft, a powerful motor-boat of some sort, took off at a rate of knots, and I couldn't properly make out the chap at the wheel. But there was something familiar about his body language and the foul-mouthed tirade he aimed at me.

I have a suspicion it was the lunatic Bogus-Unearthed. I don't mind telling you, very frankly, that it has spooked me. He came at me out of nowhere, deliberately tried to ram me, and then hightailed it like a scalded cat. If my suspicions are confirmed he's clearly got it in for me. Why that should be the case I have little idea, except that I was one of those who presided over his Courts Martial. I hope you don't mind me writing to you, but I thought I'd just mention it. If you hear anything, I know you'll come back to me.

Lancing-Lancing

-

A while later, Sophie found an anonymous scribbled note dropped through the letterbox of The Nest. It read: 'Watch your back Lancing-Lancing. First it's you, then her, then the dog gets it.'

The Nest

Dear Chief Inspector Blow,

It was good of you to drop by the other day and I feel more secure now that your chaps are keeping an eye on things. I am still mystified why Albion, Sophie and myself should be targeted, except, as I mentioned, the proceedings of the Courts Martial, if, indeed, it is the same fellow. I must stress again, however, that I have no real evidence that the miscreant on the tearaway boat was Bogus Unearthed. As I said, I am most concerned that Sophie is also being 'stalked,' if it is that which is happening.

Lancing-Lancing

-

Gone to the Dogs

Dear Admiral

The other day Catharine came across a note on the Net that you had sent to Danny Lodestar, or Yodelling, or whatever his name is, your would-be publisher chap. In it you had criticised Bogus-Unearthed and his autobiography. For the life of me, I cannot see how your remarks found their way on to the worldwide Net, but these things happen, unfortunately. I would think the comments must have been seen by Bogus Unearthed and it is that which has driven him demented. I'm working now, on your behalf, to get it taken down by the powers that be. Good luck with your travails.

George

-

Truro CID

Dear Admiral

You have been previously dealing with my colleague Blow. He is now caught up in the case of the quadruple acid-bath murders in Looe, so I am now leading the manhunt for your stalker. We have had a word with your publishing house and it transpires that it had a burglary in which a number of computers were stolen and which contained confidential letters and information.

The letters, including yours, have been leaked on to the Net by a group known as Tell the World, a shadowy coterie which believes privacy is theft. It also thinks that the Twin Towers in New York were made of Lego and people jumping from them were tailors' dummies launched into the air by the CIA.

My fellow policemen have been looking into the background of the Lord Vice-Admiral Jackson Ogle-Worth (to give him his full title, and who is known to you as Bogus Unearthed). After he was cashiered from the Navy he was sectioned, spent four years in Broadmoor, five years in the Scrubs for grievous bodily harm, and put on the Sex Offenders List for some unpleasant business involving two sheep and a goat in the members enclosure at Kempton races. Shortly after this that he was elevated to the Peerage.

I will keep you informed about developments. Rest assured that The Nest will be kept under close surveillance. One of my most trusted men will be stationed at the top of the large Oak tree by the five-barred gate at the bottom of your drive.

If anybody should look up and be curious about why he's there he will say he is the chairman of the Cornish Squirrel Society, hiding in the branches to see if reports of red squirrels in the neighbourhood are true. Polperro police are used to this sort of thing. The place is stuffed with nuts, and they're not all squirrels.

Yours vigilantly, keeping a beady eye on things

Chief Insp. Magnus O' Shea
-

The Nest

Dear Chief Insp. O'Shea

This is very distressing, especially for my companion, Ms. Sophie Collingwood. She and I had no idea that there was a sexual element to this matter, let alone one to do with sheep. Could his proclivities even extend to Bulldogs? Albion now wears a permanent, worried frown. Nor were we properly aware of the gravity with which you are viewing the case, using such terms as *manhunt*. As you mentioned on the telephone, the fact that Bogus Unearthed has gone to ground, exacerbates our worries. Quite naturally, Sophie and I are exercised by the thought that he might suddenly materialise in our neck of the woods.

I am grateful for your intervention and for the continued presence of your colleague up the tree. We feel rather sorry for him. He's up there for hours on end, in all weathers, with little in sustenance beyond a flask of tea and a few sandwiches. Very few locals have mentioned his presence. They glance up sometimes and then walk on, as if it's the most natural thing in the world to see a burly six-foot copper perched in the top of an Oak tree eating Marmite sandwiches. If you have any sort of breakthrough I would be grateful if you could me fully posted.

Lancing-Lancing

Truro CID

Dear Admiral

There's no need to worry about my man PC Butter. He's a 16-stone former paratrooper and well used to roughing it. My main concern is that the branch might give way. Being an Oak, fortunately we don't have to worry about Dutch Elm or Ash die-back.

Butter's hobbies include heavy-weather yomping. He is widely regarded as the Bear Grylls of Bodmin Moor. Butter's survival methods include catching hares and strangling them with his bare hands, then roasting them slowly over a peat fire. If the weather turns nasty he has been known to dig an outsize fox-hole, into which he descends, covering himself with earth and bracken, and breathing through a straw, a survival technique employed successfully in the past by the Vietcong. Even at home, he spends rain-lashed nights in a tent on his lawn, to ensure that he would know what to do in the event of flooding.

A public speaker of repute, Butter gives lectures on cruise ships. On an Alaskan voyage passengers had been unaware of the threat posed by Eskimo terrorists and the very real danger of Inuit boarding-parties. His warnings about soft-targets to members of the Women's Institute knitting circle, about what to do in the event of a Jihadist attack on Mevagissey, led to a surge in membership of the Cornish Liberation Front.

Yours vigilantly, keeping a beady eye on things

Chief Inspector Magnus O'Shea

-

The Nest

Dear Chief Inspector O'Shea

We are grateful for your actions, though I confess that neither Sophie nor I know what it is that we are more worried about: having a sheep-shagging crackpot on the loose, or a hare-strangling survivalist living up our tree. Is there any progress yet?

Truro CID

Dear Admiral

We are hot on the tail of Bogus Unearthed. We have conducted dawn raids on three properties and only narrowly missed him. In the first, he had been working as a sales assistant in a ladies dress-shop. Several pot mannequins had been meddled with. Without being too anatomical, we are now hunting a stalker who has in his possession a hammer, a chisel – with which he performs operations of a delicate nature on the pot models – before making love to them. On the advice of our scientific colleagues in Forensics, A&E departments at hospitals in the region have been advised to look out for a crazy with lacerations to their undercarriage.

The second swoop was on the practice of a veterinary surgeon where Chummy had been put in charge of the incinerator. He was fired when the vet noticed a sudden leap in the number of goats being sent to the big herder in the sky. A third raid was on a remote farm on the moors where he had been working as a sheep shearer, allegedly.

Trying to hide in plain sight like this will not help Chummy for long. He will discover that in Cornwall there is no hiding place, and for the police there will be no rest until he is brought to justice and has to face the full majesty of the Law.

Yours vigilantly

Chief Inspector Magnus O'Shea, keeping an eye on things.

-

Summer turned to autumn, autumn to winter, and though PC Butter remained in his tree, the Cornish dragnet still produced no results. The Admiral and the police were beginning to think that Bogus Unearthed had found cover in another part of the country. Without warning, however, there came a break through.

Truro CID

Dear Admiral

I'm delighted to be able to inform you that we now have in custody the errant sailor, sheep shagger and pot-model abuser, the Lord Vice-Admiral Jackson Ogfe-Worth, aka Bogus Unearthed.

In the middle of the night he was spotted in a boat by the eagle-eyed PC Butter who, fortunately, was surveying the sea in a north-north westerly direction, from the elevated vantage point of your Oak tree, using his ex-paratrooper infra-red binoculars which allow him to see in the dark.

Under Butter's impeccable surveillance, Bogus Unearthed brought his craft to shore and moored it at Deadman's Beach. He then scaled the cliff and proceeded in a south-south-easterly direction, making his way along the cliff-top path to your cottage. As he opened your five-bar gate Butter dropped on him, like a giant conker (or is that a Chestnut?) all sixteen-stone of him. Bogus Unearthed was taken to hospital with cuts and fractures and is now being held on remand in Exeter Prison awaiting trial.

We found various items of interest on or about his person, including a bumper-pack of poisoned Bonio biscuits, carpenters tools and a photograph of you and Ms. Sophie Collingwood, as featured in the Polperro Packet, when you were guests of honour at the Penzance Odd Fellows Ball. His nether regions were in a bit of a mess.

Had Bogus Unearthed managed to enter The Nest, which he confessed was his intention, you might have found his appearance alarming: he was wearing a sheepskin coat, ladies knickers and a goat's head mask. As Butter observed, Chummy was also blue with cold, as there was a strong wind off the Atlantic on that starless night.

Butter will receive a police medal for his diligence, but he also broke his nose when he fell on his victim.

He's a tough chap, though, and believes strongly in the healing power of bananas. So he's eating several bunches a day, and instead of discarding the skins in the ordinary way, he uses them to dress the wound. Being on patrol, with a banana skin stuck on his nose, can look a little odd, but his already formidable arrest rate has rocketed. The Chummies are so frightened by his appearance that when he approaches them they instantly confess to everything.

Personally, I had never heard of the amazing medicinal properties of a banana skin, but his recommendations are being taken seriously, and are now to be included in what we boys in blue lovingly call the Coppers Bible, the Police First Aid Manual (first published by Robert Peel in 1829 and now about to be sponsored by Geest).

We are certain about the evil intent of Bogus Unearthed. It would not have been pleasant for you, Ms. Collingwood, or Albion the dog. It's as well we've nabbed BU as we in the Force have come to call the little fruit-cake. In Cornwall, Sir, we *always* get our man.

Incidentally, you will be pleased to know that the Director of Public Prosecutions has decided not to press charges against Albion, given that the canine psychiatric reports said he couldn't resist anything or anybody in black.

At the time of the Albion incident, if you recall, several weeks before Bogus Unearthed turned up, PC Butter had come down from his tree to use the facilities. It was then that Albion pounced. He had, it seems, been lying in wait in your rhododendron bushes, knowing that sooner or later Butter would have to answer the call of nature.

As is his way, Butter dressed his own wound, which as you can imagine was on an especially painful part of his anatomy, using another unusual poultice of garlic, tea tree oil and, to make it stick, Wrigley's juicy fruit chewing gum. I am pleased to report that the bite marks are now beginning to fade.

Yours vigilantly

Chief Inspector Magnus O'Shea, keeping an eye on things.

The Nest

Dear Chief Inspector O'Shea

We are most grateful for the superlative efforts made by you and your colleagues, particularly the amazing PC Butter. We are now more relaxed knowing that Bogus Unearthed is under lock and key. Albion seems to be immensely relieved. He had lost his bounce and taken to moping around while always keeping his back to the wall.

Clearly the problems suffered by Bogus Unearthed must stem back to the time when we had to kick him out of the Navy. He had taken a warship up the Mersey and opened up his big guns on Liverpool, his explanation being that his ex-wife came from there and he had developed a dangerous attitude towards scousers.

It seemed a pretty slim defence at the time and we should have recognised that he had underlying problems. Though he and I could have drowned as a result of his caper off the coast, when he tried to ram my yacht, I shall probably give evidence on his behalf, saying that the poor fellow is clearly demented and needs help. It's the sheep I really feel sorry for.

Lancing-Lancing

**

As the months passed into years, the fondness between Lancing-Lancing and Sophie grew. One cold and snowy winter's night, as the Admiral was changing into his night shirt, he found a letter on his pillow.

Our Home

Dearest Ted

I wanted to put the following in writing, though it makes me feel wretchedly awkward, so that you can sit and think about what I am trying to say. A letter is so much less flimsy and transient than

129

our daily chatter. You will be able to read it time and again, and if you don't think it too trite, you can mull over each word in your own time, while trying to judge my real sentiments.

As you know, after Mummy and Daddy died, I found myself in what had the makings of a disastrous relationship, from which I managed to extricate myself, but at no small emotional expense to myself and, in fairness, the chap in question.

It has taken me a long time to get over my broken heart. I was at a desperately low ebb. When I saw your advertisement for a live-in nurse, I applied with some trepidation, knowing nothing of you or what the task might entail. I was, however, a nurse and understood the navy way of things, especially through my parents, and a distinguished association with the Senior Service, which as you know, in my family, stretches back several generations.

This is really a roundabout way of saying that I have never been happier, and that you have given me a sense of belonging and security which I thought I would never find. When I took the job I had no idea that it would lead to such fulfilment or contentment, or that you and I would strike up a bond of such joy; at least, that is how it seems to me, and I pray you find it the same.

I know you are a little older than me, and that the presence of Charlotte is forever in the cottage, and that you still miss her with a terrible intensity. I understand that, and I feel for you, and it is entirely as it should be.

Nevertheless, though you are still my employer, I think it only right to tell you that my affection for you has grown on a daily basis. I hope this letter doesn't sound too forward, sloppy or silly. I am old-fashioned. I was raised in a household which insisted on courtesy, modesty and discretion. Today, it sounds Jane Austen. I hope you will forgive me for writing with such candour.

Thank you for all that you have given me. These are things in my head and my heart, and I so wanted to share them with you.

Sophie

Our Home

Dearest Sophie

I too am happier than I have been for years. You have brought a great and entirely unexpected bounty of kindness and warmth into my life. You have been supportive of my endeavours, and forgiving when I get into foolish scrapes which, if I'm being honest, are so often of my own making. I no longer see you as an employee, but as my closest, dearest friend. Though you are kind about my age I am, sadly, and as you must be aware, many years your senior.

I have wondered, and worried, without divulging my concerns, about the lack of companionship in your life. I suppose I have done this in a fatherly, protective way. Our lonely cottage on the cliffs is devoid of a young circle, bereft of companions of your own age. It is as though an exquisitely beautiful young woman is trapped like an exotic bird in this solitary eyrie. I have been greatly exercised by such worries.

Perhaps you need more lively company, younger people, with whom you might choose to share your life. Much as I adore you, I fret that you are cut off up here from the fun and gaiety which are the rewards of the young and the vivacious. Having said that, there is little point in denying the fact that my feelings towards you have grown quite immeasurably. I would like to ponder a little longer on your most touching letter.

As ever

Ted.

-

Our Home

Dear Ted

Your presence is convivial enough for me. I know we have little here but the cry of the seagulls and the ocean crashing on the rocks at the foot of the cliffs. With your friendship, who could want for more? Age is not a hindrance. It brings wit, worldliness and maturity. Callow youth holds no appeal.

Sophie
-

Our Home

Dearest dear

But Sophie, it is my age which makes me shy about pressing my affection on someone younger and so attractive. I am old, with a gammy leg. Perhaps I would have sought to further our friendship had I not been inhibited by such factors. With age, the boldness of youth is replaced by a wish not to burden others, or to make overtures which could prove unwelcome, even embarrassing.

Ted
-

Their relationship continued to blossom. They took long walks together, along the shore or high up on the cliffs. They explored the countryside in the Jaguar. They sailed for hours, mooring at pretty hostelries for lingering lunches, or candlelit suppers. And when the sun burned gold and strong they swam in the ocean and lay on the warm sand; or lunched alfresco, taking impromptu picnics of champagne and smoked salmon, amid the purple heather on the Cornish moors.

They talked and laughed and chattered about silly things in which others, not party to their secrets, would see no joy. Theirs was the special laughter of those who have become close. They enjoyed the comfortable quietness of friends, content in their solitude. One night, aboard The Lily and George, they clutched at one another, and the stars fell from the sky ..

The Nest

Dear George and Catharine

This will come as a shock, but Sophie and I would like you to be witnesses at our wedding. I know marriage sounds mad at my age, especially to someone who is so much younger, but I have at last found some real happiness, as has Sophie, or so she assures me. I cannot believe my luck. Sophie is a delight in every way. We haven't yet fixed a date, but it won't be too far distant.

Very best wishes to you both

Lancing-Lancing

-

Gone to the Dogs

Dear Admiral and Sophie

A thousand congratulations to you both. We are honoured to be asked and delighted to accept. You're right in that it came as a surprise. But wrong to worry about your age, Ted, which is an irrelevance in matters of the heart. Of course, you're old and doddery and sometimes as mad as a March hare .. but we all are. So who cares? To Hell with it! We are over the moon for you and Sophie and we want to wish you the very best of luck in the future. As soon as you come up with a date, we'll clear the decks and help to get you launched.

As ever

George and Catharine.

PS: Can we take it you won't be honeymooning by balloon?

The wedding was followed by a reception held in a candy striped marquee on the lawns which surrounded the cottage. It was a large and eclectic gathering, which began quietly and ended less so. At 10pm the Mousehole Mozart string quartet left the stage, allowing Lancing-Lancing to give an inimitable version of Stars fell on Alabama on his trombone.

Dad dancing ensued, with music by Down the Looe, a rock'n roll band led by Reg Peabody (their novelty dance song, Do the Wad, reached number 137 in the national charts).

Lancing-Lancing was well-known and the event had been widely publicised, which led to the presence of several gatecrashers. They included McButtocks of Boat Puffery; Stag Hake, the Knot-in-Chief; Guiseppe Falconetti, the Italian man about town; Herman the German, who arrived by helicopter, saying he'd jetted in from Paraguay, where he was working on a secret mission, primarily concerned with taking over the world; and William Two Fingers Maltby, who sailed to Cornwall from Monaco, with a crew of three long-legged blondes, one of whom, Candice, stripped off in the early hours, whilst the party was in full swing, and gave Lancing-Lancing his own, personalised, lap dance, saying she loved it as she had never previously done it with an Admiral.

Sophie, in the meantime, had to fend off the attentions of Two-Fingers, who kept telling her that all he'd ever wanted was the quiet life and that he was desperate to settle down in Polperro (it had been, apparently, his life-long dream) especially if she would care to join him for the occasional weekend. Falconetti said he'd give Sophie turns in his speedboat if she'd spend time with him at his apartment in Port Hercule in Monaco. Buttocks said she found Sophie irresistible, and if she ever discovered gay tendencies she'd be pleased to offer her hand in marriage.

As dawn broke, Stag Hake said he'd had a belly full of Buttocks, who at the time lay comatose after consuming generous quantities of Lancing-Lancing's gin and crème de menthe punch, and proceeded to tie her up in a Uruguayan quadruple hitch, before hanging her upside down from the large oak tree near the cottage gate, which had last seen service with PC Butter.

After a couple of days, Lancing-Lancing drove his Jaguar from Cornwall to the Norfolk Broads, where he and his new bride holidayed on 'Puck', George and Catharine Steel's sail boat. They moored on Hickling Broad and Horsey Mere and ate romantic, simple suppers, cooked on the little gimbal stove, beneath Norfolk's vast, uninterrupted skies, with Swallowtail butterflies, swans, ducks and the low boom of the shy Bittern, as their only company.

Hickling Village

Norfolk Broads

Dear George

A quick note to tell you and Catharine what a wonderful time Sophie and I are having and to thank you, once again, for letting us have the use your boat, *Puck,* for a few days. Norfolk has been sun-kissed and the Broads sailing is sublime. I got caught once on a reed-bed, but came to no harm, thanks to your lifting keel. One has to turn and tack almost constantly, of course. They say if you can master Broads sailing you can sail anywhere. After all, it was Nelson who learned to sail on these waters.

Here, in the Northern Broads, we have had excellent winds, being only half a mile or so from the sea. Hickling, Horsey, Meadow Dyke, Heigham Sound and Somerton; they will always have a very special place in our memories.

Lancing-Lancing and Sophie

After their Broads break, the newly-weds continued their honeymoon at the legendary Carlton Hotel, in Cannes, on the Cote d'Azur. One evening, Two Fingers Maltby entertained them to dinner at the Yacht Club de Monaco. At one point, Sophie visited the powder room and, a moment later, Two-Fingers suddenly and unexpectedly materialised from behind a gilded pillar. Known as one of the most persistent gropers on the Riviera, where it's a fine art, he said he was mad for her, and that he wanted them to instantly sail away, his yacht being tethered just outside. When they rejoined the Admiral, Two-Fingers had a bright red cheek.

"What's happened ?" Lancing-Lancing said.

"Nothing really, old boy .. ran into a former flame. She always had a bit of a thing about me," he said, giving Sophie one of his lizard smiles.

In the taxi going back to The Carlton, Lancing-Lancing asked Sophie what had gone on.

"Oh, nothing at all. He just tries it on with every woman he meets. Can't help himself."

"So you slapped him?"

"'Fraid so. Well and truly."

"Good for you."

"You know what it's like. Sailing's full of people like him."

That night, unbeknown to Sophie, Lancing-Lancing 'phoned Guiseppe Falconetti.

"I've a favour to ask," he said.

The next day, two Italians, built like the Coliseum, button-holed Two-Fingers at the bar of the Yacht Club de Monaco.

"Go near Admiral's wife again," they whispered, "and we break two legs, pull arms from body with crane and take teeth out mouth with big pliers. Understand?"

Two-Fingers nodded.

"OK" he said, white-faced and shaken, gulping down his Campari, watching them roar away in a scarlet Ferrari.

**

Among 'legitimates', as opposed to gate-crashers at the wedding, were Lancing-Lancing's friends and neighbours, Lord Edward and Lady Amelia Claremont. Minnie Claremont is a stalwart of numerous voluntary committees, for which she is always seeking help and support, and constantly trying to inveigle people into joining her in her different charitable enterprises.

Rose Hall

Polperro

Dear Admiral

Many congratulations on your wedding, and thank you so much for inviting us to your party, which turned out to be such a lively affair. Sophie is such a lovely young woman. You have some wonderfully exotic friends. Eddie was fascinated by Herman and his military ambitions, although, of course, he has always had reservations about Germans, especially ones who look as astonishingly young as Herman.

As you may know, I am the chairwoman of the Distressed Householders Fund. It tries to help those people who have inherited houses which are so large and run down that the National Trust won't touch them with a barge-pole (bit like our place). There are several estates round here whose occupants are facing ruinous bills and who don't know which way to turn. Most of them are living in something close to penury.

On the Distressed Householders Fund we try to think of ways that can help them generate money. With your wide experience, your circle of friends and contacts and, if I might add, your fertile imagination and reputation for novel thinking, it is my view that you would make a most excellent member of the committee. What do you think?

Do pop over to the hall for some port with your lovely bride. I'll fix a date. When you have a moment, please let me know what you think.

Toodle-oo for now!

Minnie

-

The Nest

Dear Minnie

This isn't the sort of thing I normally get involved in, but since it's you, I don't mind giving it a go. Thank you for asking me.

Lancing-Lancing

-

One of several mouldering estates that the committee tried to help was Nut Bake Towers, once home to the 19th century pastry chef turned industrial philanthropist, Titus Nut. Titus Nut built pioneering steam-driven flour-mills and founded a bread and confectionery empire. Nut Bake Towers is at the centre of Nut Bake Village, which Titus built for his workers.

In its treatment of its employees the company was ahead of its time, the village having better facilities than most with its own chapel, school, clinic, communal wash-house and rows of neat little terraced houses heated by surplus steam from the flour mill.

Sadly, in 1921, the business went bust. The workers had to move away to seek employment elsewhere, and Oliver Nut, who was in charge of the company at the time, lost his fortune on the stock market in the Wall Street Crash of the same year.

Over the decades, the mansion and the village fell into disrepair. When committee members went on a fact-finding inspection they found a ruinous wasteland of collapsed homes and mountains of rubble.

The latest Nut in a long line, The Hon. Proctor Nut, works as a Strategy Profiler with the Far West Chapter of Druids, and his wife Halo Boo, who makes Peruvian prayer rugs for the Summer Solstice, are the current residents of Nut Bake Towers. They share it with their three small children Boo, Boo-Hoo and Boo-Peep, who Proctor calls his darling little Nutties.

Only the south wing, with its two decaying kitchens, a larder as big as a barn, eleven decaying bedrooms and one partially-functioning bathroom, is habitable.

The Nest

My dear Minnie

I am not convinced about the idea of Nut Bake Towers being turned into a Bed & Breakfast. I know Proctor Nut says he could do up the three unused wings, and their twenty-seven ravaged bedrooms, but I think it is beyond his do-it-yourself skills. Indeed, it would be beyond Brunel.

As for the alternative scheme, my view is that it would be cheaper and easier to move the Alps than to try and flatten the entire village and clear the site so that the Nuts could erect a Big Top from where they could sell Cornish pasties, scones and clotted cream teas, in the summer, while using it in the winter to house a circus.

There are an awful lot of people selling Cornish pasties and one would have to sell several billion clotted cream teas and pasties to recoup their monies. As for Proctor's idea of running a circus and zoo during the winter months, can he afford to buy, feed and house elephants and zebras? Anyway, don't animals hibernate in the winter? Such notions are, shall we say, woolly in the extreme.

There is a less costly solution to the Nut's impoverishment. Why not rent the estate to the army and let it blow it to pieces?

Since Putin and all these Jihadists started playing silly buggers the military is desperate for battle training grounds. It already looks like a war zone, so why not give it official status? The Ministry of Defence would pay a handsome sum to get their hands on it. They could blow everything around Nut Bake Towers to Kingdom Come, apart from the house itself. What do you think?

Lancing-Lancing.

-

Rose Hall

Well, Admiral, that was *so* jolly: the liveliest committee meeting we've had in ages, and largely down to you and your spirited presentation. Naturally enough, Proctor and Hallo Booboo, is that her name? still have reservations. But, frankly, as Eddie always says, beggars and buggers can't afford to be choosers.

As you maintained, they'll get a fair amount of dosh from the army chaps and General Axeblood's appeal at the meeting was persuasive. Isn't that the most wonderful name for a soldier? It's so redolent of the Viking hordes. As you know, *A Brief History of Nordic Facts and Myths* was one of the courses which I ran at Rose Hall, when, for some unaccountable reason, the Friesians were failing to produce their quota, and Eddie and I were facing something of a financial dilemma ourselves.

As General Axeblood said, Proctor will not only make money, but he'll do so in a way which is admirably patriotic. Given the motley assortment of lunatics currently running around the globe with their bad manners, tatty flags and AK47s, we're all obliged to do our bit.

The rows of terraced homes are perfect for Axeblood's men to bone up on their house-to-house fighting, and the creation of a sniper alley through the old piggeries and wash-house sounds very realistic. After all, the contract with the Defence Ministry would only be for three years, the army chaps will tidy the place up when they're finished, and Proctor will have enough money to refurbish a goodly portion of Nut Bake Towers and open it as a Bed & Breakfast, if that is what he and Hallo Booboo have set their hearts on.

Well done Admiral! I can see that you are an outstanding strategic thinker.

Minnie.

-

General Axeblood, a seasoned campaigner, had played down the cost of turning an estate over to the military.

Having learned to be wily over the years, he had omitted to mention the night raids, rocket attacks, land mines for practice runs by the Bomb Disposal Squad, helicopters with searchlights coming and going day and night, tanks, flame-throwers, howitzers and miles and miles of search lights and barbed wire which would ring the Nut Bake Towers estate.

Things came to a head when a bomb detonated in the old orchard and caused such tremors that the entire East Wing collapsed and dropped off the main body of the house.

Halo Boo Nut said the cacophony was intolerable, and that she was distracted she couldn't even summon up the concentration necessary to weave her Cornish Peruvian prayer mats. It was alright for Proctor, her old man, Halo Boo told Lady Claremont – "Oh please! everybody calls me Minnie" – because he was away week in, week out, poncing around at Stonehenge with the Druids, while she was stuck in what was left of Nut Bake Towers, with three screaming kids and bombs going off all day.

Rose Hall

Dear Admiral

I paid a site visit to Halo Nut the other day, wearing tin-helmet, flak-jacket and carrying a gas-mask, all of which is now de rigueur when one calls at Nut Bake Towers.

The poor creature is at the end of her tether and, I must say, it was the most awful racket when I was there. She was upset because Axeblood had lost his temper and called her Fruit 'n Nut. When I was in attendance, several rockets whooshed overhead and a mad-eyed sapper with a flame-thrower incinerated an ancient, scented Elaeagnus Ebbingei hedge (commonly known as Oleaster) with its lovely silver leaves.

She wanted to make me a cup of coffee. But the place reeked of gas and she said she couldn't use the stove for fear of blowing up Cornwall. The gas line had been punctured by tank tracks and a platoon of Royal Engineers were trying to find the leak.

General Axeblood was nowhere to be seen. Mrs. Nut insisted he was around, but that he had taken cover in what is now being called Axeblood's Siegfried Line, a run of trenches, tank-traps, barbed-wire and bunkers that start in the old tennis court, cut through the kitchen garden, and continue out into the historic Nut Bush Copse, via a septic tank – the last being deeply unpleasant – but which Axeblood describes as just another hazard of war.

As a former military man, might it be possible for you to have a word with Axeblood and ask him to cool things down a bit? He'll have more respect for you than he has for me. When I tried to confront him, his batman stepped in and instructed me to 'calm down, dear,' which I thought very impertinent. When I told Eddie about this he immediately went for his twelve-bore and wanted to lead what he ominously called a 'raiding party.' I managed to restrain him, or we'd have had a new front opening up in the Battle of Nut Bake Towers.

I am at an absolute loss to understand why it's all gone so frightfully haywire. I had great faith in this. I thought we were throwing the Nuts a life-line. But, as Eddie says, in his no-nonsense way, the best-laid plans often end tits-up. Being an ex-paratrooper, he knows about this sort of thing. He says you only have to look at Gallipoli, and that the road to Hell is paved with good intentions.

Minnie

-

The Nest

Dear Minnie

I had a word with General Axeblood, as you suggested, but he gave me short shrift. He said Navy types couldn't be expected to know anything about land wars, or to understand the need for battle-hardened troops who learn the basics at places like Nut Bake Towers. He said soldiers couldn't pad around in bedroom slippers and that bombs, machine-guns and mortars, couldn't be fitted with silencers. He went into a rant about it not being a finishing school for debutantes and said Mrs. Nut and her tribe were off their rockers, which, coming from him, seemed a little rich.

The easiest solution, Axeblood felt, would be to blow up what was left of the house or turn it into his headquarters. As for the East Wing collapsing, he described it as collateral damage, saying worse things happen in war, and it would have blown over anyway in the next high wind.

Our summit had to be curtailed when we came under sustained grenade attack and were obliged to make a run for it, having been mistaken for the supposed enemy. When I mentioned to Axeblood that it seemed a little over the top to be using live ammunition, he merely grunted and said that practice runs had to be realistic.

All in all it was not a helpful negotiation. Axeblood clearly has a problem with Navy people, so perhaps he would have more in common with your Eddie – being ex-army. On the other hand, as you alluded, it could end in a fracas. I'll talk to Sophie to see if she's got any bright ideas.

Lancing-Lancing.

-

The Nest

Dear Minnie

Well, to bring you up to speed, Sophie offered to try and charm Axeblood herself. She's very personable and there were rumours about him having an eye for the girls. I told her to be discreet about her own naval lineage, as anything even vaguely maritime seems to be like a red rag to a bull.

Unfortunately, our little ploy didn't work. He invited her into his quarters, a tent pitched in the middle of Nut Bush Copse, some distance from his Siegfried Line, and after pouring her a generous Bristol Cream had the damn nerve to try it on with her. She ended up kneeing him in his soldierly weak spot and giving him a wallop across the kisser. For one so gentle, she's well versed in capers of that sort. Being a pretty girl has given her extensive experience in fending off unwarranted overtures. She delivered her knee-jerk with such ferocity that Axeblood had to be stretchered off into the field hospital, groaning in agony and cursing, much to the merriment of his troopers.

We'll have to come up with another plan. Sophie said Mrs. Halo Nut was now utterly frazzled and pulling her hair out, literally. The children were running wild and Proctor was wandering around in his Druid robes singing canticles. They're all suffering post-traumatic stress disorder. The bangs and rat-a-tat-tat of machine-guns would drive anybody nuts.

Lancing-Lancing

-

Further attempts to persuade Axeblood to abandon his siege of Nut Bake Towers were destined to fail. The Bishop of Trabant, taking a surfing holiday away from his diocese in Montenegro, called in at the

Towers and begged Axeblood to see the light and show a little humanity. But Axeblood turned nasty and said national security was at stake and he'd have no hesitation in torturing a churchman, especially a foreigner, before giving him a finger-wagging about Makarios once having a machine-gun up his cassock.

The leaders of several environmental groups dropped by, but Axeblood told them they were all half-men and needed haircuts.

A deputation by Lancing-Lancing and Lord and Lady Claremont, to the Ministry of Defence, also proved unsuccessful. The Minister of Defence, formerly the finance director of Marks & Spencer, told them that the army had paid good money for its lien on the estate, and that it wanted to see a worthwhile profit on its investment. The army would not achieve a proper margin on the outlay if its three-year contract was in any way modified.

The Polperro Inquirer carried the story which stirred strong and ancient sentiments in the neighbourhood.

Ministry of Defence

Dear Lancing-Lancing

Re: Operation Nut Cracker

I thought I'd have a word about the other night, one military fellow speaking confidentially to another, if you see my meaning.

The Druid attack on General Axeblood and his men was quite unwarranted. I gather it's this crackpot Proctor Nut who's leading the Druid Brigade. There were several hundred of them, backed up by Fifth columnists, well-known trouble-makers, most of whom were in saffron robes pretending to be Buddhist monks.

As the Druids charged, armed with pitch-forks and firing potato-guns, a Peruvian band playing the pan-pipes turned up. The local police, who incarcerated the Peruvians overnight, said the Peruvians didn't join in with the Charge of the Druids, but had a quite different gripe, something about foreigners stealing their rug-making trade.

I had always thought Druids were a peaceful lot – the post-Joan

Baez crowd – but they were all as mad as Hell and kept chanting about the sun.

The thing that the Nuts must understand is that they signed an agreement and received a sizeable amount of money. There must be something we can do before this business gets dreadfully out of hand, and we end up with a full-scale Druid War.

British Intelligence is on its toes and our agents in the field tell us that a top-level, hush-hush terrorist summit, has been fixed between the Druid Brigade, the Joan of the Wad Collective, the Pisky Movement and the Free Polperro Liberation Army (FPLA). Our agents have collated intelligence which suggests that the FPLA is capable of desperate tactics. It is pledged to rid Polperro, Mousehole, Mevagissey and other such places, of what it calls 'the abominable tourist plague,' and says it will rehouse gypsies and travellers in second-homes, of which there are many, and which are owned and lived in largely by rich 'foreigners' from London who only occupy them at weekends.

The real threat, as we perceive it here at HQ, is if these shadowy groups get together as a combined fighting unit.

At the Ministry of Defence we don't want to find ourselves suddenly caught up in another Vietnam. Intelligence suggests that many of those involved were in the student protests and anti-Vietnam riots back in the 1960s. They're all older, fatter and balder, but we still don't want chants of Ho! Ho! Ho Chi Minh! turning into Ho! Ho! Ho Chi Nut! I implore you to use your best counsel to nip Flashpoint Polperro in the bud, before it descends into a cockpit of tumult and riotous dissent.

Next time you're in London, do try and pop into the Army& Navy Club for a quickie. Haven't seen you for an age, but loved reading about you and your dog in the great balloon adventure.

Incidentally, I always felt you were harshly treated over that invention of yours – the one where you had elastic running down your trouser leg when you're trying to have a Jimmy Riddle. Who knows? If we can quell this rather bizarre insurrection, perhaps we could resurrect your novelty device in some way.

Ambie

Lieut.-Col. Ambrose Marlowe-Drew (Counter Surveillance)
-

The Nest

Dear Marlowe-Drew

You're right, it's been an age. Last time I went to the Army& Navy I got food poisoning. We could probably do something at my club, The Reform, a nicer building, with courteous members and first class gourmet dining. Let me be candid: I think your letter smacks of panic. I do not foresee a Pisky uprising, nor do I see this relatively trivial matter (though not for the Nut's, of course) as another Vietnam.

Proctor has no ambitions to be the new Ho Chi Nut. I have tried to reason with Axeblood, as has my wife, who concluded her meeting by kneeing him in his medals. It's up to his superiors at the Ministry of Defence to tell him to be more scrupulous and circumspect about the way he conducts himself and his military forays.

If you could find alternative accommodation for the Nuts that might be the answer, especially as Axeblood hinted that the length of time that the army will be in occupation, so to speak, might be shorter than was first expected. This is because he and his men have been particularly energetic and blown up everything in sight, rather more quickly than was initially anticipated. There is hardly anything left to bazooka, machine-gun, detonate or explode, all buildings having been reduced to mountains of rubble.

The only structure still recognisable – *well*, two-thirds of it – is Nut Bake Towers itself.

But I am not happy about the way Axeblood has trained his Howitzers on it and was telling his troops to imagine they were in Berlin and had Hitler's bunker in their sights. He is urging his men to conduct what he terms a scorched earth policy, saying that it's a long-term strategy which will be for the eventual good of Cornwall.

It only needs one over exuberant gunner and the MoD could find itself facing a tragedy, which would be the catalyst for the unification of the disparate bands of freedom fighters that your spies have identified.

As for *Zip Ahoy* – what you call my Jimmy Riddle novelty – I am still, *ahem*, sore about the matter. I cannot believe the MoD will ever cough up what it owes me for that, anymore than it will offer me the Cornish Nobel Peace Prize for trying to negotiate a ceasefire in the War of Nut Bake Towers.

Lancing-Lancing

-

Ministry of Defence

Dear Lancing-Lancing

Interestingly, there are some spare lodgings that the Nuts could be moved into, on the old RAF Flit Wick base near Barnacle Cove. We had to put it into moth balls because of the government cuts.

You're quite right in thinking that Axeblood plans on vacating Camp Nut Bake in a few months, there being nothing left to blow up. We've found another site for him in Scotland. It's perfect, just heather and sheep and the odd croft at which to blaze away. One wonders what the Scottish Nationalists will have to say, but some American waste-disposal king was going to develop it anyway, as a golf course and grouse-shoot for billionaires. The Save our Sheep lot were also polishing up their placards, *of course*, but we can always harp on about defence interests and play the patriot card.

Anyway, you might want to mull it over with the Nuts – very unofficially, for goodness sake never put anything in writing. It would only be for a relatively short space of time and they could move into one of the sizeable and rather comfy senior officers' houses. It's a bit windswept, down there in Flit Wick, you know what airfields are like. But if it's peace and quiet they're hankering after, they'll certainly get it there, being surrounded by two hundred empty houses, plus the disused cafeteria, offices, watch-tower, workshops, stores and so on.

Mrs. Nutty could relocate her rug business to one of the hangars. There'd be enough room in there for a thousand spinning Jennies, or however you make Peruvian doormats. They'd also feel nice and safe. There are huge gates on the base and one of those red and white poles that lifts up and down in front of the guard house (nobody to man it, so they'll have to do it themselves). There's plenty of room for the little Nuts to run around: the whole kit and caboodle covers several hundred acres and it's surrounded by a 12-foot- high electrified wire fence.

The more I think about it, the more I feel it could be just what we're looking for. I'll be interested in the Nut's response. It could be a handy solution. Wherever possible, we try and be accommodating in the MoD. There's no doubt that the Nut Bake Towers saga had all the makings – if not of a war – then, certainly, a public relations fiasco. So if we can reduce the temperature, all well and good.

'Twixt you and me and the Quartermaster, this would not have escalated were Axeblood sane. He should have been shot years ago. But they hang on like grim death for their pensions. Let's have that drinky-poo sometime. On the other matter, the Jimmy Riddler, don't be too downcast. I understand why, after all this time, you're still smarting, but I have a feeling in my waters about its future recognition.

Ambie
-

After protracted negotiations, brought to an abrupt end when Axeblood's sappers inadvertently let off a Bloodhound missile, which obliterated the little that was left of the estate chapel, the Nut's locked up Nut Bake Towers, and with their three children moved to the abandoned RAF Flit Wick. But after some weeks there was an unexpected development.

Ministry of Defence

Re: Operation Nut Cracker

Dear Lancing-Lancing

I do think the Nut's have been unreasonable and unappreciative. The illegal occupation of the empty houses and other buildings at RAF Flitwick by hundreds of foreign Druids who have gathered from all over the world is causing consternation at the MoD. As you know, only bona fide druids are being allowed in via Dover and the different airports, but aerial surveillance by drone indicates a Druid invasion of the base of quite staggering proportions.

Huge numbers of Gipsies and travellers have swollen the druid ranks and set up permanent camp, which seems odd given that they call themselves *travellers*. It is going to be difficult to re-conquer the territory. Guards from the Druid Brigade patrol the electrified perimeter fence armed with potato-guns, which don't sound much, but believe me if you get a King Edward pellet in your eye you know about it.

Intelligence have a plan to infiltrate Flit Wick with Fifth Columnists. They'll pass themselves off disguised as assorted fanatical druids, Buddhist monks, Peruvian pan-pipe players and every imaginable type of Polperro Liberationist.

Their task will be to sow dissent, turning the assembled against one another. Guerrilla tactics will cause havoc with the day-to-day functioning of the squat. It'll be the usual Special Op's stuff: blocked lavatories, vandalism in the prayer-mat hangar, mystery blight wiping out vegetables in the allotments they've dug round the runways, poisoned carrots guaranteeing salmonella.

It'll be made to look as if it's all the fault of the travellers. We'll foment friction and dissent between the factions, so that eventually they will all turn on one another. Divide and rule, that's the kernel of the Stop the Nut strategy. Hopefully, most of the incursors will lose heart and then beetle off back to wherever they came from. Any stragglers who choose to remain we can mop up later without too much fuss.

The boys and girls in Intelligence are being given intensive training. They love a bit of pantomime.

They're building horse-drawn gipsy-caravans and painting them in garish colours. They're learning to light camp-fires, smoke shag in clay-pipes and sing Romany folk songs. They're being shown how to handle pie-bald ponies (notoriously wilful) and how to cross palms with silver and read crystal-balls. They've taken to wearing big hoop earrings and red and white dusters on their heads. They're getting their tongues round Romany, though their accents are still a bit cut-glass, and they're learning how to make pegs.

They've been told time and again that real Romanies are thin on the ground, and that today's travellers are likely to be big in scrap metal and drive Mercedes'. But Intelligence comprises Oxbridge to a man. They think they were born to rule and they're all chippy as hell because they really wanted the diplomatic service. But the Dip Corr has been cut and embassies are as rare as knife-sharpeners on bikes and peg-sellers in spotty headscarves. The problem with today's Spooks is that they don't listen. Hey-ho! What can one do? It's the highly-educated younger generation. We'll have to see how the Stop the Nut campaign pans out.

Ambie

-

The plan was eventually successful. The Druids and Piskies were hit by a series of mystery misfortunes and consequently fell out spectacularly with the Gipsies and travellers, most of whom were entirely counterfeit insurgents led by the likes of MI5 officers Jake Snipe and Angie Jutting, deep cover-names for Jonty Bottom-Hogg and Tiggy Bracing-Lusty. The travellers became fed up with being blamed by everybody and departed RAF Flit Wick in a convoy of lorries, caravans and Mercedes', to sell as scrap that which they'd pinched off the base, including two hangars. The different species of Cornish liberationists gradually ran out of steam and returned to their homes. Axeblood and his squaddies went north to re-live the great Clan battles of the Highlands.

The Nuts today have a prosperous enterprise at Nut Bake Towers. Its biggest asset is that it's still in a state of total decay with hardly a roof, no running water, heating or sanitation. The Nut's now run it as a management survival school – advertised as the toughest and most deprived in England – where companies send their managers to learn about leadership. Promising students can progress to a Nut Bake MBA, a two-year-course described by its graduates as 'two years of sheer Hell'.

Candidates have to cope with no showers, sanitation (a hole on the moor, even in winter) de-hydration, sleep-deprivation and starvation but for a daily bowl of Halo Boo's Tibetan lentils cooked in a goat's spleen. On Sundays, she or her managers serve candidates a special treat of cow udder melts flambed in an Indonesian love jus and pickled walnut dip.

Nut Bake Towers is widely regarded as the Eton of the business survival schools, with fees to match. The esteemed company organ, Management Now! described it as 'the best of the best .. so gruelling corporate high-fliers are reduced to weeping wrecks.' With its motto 'Hard Nuts aren't born, they're forged,' it recently went public, its flotation proving to be a Stock Market sensation.

The chairman, Proctor Nut, who forsook Druidism for the City, told eager investors that Nut Bake Towers was a business with no downside. 'We have no outgoings,' he said. 'It's the perfect business. All incomings and no expenses. We don't offer food, beds, rooms or much of a roof. We don't have any utilities so there are no plumbing, gas or electricity bills. There are no laundry bills because we don't have any sheets or linen because we don't have any beds, apart from one or two, without springs, and they're just for those softies who fall ill.'

Proctor and his family have left the house and now live permanently in the penthouse suite of the five-star Alhambra Continental in Padstow, from where they are helicoptered back to the Nut Bake Survival School on the rare occasions when their presence is needed by their team of ex-SAS managers.

Jason Probe, in his influential share-tipping column, 'Coining It In', in the 'Wall Street Packet', wrote: 'Everybody should do it. You torture people half to death, give them accommodation you wouldn't *keep a dog in, and fleece them for a fortune. The Nut Bake Survival School (NBSS) run by Proctor Naylor, once a foremost Druid and now a hard-driving Capitalist, is one shrewd operator. As long as companies make so much money they don't know what to do with it, the NBSS represents non-stop profit. Investors everywhere should fill their boots and buy, buy, buy.'*

**

Those closest to Lancing-Lancing, especially George Steele, kept up a stream of letters, knowing that the Admiral relished getting all the news. Steele understood that his friend had led an exceptionally full life, and that he missed not being quite as active as he had once been. Whenever something untoward, amusing or unexpected happened to Steel, he would always send a letter.

Gone to the Dogs

Dear Admiral

How the devil are you? Thought I'd just drop a note complaining about life in general. Things have been frightfully tedious since your magnificent nuptials. Did anybody let Buttocks down from that tree? Or is she still hanging around?

Catharine and I did have one spot of fun, though, when the owner of Balzak Dynamo invited us for a weekend on one of his boats. As well as his football team he's got another nine yachts, a couple of submarines and the odd helicopter. Doesn't pay a bean in tax, of course, and is wanted all over Eastern Europe.

His estate in Mole Valley in deepest Surrey looks like Guantanamo Bay. Used to be a golf course but he's converted it into a fortress. He's keeps a string of racehorses there and the odd camel. I think he's Albanian, but when you ask him about his background and his nationality he gets rather shirty. Everybody calls him Erik. Catharine's good at languages and says that it means 'ruler of everything'. So I'm not sure who or what he is,

152

except that he's colossally rich and for a chap on the run seems to be hiding in plain sight.

I'm uncertain, even mystified, why Erik the Ruler invited us, though he hinted that at some point in the future he might buy a newspaper, or four, and a few TV and a radio stations, as one does. He also wants his yacht written up. It's the sort of thing Buttocks likes to run in *Boat Puffery*. Such pieces are more like *Homes & Gardens* on water, rather than *real* journalism, but fees being a little thin on the ground, currently, I've had to temporarily soften my opposition to writing advertorial. As Catharine the Pragmatist says, though such pieces go against the grain, it's a case of *if needs be*, and they all help to pay the bills.

It would be ungracious to knock Erik's generosity, and there's no question that he knows how to throw a rip-roaring party. Catharine and I woke up with dreadful hangovers in a king-size bed in the Erjon Suite (Catharine said it meant wind, which was worrying). Neither of us has a clue how we arrived in the windy suite. We must have had more vodka and champagne than we thought. My mind's a blank, as is Catharine's.

At breakfast we were treated most graciously by Erik the Ruler's squeeze, the lovely Tania. It was glorious weather, hot and sunny, and I've never seen anybody fill a bikini like Tania. Erik kept calling her Tits in that extraordinarily charming way so many East Europeans seems to have. She said she was from Smolensk and married to Yuri Schlopski, the Balzak Dynamo goalie, and that she hoped Yuri wouldn't twig that she was carrying on with Erik, as Yuri was prone to psychotic fits.

After breakfast (smoked salmon and another vat of Cristal) we were helped off the yacht – about as big as the *Titanic* – back to Portsmouth. Most enjoyable, but we had to hole up for the night in the Fizzy Snapper (converted Napoleonic watch tower, and still pretty basic) as neither of us were fit to drive.

Lots of love to Sophie. Married life treating you well?

George

Nest

George, dear boy

Since you ask, Buttocks was rather forgotten at the wedding party, so I'm afraid she did an overnight hanging around in the Oak. She was in a Hell of a rage when we cut her down the next morning and said that by the time she'd finished with Stag Hake his own mother wouldn't recognize him (polite version).

Your party sounds a winner. Erik the Ruler must be a rarity. There can't be too many football-crazy Albanian camel-breeders. Perhaps he was sounding you out for an editorship? One never knows what these people have in mind, if anything.

Yes, thank you, married life is excellent. Sophie has had a mellowing influence. I've even started wearing after-shave and she says I ought to use moisturizer as my skin's brittle from being up on the Bridge for all those years. It'll be tattoos and blonde streaks and piercings next. Fortunately, that's *not* Sophie

Keep your futtocks oiled

Lancing-Lancing

-

Boat Planet

Dear Admiral Lancing-Lancing

The treatment meted out to me by a guest at your party, the unspeakable Hake, was shocking. I would hope, at the least, that you have reprimanded him.

I have spoken to the police, but their view is that the party was on private property and that everybody was so inebriated I was rather asking for it, which, as I am sure you will concur, is appalling, sexist, misogynist and all the rest. I was, after all, helpless and without defence when I was set on by that foul-mouthed knot-head. At some point he will *have* to come out of hiding. When he does, I'll be waiting. How would you like to have been tied upside-

154

down in a tree all night?

Nicola McButtley

-

The Nest

Dear Ms. McButtley

I too think it was disgraceful behaviour. Had I been aware of your plight I would certainly have cut you down. As for you being defenceless, I gather you played a blinder at scrum-half in the winning rugby team in the afternoon, when celebrations were still at a playful stage. Shortly afterwards you were instrumental in winning the tug-of-war, with the opposing team being very nearly wrenched over the edge of Deadman's Cliff. As the evening wore on you challenged the 'biggest b*****d in the room' to take you on at kick-boxing, which resulted in my frail and elderly odd job man, Trumble, being ambulanced away, when you mistakenly imagined he had stepped forward to accept your challenge. In fact, he was merely acting as a waiter, and was kindly offering you a Daiquiri Sizzler (your seventh, according to Hake).

If you had not so conclusively beaten Hake at arm-wrestling, and then thrown up over him, the incident to which you refer would not, in my view, have occurred. I think demonstrating your considerable prowess at rugby, excelling in the tug-of-war, being lethal at kick-boxing and virtually twisting Hake's arm from his shoulder, makes your claim about being a 'defenceless' little person, rather hollow.

Further, if you will allow me to point out, you, Hake and several more, were gatecrashers. You had not been invited. Your presence and behaviour, and that of other imposters, could easily have upset my bride and wrecked what for both of us was a special day.

Fortunately, Sophie is made of sterner stuff. She is not easily perturbed, having come from proud naval stock, unlike others I can think of who make a good living out of maritime affairs, but have little or no background in the subject. I also think it

155

inappropriate that on her wedding day you had the gall to ask my bride to change her nature and run away with you to be your wife.

None of this, admittedly, excuses tying you upside down and leaving you hanging in a tree overnight. The squirrels are active at this time of year so, looking on the bright side, it could have been worse. Though you weren't invited, I would still like to apologise. This was a terrible way to treat anybody.

Lancing-Lancing

-

Gone to the Dogs

Dear Admiral

Something shocking has occurred. A bunch of photographs arrived the other day showing myself, Catharine and Tania, the goalie's wife and mistress of Erik the Ruler, in a state of undress. They purport to show a threesome going on in the Tirana Cabin of Erik the Ruler's yacht. Attached to them was a note from Erik saying that he thought I would like them as a souvenir of our pleasant sojourn. He says he'll be in touch shortly as he wants to ask a favour. I can't think what it might be and, in truth, neither Catharine nor I can remember a damn thing about threesomes (it's really not our scene) or the photographs being taken.

If you look closely at them it appears we were dead to the world. We had a drink or two, but in all seriousness not that much. All we can think is that we must have been out cold, drugged to the world in some way. I'll keep you posted, but we're spooked at the moment.

George

-

The Nest

Dear boy

I don't blame you for being a little uneasy. Funny lot some of these people. It's gone on for years but I thought such capers had died out when the Cold War started to thaw. Do you want me to have a quiet word with my pals in security? Be pleased to help if I can. Try not to worry about it too much. When you're rich as Croesus it's inevitable you end up barking. Erik the Ruler is clearly a head banger.

All the best

Lancing-Lancing

-

Dogs

Dear Admiral

Well, Erik the Ruler has been in touch again. He wants two things: Catharine, and a glowing write-up in *Boat Puffery*.

He says if I don't play ball he'll send the snaps round Fleet Street and we'll be a laughing stock. Killing him is a distinct possibility, and one that Catharine rather favours, but only if we could get away with it. I have been unsure about what to do. I think, however, we have now agreed on a plan of action.

We're going to give Erik a roasting. It's a good story and I can make more than a few bob out of it. So I'm going to have a word with a friend on *The Sunday Times*, Marty McNiece, and offer it as an exclusive. We're not too concerned about being seen in the buff, and anyway, Marty will blank out the naughty bits.

Erik the Ruler's dodgy enterprises will get a public airing and be nicely raked over. He runs an iffy portfolio and he's already despised as the king of the tax-dodgers. He'll find out that I won't roll over quite as easily as the supine planners who are letting him build a three-storey underground extension beneath his Grade I West End mansion. It will have two nuclear bunkers, a vault because nobody trusts Hatton Garden anymore, ballroom, swimming pool, library, a wine cellar as big as Burgundy, and stables for his horses so that he and Tania can continue their post-boudoir galloping in Hyde Park each morning.

I must remember, incidentally, to take a close look at how many planning officers are being bribed by the likes of Erik the Ruler. When this attempt at blackmail makes the headlines, doubtless Tania will be offered a presenting role on a TV reality show, so at least she won't lose out.

I confess, Admiral, to being angry. Perhaps dangerously so. You can no doubt sense it in this missive. Killing him, after torturing him slowly, still seems an attractive option.

Heavy weather ahead.

George

-

The Nest

My dear boy

Now hold your horses. Don't be too precipitous. Before going to the 'papers why not warn him of your intentions? You don't know what he might offer. It could be something to your advantage and won't have involved you in all these other capers. I'm an older hand than you, have a think about what I say. Don't do anything until you've calmed down and given the whole wretched business some very careful thought.

As ever

Lancing-Lancing

-

Dogs

Thank you, Admiral. You helped pacify me and it was wise counsel. I'm grateful. I have taken your advice, and rather than putting anything in writing – you know how bits of paper can boomerang on one – I had a quick word with Erik on the 'phone. He was pretty taken aback when I told him that I was going to go public, that I didn't give a damn about his two-bit threats, and that I was going to give the 'papers the whole story. I think he realizes he has more to lose than me.

I mentioned that it would be enormous fun if swarms of journalists began prying into his affairs. They'd undoubtedly turn up some very readable stuff. Drugs, for instance? It certainly wasn't aspirin that he gave Cathy and I. Orgies? Dubious tax affairs? Offshore companies nobody knows about? People trafficking? Bribing planners?

George

-

Gone to the Dogs

Well, Admiral, it didn't take long for Erik the Ruler to come back to me. He says he'll give me anything I want, including Tania. It seems a shame to let such an unpleasant piece of work go entirely Scot free. This is just to thank you, once again, for your advice about showing restraint. It seems to have paid off.

George

-

The Nest

Dear George

One of our village football teams down here is having a bad time. It's a non-League outfit, strictly amateur stuff. The changing rooms are falling down, the pitch needs levelling and turfing. It had two small makeshift stands, but one is now cordoned off for fear of collapse. The players can't afford new boots or strip and the one football it possesses is punctured. Things can't get much worse.

It's in Gigglesperm, a dot on the map in the middle of nowhere. The pub's closed, the post office has gone, the grocery store shut down years ago and the bus service is a joke. The ups and downs of Gigglesperm Rovers (mainly downs) is the only thing left.

I wonder if your new intimate, Erik the Ruler, might bring

his multi-million pound footie team down for a bit of a kick around? It would cause a sensation, bring in the crowds and boost Gigglesperm's coffers. As you're now in the happy position of being able to subject Erik the Ruler to a little gentle coercion, rather than the other way round, perhaps it might be worth suggesting this to him. What do you think?

Lancing-Lancing

-

Gone to the Dogs

I think it's a dandy idea. Erik won't dare say no because he knows I'll be off to the 'papers with the sensational story of his dirty pics and his clumsy attempt at blackmail. Be in touch soon.

George

-

Gone to the Dogs

Erik

Now that we understand one another, I have a suggestion that will not only stop you being splashed all over the newspapers, but which will also win you considerable kudos in the community. Meet me in The Gibbet pub, on Wet Bog Lane, near Mudchute Docklands Light Railway station, on the Isle of Dogs, at 1pm tomorrow. Come alone. Leave your henchmen behind. Nor do I wish the presence of Tania, charming though she is – or the deal is off, and I will write the story and submit the photographs.

George Steel

-

Gone to the Dogs

Well Admiral, great news.

Erik the Ruler is to bring his star-spangled team to play your lot.

It will be an epic occasion and should raise a fortune. I twisted his arm and he also agreed to put a chunk of money into Gigglesperm FC. It will pay for a new club house, new stands, a new pitch, changing rooms and showers, massage facilities (he said Tania might be interested) and a full-time physiotherapist. He will also hand over sufficient cash to enable Gigglesperm to buy some decent players. It sounds costly, but to him it's petty-cash. He knows he's getting off cheaply.

Curiously enough, Erik seems to be looking forward to what will undoubtedly be the fixture of the decade. I dropped a hint that he might get a Gong, or the Grand Order of the Golden Boot. With the thought of that, he became very excited. I've no idea if his nationality and domiciliary status (transient) would qualify him, but he's content with the idea that one day he could even meet Brenda. He wanted to know how much it would cost him, and to whom he should his money. I told him it didn't work like that, or it's not supposed to, which he found astonishing. One is bound to encounter these minor cultural differences.

To spur him on, as an extra little sweetie, I mentioned *en passant* that it might result in a weekend shooting-party at Balmoral. It's the sort of tosh in which he delights, and he has already had himself measured up for tweeds, plus-fours and a deerstalker. The one thing we know for sure is that he really enjoys shooting things.

He even apologised for what he called our 'little misunderstanding'. I told him that trying to buy somebody's wife, undressing and drugging his guests, mocking up photographs suggesting that we had been in an orgy, was hardly small beer. He shrugged his shoulders and said everybody did business like that where he came from. He didn't seem to understand that it wasn't the English way (generally). He also hadn't appreciated that we have a free Press (well, relatively) and that scrutiny of his affairs would make juicy copy.

I'll do the necessary in terms of publicising the event. I think the injection of new money and facilities should take place *after* the match; it's a better story with stronger pictures if Erik's Balzak

Dynamo, the world's most expensive team, has to play on a bomb-site, with all its clapped-out facilities. It gives a whole new meaning to the Beautiful Game. Just imagine: Erik the Ruler's spoiled brats up against eleven hearty Cornishmen more famed for boldness than their balletic skills.

Kindly airs

George

-

Nest

My dear George

Well, the big day draws close. The crowds are going to be phenomenal. There's been a lot of advanced publicity, which I'm sure you're behind. So well done. The various profiles of the Gigglesperm players in the newspapers have been fun, if a shade overblown. There have been shoals of letters in the newspapers saying what a pleasure it is to see football getting back to its grass-roots.

It's good to read about the Gigglesperm goalie who's a cheesemonger by trade (not that Gigglesperm has such a thing, and he lives thirty miles away in Spittington). And, too, the bionic pensioner at left back, who discards his stick before every match and plays with a wild, uncontrolled energy. The Michael Buble impersonator, Reggie Brightside, is an outsize personality with a big following. He drives a laundry van and plays centre-half. Not many people realise that Robbie Cresswell, the former prison-officer at centre-forward, has a physical approach to the game. He's not called 'Clogger the Screw' for nothing. The inside-right, Cy Lear, is known as the 'Knee-Capper,' because of unpleasantness when Gigglesperm lost to the Saltash Tin Men (officially 7-0 but the Ref said it was probably more; he ran off the pitch and stopped counting when a melee broke out). On the left-wing, Baltic Bertie, runs like a scalded cat. A persecuted Lithuanian, he doesn't speak English and he doesn't like Albanians, so it would be prudent to keep him away from Erik the Ruler.

All in all, I think it has the makings of a memorable fixture.

Kindest regards to you and Catharine

Lancing-Lancing

-

Gone to the Dogs

Dear Admiral

Erik the Ruler says Enrique Farago, his star striker, wants to drive down to Gigglesperm. Farago says his team-mates don't know anything about tailoring and he wouldn't be seen dead on the team coach with them. In fact, he says he wouldn't be seen on any bus, ever.

The Ruler wondered where Farago could park his Bugatti Veyron with a reasonable degree of safety? He smashed his first one up in the Blackwall Tunnel, the second he gave to a jilted boyfriend and he doesn't want anything untoward happening to his current banger.

Could he leave it at The Nest and you could run him over to Gigglesperm in the Jaguar? His car costs as much as Herefordshire and from what Erik says it's the only thing Farago loves more than himself. Farago says if it can't be kept safe and warm he won't come. He's a cry-baby but a big attraction and it would be a pity not to see him. I hate cow-towing to the spoilt little bastard but we seem to have no choice.

Hey-ho! Such things are sent to try us.

George

-

Nest

George

No trouble at all.

Lancing-Lancing

The big day arrived and Gigglesperm was swamped with tens of thousands of supporters from all over the country. There was rowdy behaviour from Balzak Dynamo's large army of travelling fans who rampaged along Dead Man's Sand before descending on the Boscowan Arms and throwing Len the landlord into the Atlantic.

A major disappointment was the non-appearance of Farago. Police clocked him at 172 miles an hour on the A30, while checking his lipstick in the rear view mirror. He was arrested and detained, as was his passenger, his new husband Bunny, who police said had aided and abetted the offence by egging him on.

The Mouse Hole, a local free sheet, noted for its impartiality and fairness, was forensic in its dissection of the two sides: 'Eleven prissy, over-paid, narcissistic, brain-dead fancy boys who couldn't kick their way out of a paper-bag, versus a Cornish team oozing talent: bold, gifted, humble, manly, penniless and cerebral (until government cuts the right-half, born in Cardiff, drove a mobile library on Bodmin Moor and was known as Jones the Book)'.

Dogs

Dear Admiral

The thing that swung the match, before the riot, was the Knee-Capper and Cloggers ganging up on the linesman. Tempers were already fraying when the linesman flagged Cloggers off-side for what would have been a vital goal. When Cloggers remonstrated with him and found out that he was a 'foreigner,' in other words, a Devonian, well, that was it, Kerboom!

There's always been competition between the two counties, it goes back to the Tin Wars. There was that nasty incident when tacks were left on deck-chairs in Ilfracombe and the Devonians hit back with an oil-spill round St. Michael's Mount.

Erik the Ruler said the match proved more expensive than he had anticipated. Farago could be jailed for a month depending on the Beak's mood. He hasn't helped himself by saying he can't be in court because it's the grape-harvest at his estate in Tuscany.

Erik didn't reckon on having to pay for a helicopter to fly three of his star players to the Royal Cornwall Hospital in Treliske. The Knee-Capper ensured that they'll miss an axial fixture with Real Madrid.

Catharine and I were near the Balzak goal. When Yuri Schlopski, the goalie, was hit on the head by a bottle of Joan of the Wad brown ale, hurled out of the crowd, he fell as if he had been axed.

Tania, Yuri's wife and Erik's lover, became hysterical and ran on to the pitch screaming in Latvian. Her faint was very Gone with the Wind. With precision timing, a bevy of photographers, some of which had travelled down with her in Erik's jet, just happened to be on hand when she came round and surprise, surprise, the top of her dress had been strategically dislodged, revealing the two-up front formation which Erik favours.

It was all a little fractious, but it will go down as a momentous day in Gigglesperm's history, of which there have not been too many.

As ever

George

-

The match marked the start of the rise and rise of Gigglesperm Rovers. With new facilities and enough money to buy big-name players, it first entered the Alfonso Ice-Cream Cornish Sundae League, moving up to the Princetown HMP Dartmoor Conference. It's now in the Championship and its Glaswegian manager, Mick McFarlane, told the BBC's Match of the Day, that he's optimistic about getting Gigglesperm into the Premiership. 'Och aye the wee banashotty is a gud chance for us, nee doot aboot it. Hae a gud rin. Thenk ye.'

**

Away from the rigours of football, life on the home front, high up on Dead Man's Cliff, continued on its pastoral course, with Lancing-Lancing and Sophie enjoying their new found happiness at The Nest. Lancing-Lancing, Ted to his adoring wife, and now Teddy, had been given momentous news.

Our Home

My darling Teddy

Before we were married, I put down in writing how my feelings for you had grown. I now want to say, on paper once more, how happy I am with our latest, most wonderful news. As we said in bed last night, I don't mind if it's a boy or a girl, as long as they are well and they are happy.

Our life will change, of that there is little doubt, and it will definitely be for the better. I never thought I would have children, and now I am delirious with joy. I am so pleased that your own children, Elizabeth and Jack, are as delighted as we are. I had been a little nervous about how they would take the news, especially when they thought about their own late mother, your beloved Charlotte. I am blessed to have married you, and to be part of such a warm and loving family. Teddy, I am so excited. Forgive the soppy nature of this billet-doux. I am just a doe-eyed ninny.

My love, as ever, Sophie
-

Seven months later, Sophie gave birth to a boy, weighing just under eight lbs. George Edward Jack (the latter after the Jazz trombonist Jack Teagarden). Lancing-Lancing played Moonlight Serenade on the trombone in the delivery room, which Sophie said helped to relax her, though Lancing-Lancing knew in his breast that she was merely humouring him.

The Nest

Dear George and Catharine

We are so pleased to have you as the godparents, and we are looking forward to seeing you at St. John's in the village. We'll have one or two glasses of bubbly and as you're staying a few days we'll get in a spot of sailing. Who would believe that I am, once more, a doting dad? Even my trombone playing has improved (marginally).

We've paid you the ultimate compliment, George, by naming the little chap after you. It's a fine name when one thinks of the flag, slaying dragons and all that. I know several George's, and they're all excellent, plus the fact that George Gershwin is a favourite of both of us (who could not be moved by Rhapsody in Blue?).

I have a sense that little George will be a fine sailor. Britain's skipper on an Americas Cup entry? Or is that being a shade precipitous? Talking of which, do you fancy a go at the Three Rivers Yacht Race in Norfolk? I thought I might sail the *Pegasus* up the coast and on to the Broads. Or we could enter your *Prelude*, since it's already moored there.

What do you think? It's some while after the Christening, so we've got time. It could be a lot of fun.

Lancing-Lancing

**

Lancing-Lancing has served on numerous government bodies and charitable committees. As well as playing the trombone, he is also an amateur painter and, characteristically, has always been self-deprecating about his abilities. Many years ago his artistic inclinations led to his involvement with the National Museum of Maritime Art in Greenwich.

National Museum of Maritime Art

Dear Lancing-Lancing

Good to see you at the Museum's recent do. We've had to take out more insurance after that crackpot threw paint at the Turner. He told the coppers he did it because Turner was 'nautically inaccurate,' had his sails going the wrong way. When somebody said Turner was a painter, not a naval architect, he threw a wobbly.

This is just a quick shot across the bows to tell you that the new wing is going to be named after you. It's a just reward for your years of dedication. The powers that be want to trumpet it in their own time, but we've known each for donkey's and I wanted to be the first to congratulate you. Knockout news about little George!

Bye for now

Beamy (Harry Beamish, curator NMMA)

-

Nest

Dear Beamy

Good of you to tip me the wink. It's undeserved and I'm flattered. Entirely agree about Turner. There's nobody in his league. As you know, the Nest bursts with pictures which Charlotte and I picked up over the years on my different postings. They're not worth much but they've given us great pleasure, and now Sophie enjoys them too. It's obscene to buy pictures to watch them appreciate or to match the wallpaper.

Lancing-Lancing

-

During his years at sea, Lancing–Lancing spent any free time he had in his cabin, drawing and painting the exotic places and people he encountered on his different voyages. His enormous collection of canvases that he painted himself – what he calls his 'multi-coloured daubings and lash-ups' – he stores in a barn at the Nest. He told Sophie he had no intention of inflicting them on her by hanging them in the cottage. Harry Beamish and his wife were among the guests that Lancing–Lancing and Sophie invited to baby George's Christening.

National Museum of Maritime Art

Dear Admiral

George's Christening went well. Thank you so much for inviting us. It was good of you to let me see your own pictures. I felt privileged when Sophie said very few people were allowed to look at them.

You really should value the stuff you've collected to see about getting it properly insured. Ziggy Meinwort is an old friend. He runs a gallery in Cork Street and he's had an association with Cornwall and the St. Ives School which goes back years. He's often down your way so he could easily drop in and give you a valuation. He's got a dry sense of humour and I'm sure you and Sophie would like him.

Beamy
-

Subsequently, Ziggy Meinwort called at the Nest. In addition to valuing the pictures on display in the cottage, including various Peter Burman's, Peggy Somerville's and Leslie Rackham's, he persuaded Lancing-Lancing to show him his own pictures hidden in the barn. 'They're not too bad,' Ziggy said, 'and I know how to turn them into the next big thing. If you go along with me, it'll be fun.'

He outlined the nuts and bolts of the art market to a fascinated Lancing-Lancing and Sophie and told them he was in despair at today's 'crass rubbish' which was achieving astronomical prices. 'It's not art,' he said, 'just vulgar sensation. Find something shocking, unpleasant or bizarre, and think advertising'

For years he had run a gallery specialising in Old Masters, especially Aelbert Cuyp (1620-1691). But he found that his business was losing ground to more avant-garde galleries. Deciding that if he couldn't beat them, he'd join them, he changed the name from Ziggy Meinwort Fine Art to The Throb, and began staging cutting-edge exhibitions.

'You can never buck the market,' he said. His last show featured a human corpse pickled in formaldehyde being slowly devoured by bluebottles. The corpse was that of his Auntie Hildegard, an avid

169

collector of contemporary art. She had begged Ziggy that on her death he would pay her the ultimate compliment by turning her into an exhibit. The resulting work, 'Auntie Hildegarde, dead,' sold for several million dollars to Houston's Dick Museum, with its controversial vulva roof, which leaked, designed by Sir Norman Bocker, the enfant terrible of international architecture.

Ziggy told Lancing-Lancing and Sophie that he wanted to launch 'dog art'. It would necessitate Albion and his muddy paws padding around on Lancing-Lancing's canvases. The Admiral and Sophie took his idea none too seriously but allowed him to return to London with a hoard of pictures trampled on by the bulldog.

The Throb

Cork Street

Dear Lancing-Lancing

The First International Barking Mad Exhibition will be held next month with the world's finest examples of Dog art. Dog has rarely been seen outside the tepees of Oklahoma where the little-known Paw Paw Indians lived. Persecuted and secretive, this once proud tribe was wiped out by poisoned Buffalo meat in the early 19th century.

I include your invite, but it's better if we do a Banksy and don't reveal anything about you, or the dog. I can predict with an absolute certainty that we will not be out of pocket. The worth of a painting has nothing to do with its quality, but is entirely to do with fashion, public relations and marketing.

I have taken on the PR agency, Tainted Love. It's a one-woman band comprising Cammie Winstanley-Short. She prances like a pony and gives good dog, having being reared at gymkhanas and shoots. Her father made the headlines after a funny do with a rent boy in Dolphin Square.

Cammie's none too bright but she shrieks a lot, and her circle will be mad for Dog. Cuyp would turn in his grave but you'll be able to buy Albion a diamond collar.

Shalom

Ziggy.

-

Cammie activated her circle and an excited throng gathered at The Throb.

Ziggy had to send out for more canapes and champagne (after 9pm it was Prosecco). 'Keep the serviette round the label,' he told Kristiana, two weeks in London from Bulgaria. 'They're well coked up. Nostrils like the Blue John mine in Derbyshire.'

The paintings included a large canvas by Lancing-Lancing of an Egyptian market scene, almost obscured by Albion's paw prints. It was so heavily smeared with mud it looked as if the dog had rolled on it. 'He'd been in the stream and was trying to dry himself,' Lancing-Lancing confided to Sophie, keeping his voice low.

Another picture which attracted a great deal of interest was of a canary in a cage, being eyed by a kitten, but so pawed that it was difficult to discern the subject. 'The worst I've ever done,' Lancing-Lancing whispered. 'One of my first.'

A third painting, catalogued 'Dahlias, mixed media', was what it said, the vase recognizable, but the flowers obliterated by a paw print. Connoisseurs, their heads bent to within an inch of it, scrutinised the brush strokes, before quickly stepping back, blanching at its scent. 'Albion wet himself on it,' Ziggy murmured.

It-girls Binky Leicester, and her twin sister Fruity, bought several large examples of Dog.

Binky did art history on a ski and paint course in Zermatt, and was the ex-lover of a Lichtenstein royal. Fruity is the Executive Director of Colour for the Small is Beautiful hotel chain. It was founded by her father, Bernie, who for years struggled with a B&B in Wigan (two small bedrooms and a shared bathroom) before hitting on the idea of calling it boutique.

He went on to make millions with a chain of miniscule hotels with midget rooms, which, as the acid food and hotel critic, 21-stone Claude Forgoe wrote, in his column in the influential Scoff and Stay magazine: 'Rabbit hutches where pretence is the only excess'.

Bernie sued him saying Forgoe (behind his back hoteliers called him Black Forest Gateaux) was waging a vendetta because he once got stuck in a Small is Beautiful bath.

At the exhibition, Binky told a reporter from Le Scald, the design-bible: 'Dog is real.' And Fruity said: 'It's so ethnic. All those poor people in earthquakes and things. There's no shopping or anything'. The exhibition was a huge success with pictures being sold for thousands of pounds.

Consequently, faced with an outcry, The Department of Culture had to intervene to stop Houston's Dick Museum, with its vulva roof, buying too much Dog. In Parliament, the firebrand Scottish Nationalist, Fanny Fraser, the member for Arbroath and Smokie, told the Minister for Culture, the former vicar Bertie Small, that it was a disgrace that Scotland's cultural treasures should be sold to America. When Small asked her what Dog art had to do with Scotland, Fraser shouted that he knew perfectly well, and that he and it were all shite, for which remark she was ordered out of the House by the Speaker.

Art Eye

Great Windmill Street

Dear Ziggy

I wish to write a major feature on Dog, but, sadly, I am unable to find out much about its history. Could you furnish me with a little more detail? Congratulations on the show.

Cyrus Harbinger, Investigations Editor

-

Harbinger, and Jon Coward of Panorama – known in the BBC as Panamania – teamed up and filmed in Oklahoma, but found few locals had heard of Dog art or the Paw-Paw tribe. An ironmonger in Tulsa said his grand pappy was Little Chief Soft Toe, and that he had married a *Shoo Squaw, Falling Water.* But Coward thought the ironmonger was thinking about the architect Frank Lloyd-Wright.

The Running Bear Memorial Society, of Dakota, laid claim to the pictures, saying they were stolen from the Running Bear tribe in 1870 by Chief Crazy Piebald Pony. It was further alleged that Col. George Custer (1839-1876), shortly before the Battle of the Little Big Horn (1876), stole them back from Piebald Pony and his Crazies, and then sold them to buy musket-balls, at JJ Harding's auction house, in Kansas City.

DNA analysis of the pictures was conducted by the Art Institute of Saskatchewan. It confirmed that the mud was mud, but was unable to date it with the precision for which it was renowned (some of its scientists thought it Roman, from the Bath region). The brushwork was considered so crass (which put Lancing-Lancing's nose out of joint) as to be on a par with early cave paintings found in the eastern Yemen.

Ziggy Mortenstein refused to comment on the grounds that it would betray client confidentiality.

On Panamania there were serious ructions between Professor Heinz Burglestrop, a Viennese expert on primitive art, and the leading Maoist anthropologist, Dr. Lucian Free, of the University of Dulwich and Croydon West. Burglestrop said Dog was post-Primitive and influenced by Schiel, Klimt, Oskar Kokoschka and the Fin-de-Siecle movement, at its height in Vienna at the turn of the 20th century. Dr. Free said Fin-de-Siecle comprised spoiled little bastards and child molesters who corrupted the working class so much that it led to World War 1.

The mystery and notoriety of the pictures was such that their value continued to rise. The Daub, an influential monthly with a miniscule circulation, said Dog pictures were an example of Naïve Art at its finest.

Dog today is priceless. Most Dog is in private collections, kept in the dark in vaults in Geneva.

'Dahlias, mixed media', on which Albion had wet himself, was bought by Fruity Cargill, for her hideaway in Mustique. But its odour grew so sour and pungent in the sun that she later sold it at auction,

173

where it was subject to an intense bidding war won by Houston's Dick Museum.

A Dick spokesman said it would be hung in a specially-built refrigerated gallery. Later, 'Dahlias, mixed media', was ruined, when a violent storm swept in from the Gulf of Mexico, and the vulva roof leaked, again. The trustees are suing the architect, Sir Norman Bocker.

The Nest

Dear Beamy

Sophie and I have come into an unexpected windfall. We're keeping a little back for young George and the grandchildren, but after much thought we've decided to give most of it to worthy causes: damaged kiddies, people on life support machines, impoverished sailors, the destitute and so on. There's some left over which we want to give to the museum so that it can enhance its collection. I don't want any of this shouted from the rooftops. You'll simply have to say it's come from an anonymous benefactor. Got on well with Ziggy, a very handy meeting. Thank you so much for the introduction. We'll do supper at The Reform.

Lancing-Lancing

-

Note on the fridge at The Nest

Teddy

Just a quick scribble: I've nipped out to buy more Gordon's. We're getting a bit low. I was just thinking about Dog. Isn't it fun giving money to the deserving when it's from people with more cash than taste. Of which, I'll call in at the vet's. See if they've got anything to calm Albion down. Have you seen the leg on the chaise?

S

**

Yarns and legends about the late and infamous surgeon, Dickie 'Butcher' Thrupp, crop up throughout the Lancing–Lancing files.

Gone to the Dogs

Dear Admiral

I've just returned from the launch of a new yacht built by the Birtonioni Brothers, in Saint Raphael, on the Cote d'Azur. Beautiful craft, the mast as tall as the Empire State and she went like the proverbial off a shovel. Usual free-loaders hanging around: Buttocks, Two-Fingers, Falconetti and all the rest.

The Birtonioni boys have always been a bit dodgy. I recall some years ago when old Mama Birtonioni sustained a nasty mosquito nip on the top of her head. We were a couple of miles off Balzi Rossi, on the Ligurian coast, testing a new 250-foot *Birtonioni*. It was as tasteful as a brothel and called *Keep on Gobbling*, having been bought by some fowl mogul in Britain.

Among those aboard was Butcher Thrupp. The Birtonioni's like to have medical help at hand when they're at sea (as do their oligarch customers). Butcher had stopped practising by then, but he was always eager to get the knives and the saw out if he could. He'd have made a good carpenter.

He took Mama Birtonioni into the Norfolk Bronze state-room. The cabins were named after turkeys, or bits of them. The more modest (one bathroom) had names such as Breast, Mince and Drumstick. Tasteful eh? We thought Mama Birtonioni needed just a dab of TCP. But Thrupp was always looking for something more serious. When she finally managed to stagger out of the Bronze Turkey state-room she was bent over her zimmer frame, chalk-faced and working her worry-beads.

It was obvious that Thrupp had found something sinister, as she was by now entirely bald with a large sticking plaster above her left ear. Luca, the eldest of her five boys, rushed forward to help.

'Did Butcher have to operate Mama?'

'Only a little incision,' Butcher said. 'But she wasn't too keen and started screaming. I shaved the contaminated area to ensure the infection hadn't spread. I've done a bit of stitching and I've smeared on some strong ointment that we used to use in the Navy. Looks worse than it is. Tends to sting a bit, makes your eyes water, but it'll do the trick.'

Months went by and the bite slowly disappeared. But Mama Birtonioni's hair never grew again and she had to take to a wig. An Italian doctor from the old days (the Birtonioni's hail from Sicily, 'nuff said) told Luca that Butcher had used the wrong liniment and should have known that the old lady would go bald. Luca went ape, and said that if he ever clapped eyes on Butcher again he'd give him what for.

As far as I know nothing happened, though Thrupp had to watch his back. It's unwise to make anybody go bald, let alone Mama of the five Birtonioni boys. I'm sure my memories will stir a few of your own.

Kindest airs

George

-

The Nest

Dear George

As you say, your letter invoked some memories. I recall the case of the bald Italian lady, but I'm not sure if any reprisals which could be pinned directly on the Birtonioni boys. I imagine they were pretty deft at covering their tracks. I do remember, though, that dear old Butcher went through an odd time after he'd scalped Mama.

As well as surgery, he had two other passions: an eye for the girls and fast cars. On one occasion he took an Italian nymph called Aida, who he'd met earlier that evening at the Blue Lamp Club, to supper at Ciao Bambi in Soho.

Ciao Bambi was a good Italian near Brewer Street: standard décor, gingham cloths in a red and white check, Chianti bottles in raffia caked in candle-fat. Sadly, it no longer exists. With the bookshops and massage parlours it was swept away by the sanitise Soho lot, led by the Labour MP Patrick Hollis (now a Peer), the one who later exposed himself at the Queen's garden party.

Anyway, I digress. Aida, the young lady with whom Butcher was smitten, was called away from the table by Guiseppe, the manager, to take a call (pre-mobile era) during which time Butcher sat there twiddling his thumbs anticipating a night of unbridled (or even bridled) delight. On her return, however, Aida had changed from a dead-ringer for Sophia Loren into a screaming banshee, her ire directed full-volume at the hapless Butcher.

His Italian was pretty basic, so he didn't have a clue what she was ranting about. After much gesticulation and menacing finger-signs, as is the Italian way, she went for her coat and stormed out, emptying a bowl of Gnocchi Siciliana over Butcher's head, followed by what was left of a bottle of Rioja.

Butcher never found out what it was all about, though Guiseppe said she had been using language he hadn't encountered since he worked in the docks when he first came to London. Some weeks later, Butcher was finishing a shift at a clinic in Harley Street. He earned a good living when he left the Navy, doing jobbing surgery at dodgy private clinics, all of them choc-a-bloc with monied clients, largely from overseas. A lot of them wanted cosmetic surgery, which wasn't his speciality, but he was always up for a challenge.

Anyway, as he approached his latest pride-and-joy, a svelte Lancia Flavia, it blew up, the blast obliterating the car, smashing every window in Harley Street and knocking Butcher to the ground. The Bomb Squad made inquiries – a mosque in Bradford was raided, car-dealers turned over – but nothing was discovered.

The word went round that he'd upset a Saudi princess with a post-hijab procedure that wasn't quite up to scratch. He denied all the allegations but he did wonder if the demented signorina in Ciao Bambino, and the subsequent bombing, were in some way related, though he never mentioned anything to me about turning Mama Birtonioni into Yul Brynner. Your story is probably a missing piece in the Thrupp jigsaw.

Good winds

Lancing-Lancing

**

The following note was pinned on the potting shed door at The Nest

Dear Mr. Trumble

I'd be grateful if you would stop leaning on the garden fence and abusing passers-by as they go about their lawful business. I've had yet more complaints, one of them from a young mother walking her toddler and pushing her baby in its pram. She was frightened out of her wits when you popped up over the fence, threatening her with a garden fork. There appears to be no reason for this behaviour. Do you need help?

Lancing-Lancing

-

Rookery Cottage

Dip Lane

Dear Admiral

I don't need no help. I can do it on my own.

Trumble.

-

The Nest

I was not thinking about the garden.

Lancing-Lancing

Rookery Cottage

Dip Lane

I don't need no help. The little lad was weeing up against the fence which I just creosoted and I didn't want him getting stuff on his clothes or his Mum. I didn't threaten nobody. I had the fork because I'd been digging in the new carrots. I didn't mean to upset you. I was looking after your fence.

Yours kindly

Mr. Trumble

-

The Nest

Dear Mr. Trumble

Thank you for your note. Perhaps I was being rash. It might be wise not to be holding your fork when you talk to people. The carrot patch and the vegetable garden look very good. Well done.

Lancing-Lancing

**

Lancing–Lancing has been courted by all the political parties over the decades. His lifestyle and background suggest that of a Conservative, but many of his views are closer to a Liberal or Labour persuasion. When asked about such matters he maintains that he has a low opinion of all politicians, of whatever creed, and that the qualities he values most are honesty, conscience and a sense of vision, which he feels are in short supply in the Commons. Some say his views are so contrarian, that as any colour of politician he would present the electorate with a contradictory and baffling manifesto.

Troutbeck Parish Council

Dear Admiral Lancing-Lancing

I am writing to you on behalf of the people of the West Country, namely the constituency of Troutbeck-cum-Rockside, who would like you to stand as an Independent MP. With your reputation for inventive and original thinking, we feel that you would make an admirable and worthy representative of Troutbeck-cum-Rockside in the House of Commons.

Your sincerely

Sylvia Longing, sec. to the council
-

The Nest

Dear Ms. Longing

Though complimented, I have two reservations. How can an Independent represent your views when he is supposed to be *independent*? Is that not an oxymoron? Secondly, I tend to despair of all politicians and most ginger groups, be they left, right or anywhere in-between. Accordingly, flattered though I am, I am afraid I must reject your very kind invitation.

Lancing-Lancing.
-

Months later the millionairess MP for Troutbeck-cum-Rockside, the ultra-Green Harriet de Villiers, was engulfed in what the newspapers called The Big Ming scandal. She lived with her wife, the ecological warrior, the Hon. Charmaine Clenchwarton, in Grey Goose, a moated Jacobean manor-house, in 1000 acres with the fast-flowing river Snout running through.

Grey Goose had been left to de Villiers by a former lover, smothered to death when the roof of a badger sett, in which she lived, fell in. The house was in a sorry state because of de Villier's habit of stealing

Christmas turkeys from local farms and giving them sanctuary through the run of the house. Born in New Zealand, de Villiers wanted a Maori as Chancellor of the Exchequer, saying somebody in a grass skirt with a bone through their nose would be a breath of fresh air in Downing Street. She wanted Buckingham Palace as a safe house for Crack heads, with the Queen living in a council house in Ashby-de-la-Zouch. St. James' Park would be used for allotments. All meat would be banned with car manufacturers, butchers and shoe-makers hanged.

On her parliamentary expenses de Villiers had managed to re-roof the manor, clean out the lake and educate her children, of whom she had four with three different mothers, at the Ofsted-outstanding Dirk and Sporran Co-Educational and Progressive School, in Fife, where boys wore pink skirts and suspenders, smoked pot at eight and had regular sex at nine.

De Villiers was exposed as an insurance cheat by The Daily Mail, for burying two Ming vases, a John Constable, a vintage Bugatti and the world's last Spitfire, beneath the orangery. She said in court that she hadn't been herself since her former lover died in the badger sett and, consequently, was given three-months suspended, of which the Mail said: 'Dirty de Villiers is the luckiest twister in the Kingdom. She's a two-faced Kiwi humbug', for which remark the 'paper was sued by a Blackpool rock and toffee-maker, and UK diplomatic ties with New Zealand were put under strain.

Once tipped as a future prime minister, Dirty de Villiers was obliged to abandon her parliamentary seat. She said from her holiday retreat in the Virgin Islands, that she had been misreported and that she forgave her enemies. She had now found peace and serenity in Buddhism, and occasional bouts of snorkelling.

The Nest

Dear Ms. Longing

Having seen the downfall of the dastardly Dirty de Villiers, I have decided to fight the Troutbeck-cum-Rockside by-election. I have no desire to win but wish only to keep the other candidates on their toes.

Lancing-Lancing

-

While de Villiers kept her head down on Sapphic Spit, in the Virgin Isles, her wife, the flame-haired eco-warrior, The Hon. Charmaine Clenchwarton, fought the seat on behalf of the Sunbeam Alliance. 'Charming' Clenchwarton was the daughter of a prominent pig-farmer, the late Charlie Bell, known in Smithfield Market as 'Dead Ringer,' who at one time had been the chairman of the Eat More Meat Movement. Noted for his extreme opinions, he had bred a herd of commando pigs which he said could be unleashed 'in the event of a civil war with vegetarians and people in sandals.' It was generally agreed that he would rise from his grave if he knew what Charmaine was up to, but he had been cremated.

In fighting her election campaign, Charming brought in a series of environmental breakthroughs on the Grey Goose estate, backed by the Countryside Compact, the Let's Wild the Lot Campaign, and the Endangered Species Collective, the latter notorious for its stop-at-nothing tactics.

One of her most innovative moves was the introduction of wolves. There was already consternation among villagers about TV being unwatchable after 150 wind turbines were installed on the estate, but now the mood had swung from tetchy to terror.

Charming Clenchwarton held a meeting in Troutbeck-cum-Rockside parish hall to try and pacify the locals, telling them that wolves were safe if you didn't go near them, and that nobody should feed them crisps or Mars Bars. 'They're very good at finding their own food,' she said, which added to their alarm.

Nest

George

Thank you for your note about my political pretensions. Charming Clenchwarton's determination to turn the place into a zoo have not stopped with packs of wolves. She has also introduced otters into the Snout, and even managed to breed large numbers of Beaver.

Such eco-engineering was certain to have repercussions. Nobody was surprised when the Snout suddenly burst its banks and inundated several homes, including the vet's. The one good thing about the flood was that several hundred bottles of the vet's filthy homemade wine were swept away down the valley never to be seen again. To me, it was as joyous a moment as when other bottles blew up in his shed a while ago.

The flood was caused by beaver being beaver. Some distance upstream they had gnawed through a forest and built a dam bigger than the Zambesi. Finally it burst, and the rest – including the vet's wine – is ecological history. I'll write again soon, but I have to get back to a spot of door-step campaigning.

It's awfully tedious and sometimes people are abominably rude. I knocked at one house and a chap came to the door in a kilt, which is unusual in Cornwall. He went on and on about Trident and Faslane, most of which I couldn't understand as he was a Glaswegian. On discovering I was ex-Navy he went totally Trident, his frenzy only subsidizing when Albion made a pincer-move on his left-ankle. Such are the joys of canvassing.

Top-ho!

Lancing-Lancing

-

The Nest

George, old chap

Here's another missive from the Red Riding Hood election. Not content with letting wolves roam the countryside, Charming Clenchwarton has now 'saved' the Mammoth Sea Eagle. With its twelve-foot wingspan, locals talk about the war years and how it reminds them of a Lancaster. It's a rare species, and to see it in flight is breathtaking, if a touch frightening. Every imaginable scare is doing the rounds: lambs being carried into the sky, mothers rushing indoors with infants for fear it will swoop on them, huge fish and beavers being dragged out of the Snout by giant talons.

It's hard to find voters, most being afraid to venture outside. They'll only open their doors an inch or two for fear of an otter slipping inside and making for the bathroom, or a wolf barging in and carrying off babies in cots and grannies in rocking chairs.

The good news is that there's no way I can win this seat. There's another more mainstream and sensible contender, representing what Clenchwarton calls The Really Boring Party. My views on a range of issues, especially defence, aren't going down at all well.

There are several more loony candidates, some of them in costumes. The chap from the Clean Up Everything Party walks around in a dustbin. He can't see where he's going and keeps banging into things. The most engaging fellow I met, before he passed out, is from the Forget it Party. Prior to keeling over, he told me his name was Ollie and that he wants compulsory 24-hour drinking seven days a week. He's usually out of it on a bench in Prince Albert Park. A woman who lives nearby, who said she wouldn't vote for me because she'd had difficulties with a sailor in Portsmouth, said she saw an otter sneak out of the boating lake and eat Ollie's sausage sandwich. She sits at her window keeping guard, convinced Ollie's going to be eaten by a wolf, or be carried off to some distant eyrie by a predatory sea eagle.

Mind the shoals

Lancing-Lancing

-

Cheetahs Forever

Oldham, Lancs.

Dear Captain Lancing

On seeing the success of releasing wolves in your part of the world, it would be good news for your election campaign if you were able to announce that we are going to liberate cheetahs in the

184

area. Cheetahs would add to the interest that people have shown in treating animals with the same respect as humans, and they would further enrich the diversity of wildlife in the area. We look forward to your response.

Yours sincerely

Noble Franklyn, Cheetahs Forever (Chmn).

-

The Nest

Dear Franklyn

Are you out of your tree? Have you not followed my campaign? This constituency is not a wild life park. People already gibber at the thought of being assailed by a predator from the air or a beast on the ground. I am not, let me assure you, picking on cheetahs. I would apply the same degree of rigorous opposition to the release of tigers, lions, crocodiles, cobras or bison. Incidentally, I was once a captain, a rank I greatly enjoyed. Thank you for writing, and I am sorry that I cannot endorse your plan.

Lancing-Lancing (Adm).

-

Jack Claws Cottage

Waddlebridge Bird of Prey Centre

Bodmin Moor

Dear Bosun Lantern-Lantern

Visitors don't come here no more since you and your lot let eagles fly around willy-nilly. We're up on moor and we used to be OK giving out jobs where there isn't much work. It's hard on the moor. We have bad snow and get cut off with the road blocked and the 'phones aren't good and I'm no good on the internet but my lad is. The point is nobody's coming no more while you've got big birds flying loose and wild wolves and things stealing sheep.

I hope you don't mind me writing like this but we've got to start sacking people, like old Twomin, he's been here years, and the nice young girl at The Pheasant, who did marketing and Chinese and can't get no job, so she feeds Alvin our old vulture. Alvin loves her and would miss her if anything happened. He'd start picking his feathers and end up bare. It's what happens if he gets stressed. He does it every time. He should have shiny black feathers, but he's all matted. He likes seeing people, but nobody comes now. So he's depressed, like my wife, even if she's not matted like Alvin. Alvin likes lamb so we keep sheep here. But with no customers the sheep are thin because I can't afford pellets and things. You have to watch sheep if they start munching at gorse and stuff on the moor.

We don't want to go bust. My wife's going mad about it, and says your ruddy eagle is a bloody nuisance because everybody sees it flying around for nothing, and nobody pays to see it. Others won't come up moor cos they frit about something jumping out and giving them a good maulin. I don't know what I'll do if I have to sell up. Anyway, who'd buy it? I can't go back to Africa because I'm too bloody old, and that's where I learned about birds. I don't want to have to drive a lorry. There's no money in that, and I'd be away for long runs and what would happen to my wife and kids stuck up here on moor where it's cold and snows?

We haven't got any proper electric, just gas in a bottle, and the peat. There's no way my wife and kids could cut peat, if I'm on a lorry. The moors protection lot plays up about me cutting peat, buggering up the infrastructuring they reckon. My wife's good at darning and we're all in the same bed, keeping warm best we can. She's good at clipping beaks and nails, all of us, as well as the birds. I can't afford to have the septic tank emptied. So we use the bushes and it's bloody cold. We've got hawks and a nice buzzard. He's got a bit of a temper on him cos he's got the moult. Keeps going at himself. Sorry to complain but we're worried about things.

Jack 'Beaky' Dawes

The Nest

Dear Mr. Dawes

Thank you for your interesting letter. Your wife and family sound delightful and long-suffering. Alvin, too, appears to be a wonderful creature. Chaps like you are what we need. Knowledgeable, determined, independent, spirited and providing employment where jobs are scarce. I congratulate you, and I am disturbed to learn that your enterprise is jeopardised by events in what one newspaper calls 'Wolfsville'.

I wish to assure you that I am merely a candidate in this election, and I deplore the madness in which we are engulfed. The area has been transformed from an oasis of tranquillity into an ecological Brooklyn. People are running scared and I am doing my best to see sanity make a comeback. In the meantime, all I can do is assure you of my support and urge you to cling on, as best you can.

My best wishes and kind regards to you and your family.

Lancing-Lancing

-

The Nest

Dear Ms. Ponting

Re: Disaster in the West Country

As the Secretary of State for Rural Affairs you will be aware that the constituency in which I am fighting a by-election is besieged by aerial and ground-based attackers. My message is as concise as this note: please intervene immediately and stop this madness.

Lancing-Lancing

Lancing–Lancing's plea to one of the grand offices of State failed. No written response could be found in the Admiral's papers, though there was a scribbled note on a Post–it sticker written by Lancing–Lancing after a junior civil servant from Ms. Ponting's office telephoned him to say that the administration endorsed the work undertaken by diverse environmental agencies and pressure groups, which included the 'controlled' release of endangered species back into the community. Lancing-Lancing had scrawled on the Post-It note: 'Bollocks.'

Dogs

Dear Admiral

Can it be true that in your part of the world raptors are downing pigeons and carrying lambs away? I hear that the fox-hunting lobby are now excited because they think they have a new purpose. Catharine and I both hope that you and Sophie are safe. It sounds as if you're in that movie by Hitchcock.

George
-

Nest

My dear George

The reports, sadly, are true. I had a letter from Bude Pigeon Racing Society who said that Red Kites introduced here a few weeks ago were as menacing as Messerschmitts over the White Cliffs of Dover. Every time they have a race they don't know which ones will make it, let alone win. Survivors are 'winged', like crippled planes limping back from sorties over Germany.

Pigeons which manage to reach their home lofts are in a sorry state, feathers everywhere, after bruising 'dog-fights' up in the heavens. Alacrity the 1V, the winner of the coveted Burnley-Manilla Stakes (the Grand National of pigeon racing) just made it back to its loft and was in a hell of mess. Fanciers said it was a Kite that had done for it. The future of pigeon racing now hangs on a wing and a prayer.

There was a nasty incident at Mr. Ram's Balti in Saltash. It's popular with tourists, with a terrace overlooking the water. The place was crowded when a dead pigeon fell out of the sky smack into somebody's vindaloo. As Mr. Ram said, it's not good for trade, and as well as having to offer free meals all round he had to pick up the cleaning bill for all those diners who'd been splashed by curry sauce. One chap got it in his eye and had to be helicoptered up to Moorfields. The woman Clenchwarton is barmy.

Lancing-Lancing.
-

The Nest

Dear Brigadier Chumpington

Re: The Royal & Ancient Chumpington Wolf Pack

I cannot endorse your activities in my election manifesto, as you request. I saw the hunt and its baying hounds sweep hell for leather through Piddlecum-Ugly. Your chaps in helmets, visors and suits of armour terrified the locals and sent children screaming into the arms of their mothers.

These are vulnerable people. Until the intervention of Charmaine Clenchwarton, who should be certified, they have been under ceaseless assault, including aerial bombing by giant Sea Eagles, and wolves seemingly ravenous for human prey.

While I appreciate that the Royal Chumpington has searched for a role since fox-hunting was outlawed, let me assure you, wolf-hunting is not an alternative.

I was alarmed that three Alpaca on High Ridge farm near Windlestuff, which on the whole are gentle creatures, apart from the odd spit in the eye, had been savaged by your hounds, who clearly don't know an alpaca from a fox, let alone a wolf. Without your armour, and faced with a pack of wolves, frankly you'd be mincemeat. Huntsmen and horses in suits of steel, as if dressed for a medieval jousting match, merely exacerbate, rather than alleviate, the problem.

Lancing-Lancing

Pressure groups massed in the constituency. They included the 'Wild Boar Liberty Party', the 'Spanish Black Pig Forum', and 'Woollies', worried about raptors scooping up lambs. 'Save the Whale' and the 'Old Bat Foundation', fielded large contingents, the latter exercised about too much focus being given to young bats.

Charmaine Clenchwarton spent her nights hanging around the tents and crackling campfires, breaking into song as the flute, melodeon and mandolin players of the Beak and Claw string quartet, performed Joan Baez classics, while anti-nuke protesters smoked hookahs and shouted 'I have a dream'.

Tensions rose when 'Meat Forever' arrived, a noisy contingent of butchers and slaughtermen, in blood-drenched aprons and carrying cleavers.

A personable coterie of air hostesses, members of 'Trolley Dolly', linked up with 'Runways Now', a group of mainly gay airline stewards. The most vociferous were 'Eight Lanes and More', pro-motorway lobbyists, and the 'Bugger the Green Belt Chapter', whose brickies, plumbers and scaffolders, leaped out of a canvas-sided ex-army lorry and made rude gestures at the peace-people, shouting that they'd happily shove them and their flutes in a cement-mixer and bury them under the M25.

The Nest

Dear Chief Constable

I feel I must warn you that if tensions continue to rise between animal rights people, and those not of their persuasion, then calamity is certain.

Droves of people have set up camp in and under Hobgoblin Wood. They are living in trees and in a network of tunnels. Sanitation comprises two planks and a trench, and camp fires flicker all night long (to keep warm, to sing around, to cook baked beans, but mainly to keep wolves at bay).

Reports are filtering in of a band of Syrian birds-egg collectors arriving in the dead of night by small boat in Camelot Bay, their intended prey being the Sea Eagles' eggs. Locals think this group has no interest in birds' eggs, but is a Jihadist cell. Some of the incursors are in suicide vests and bent on hunting down infidel Piskies.

Meanwhile, members of the Lancelot & Guinevere Golf Club, in Andy Pandy trousers and tartan pullovers with diamond socks, are keeping a 24-hour vigil on a cluster of bunkers around the eighth hole, where two wolves lay in wait and threatened an elderly couple who had to make a run for it in their buggy.

Something has to be done, and quickly.

Lancing-Lancing
-

The locals had taken to calling the biggest of the Mammoth Sea Eagles, 'Nobby', after it crash-landed on the tin roof of the Gents lavatory in Boscastle, terrifying retired herring-salesman Ernie Hardwick, whose irritated bowel problems were made worse by Nobby's sudden and noisy arrival.

Nobby only departed Boscastle Gents after eleven hours, by which time Ernie, stuck inside for fear of attack, was beside himself and desperate for sustenance.

Nobby flapped slowly away, in a westerly direction, casting his shadow over The Cock and Hoopla, where Bertha and Herbert Whistleton, married for more than fifty years, and Spot, their small spotty dog, were enjoying an early evening shandy in the rose garden, famous for its collection of electrified gnomes.

When they left, arm-in-arm, they ambled home along a quiet country lane, looking forward to an exciting evening, starting with Coronation Street. Spot skipped merrily along beside them. High above, partly hidden by cloud, Nobby studied them with his unblinking stare, quietly hovering, his great wings outstretched. Suddenly he swooped, as fast as a missile, carrying Spot off into the heavens. Bertha fainted and Herbert was in an unhappy state.

Later, a great Spot hunt was organised, and Nobby was seen, clutching Spot, flying high over Collamore Gap. On the ground an angry posse, comprising members of the 'Bugger the Green Belt Chapter', were all for shooting the bird.

As it transpired, Nobby simply deposited Spot back on the roof of the Boscastle Gents, entirely unharmed, and then flapped lazily away, as if saying: 'We mammoth sea eagles are always being picked on .. give us a break'.

But the incident was sufficient for the authorities to move in. The wolves were eventually rounded up, after a few close shaves, and one by one the Mammoth Sea Eagles and the Red Kites were captured, and later released on the remote Scottish island of Glonk by Aire, which delighted great numbers of people, but enraged shepherds and the firebrand Fanny Fraser of the SNP.

It had all been too much for Lancing-Lancing who abandoned the election, as did The Hon. Charmaine Clenchwarton, who went off to join her lover, Dirty de Villiers, on Sapphic Spit. The election was finally won by the very sensible candidate from the Terribly Boring Party, as Lancing-Lancing had predicted weeks before.

The Syrian birds egg collectors, believed to be heavily armed and still wearing their suicide vests, are still at large.

Lancing-Lancing's involvement with wild animals and packs of wolves led to some confusion on the part of Herman the German, who wrote to him from his recently re-located headquarters in south America (what he calls his lair) and where he was still drawing up his master-plan to take over the world.

Near fuel dump,

Behind Guzman's ironmongery, Asuncion, Paraguay

Admiral Flushing Flushing

You now is wolf man, yes. We give you big wolf medal in Paraguay freedom moovment. You win best medal PWP[2] for good busyness in England. You run our ships, yes. You rite back soon you can. We have new adress for secureety problem now fix. We redy to start

---

2   The Grand Order of the Paraguay Wolf Pack was won by Admiral Karl Doenitz who led German U-boat 'wolf-packs' in WWII. He took over when things got sticky for Hitler in at the end of the war.

up busyness anytime soon, yes. We now in Herman's Lair redy for big truble all over place, yes.

Make war soon, yes

Col. Herman Grindlevald (you call me Herman German)

-

The Nest

Dear Herman the German

Thank you for awarding me the Grand Order of the Paraguay Wolf Pack, though I think there has been some misunderstanding. My recent tribulations with packs of wolves and other animals had nothing to do with submarines. I am afraid I must, once more, reject your kind offer of putting me in charge of your navy.

Lancing-Lancing

**

Lancing-Lancing and Sophie were just getting back to their quiet and idyllic life at The Nest, after the hullaballoo caused by the Red Riding Hood by election, when their contentment was broken by disturbing news that a three-day pop festival was to be held close to their home, of which Lancing-Lancing had previous experience.

The Nest

To: Sir Bunny Snortington

Executive President Gob-on-a-Stick Promotions

Dear President Snortington

I have read in the Mousehole Messenger about the coming Snortit Pop Festival. I am worried about its increased size, from two stages to seven, the construction of an airstrip, the building of the new heliport and a 'pop-up' hotel (what is that?) and, further, that you expect 'hundreds of thousands of fans because of the pulling power of Patti and the Pink Gussets.' As the site is within yards of my cottage can you give me assurances that there will not be any more trouble?

There were two hundred arrests at the previous event and my man Trumble was pushed over the cliff. He had to be rescued by the fire brigade from where he was clinging by his finger tips to a Puffins nest. The Hells Angels employed to provide security stole the lead off the church roof and the conflagration when a pot-smoker set fire to the straw houses and tents caused mayhem.

The mass nude baptism by followers of the Maharishi of Potters Bar very nearly resulted in a drowning, and that's exactly what happened when one of the Maharishi's disciples suffered a dreadful death when he fell between the planks into an open latrine. There was, too, the nasty incident of my dog, Albion, and the deranged warbler known as the Bishop of Broadmoor, aka the Man in Black.

I realise the festival is part of the 24-hour economy, a policy as half-baked as its name, which everybody recognizes as a green-light for carnage which will stretch the Samaritans, police, ambulance, midwifery and hospital staffs to breaking-point.

Lancing-Lancing
-

No response from Sir Bunny Snortington or Gob-on-a-Stick Promotions could be found in Lancing-Lancing's files, and the Snortit festival went ahead as planned. It was the launch of Patti of the Pink Gussets' mercurial career. When she headlined at Snortit she had been in the music business two weeks. Her sudden ascent began with her influential Grunge-meets-Garage version of the 'anthemic '70s disco-hit, Screw It. Unable to sing, write, read music, spell 'lyricist' or play an instrument, gave Patti an affinity with her followers. 'It's like I'm one of 'em, innit,' she said.

Two weeks after Snortit, she won an OBE for 'outstanding services to humanity and the starving.' Days later she was made Visiting vice-chancellor and Professor of Rap and Trends, at Albright College,

Pennsylvania, where she was feted by Professor E.E de Sly, who wrote Berlin Up! widely acknowledged as the world's worst-ever book on Teutonic culture, of which, Dr. Hugo Bliss, of the faculty of German Studies, at Brazen College, Oxford, said made Albright College an academic laughing stock.

The leading rock critic, Vi P, said Patti's OBE was an act of mealy-mouthed churlishness on the part of the government, which was clearly out of step with the demands of the wider populace. It should have been the Nobel Peace Prize, Vi P wrote, arguing that Patti, 19, from Shaft Green, Oldham, where she was discovered on household disinfectant, in Morrison's, reminded her of El Greco in his disciple period, crossed with Benjamin Britten before he slept with Peter Pears and went electric.

For Lancing-Lancing and his neighbours, Snortit was a weekend of unadulterated hell.

Lord Eddie Claremont became so exercised about helicopters and singers jets flying low over Rose Hall, that he took to the skies in his Tiger Moth and conducted flour-bomb sorties over the festival.

'I'm very worried about him,' Lady Minnie, told Lancing-Lancing. 'It's years since he flew. He couldn't get into his flying-suit and it took an age before the old Moth would fire up. It was covered in straw and dung in one of the derelict cow sheds. He should have sold it when we got rid of the Friesians. He says he loves a dog-fight and thinks he's the Red Baron. I had to stop him having a machine-gun in the cockpit.'

The Nest

Dear George

Sophie says I'm becoming curmudgeonly and by way of making amends I am going to stage a small music festival at the cottage. I hope you and Catharine will come along. I know I sound like 'Outraged from Royal Tonbridge', but it's a mild response to Snortit.

All proceeds will go to Children Playing, which helps youngsters from deprived backgrounds to learn music and to play an instrument. Sophie says it's not a bad notion, though pitifully middle-class. She's right, of course, but on the whole seems supportive, seeing it as a modest antidote to Gob-on-a-Stick. Pleased, though, to see that the preening *Sir* Bunny is now facing charges for abuse and fiddling his tax. And this was the same species who urged youngsters not to bother voting in elections. I suppose it's only to be expected. He has been, after all, recently *knighted*.

Lancing-Lancing

-

Dogs

Dear Admiral

We'll certainly come to your music weekend, but we tend to agree with Sophie. Is it not rather *twee*?

George

-

Nest

Dear George

Thank you for your candour, and you're right. I've cancelled the idea. Twee summed it up. We've sent a modest cheque to Children Playing (to salve my middle-class conscience). Apart from anything else, children might have been encouraged to learn the trombone, and that would have been terrible for everybody.

Lancing-Lancing

**

Nest

Dear George

A while ago we talked about the Three Rivers Race in Norfolk. It takes in the Ant, the Bure and the Thurne, and lasts twenty-four hours.

The wind often falls in the night so, if you wish, you can soldier on, or drop the mud-weight and sit it out. There'll be all sorts of sail boats and, doubtless, the usual chaos at Potter Heigham Bridge, especially if there's a good blow and a tide. It's medieval and low, where we had our last little altercation. The race is fun when it's going well, not so grand if it's perishing cold and you're stuck in the reeds.

Lancing-Lancing
-

There was a good turnout with close to two hundred yachts competing. They were of all shapes and sizes with crews that ranged from expert to novice. After the race Lancing–Lancing received the following letter:

The Houseboat Costa Lotta

Hickling Broad, Norfolk

Dear Mr. Lancing

I am not much of a letter writer and I don't want to harp on about the incident, but I would be grateful if you could make sure that you conduct all our business, re: the repairs, through my office address on the visiting card that I gave you.

As you gathered, when your bowsprit (I believe that's what you call the big thing that pokes out at the front of a boat, like a sharp pole or lance) suddenly poked through the bedroom window of the Costa Lotta, my friend and I were at it. When she screamed out, I'd got my head down, so to speak, and I thought mistakenly that it was a cry of passion.

The thing is this: my wife was back home in Epsom at the time of the accident, being rather under the impression that I was out of the country on business. If the truth be told, she doesn't really know about my friend, or the Costa Lotta, and neither does the tax man, so I would like everything in cash and, as I say, done through my office.

I could tell straight away that you and your friend, George, were both navy types and had some sympathy with my dilemma, especially when my friend was rushing around trying to get dressed and get us all a drink. She's a lovely little thing and we have a nice time.

You may have noticed that she was younger than me by a good few years. She's a very nice girl and lives full-time on the Costa Lotta, while working in Tesco's. I don't know why I'm unburdening myself and sharing my secrets with you. The houseboat-builder says it'll be about £400 to replace the window and do some decorating. We've got to buy a new mattress as well, from where the bow-sprit speared it. I hope that's alright.

I'm glad you got back safely. At least you didn't sink your sailboat, or the Costa Lotta, which you would have done if you had hit us beneath the water-line.

I've come to regard you, through the accident, as a good friend. Every cloud has a silver-lining. When you'd gone, after you'd untangled your boat from our bed, we stuck some cardboard where the glass in the window had been, and after we'd made a cup of Typhoo, and got over the surprise, we got going again with my own little bow-sprit, if you get my meaning.

Best wishes, and nice to meet you

Ernie Green

-

The Nest

Dear Ernie

I entirely understand and, again, I would like to say how sorry I am for so rudely interrupting your devotions.

Had it not been for a sudden and extremely violent gust of wind, and being forced to make an impossibly tight turn by the antics of a wind-surfer, who clearly knew nothing of winds and currents and shouldn't have been there in the first place, and who could have been impaled on our bow-sprit, we would have continued with the race, leaving yourself and your friend in peace.

I have sent the money as you requested. Thank you for being so understanding.

Best wishes and kind regards to you and your friend.

Lancing-Lancing.

-

The Houseboat Costa Lotta

Hickling Broad

Dear Admiral Lancing-Lancing

I have now got your proper name. I've been looking you up. I said to my friend you looked familiar, what with your balloon adventures and the dog and all that. We need more like you, if you don't mind me saying so.

Something else I said to my friend (we're enjoying another little stay in the Costa Lotta while Her in Epsom thinks I'm on ball-bearing business in Taiwan) is that if we're going to have coitus interruptus it might as well be by an Admiral with a bow-sprit. She loved that!

When I last wrote I said that I thought you and I were kindred spirits and that we would be friends.

I wanted to ask you something personal, if that's OK. My wife doesn't understand a man's needs, if you get my drift, whereas my friend in the Costa Lotta understands them better than most. I know we haven't known each other long, but do you think I should leave my wife and make an honest woman of my friend?

I don't know many important people, and my friend said that with you having been around a bit you'd be able to give me some good advice. My grandad was in the navy on HMS *Bellerophon* in the First World War. Did you ever come across him? He was called Albert, but everybody called him Bert and Mum said he was very brave.

All the best

Ernie

Nest

Dear Ernie

I was interested to hear about Albert, your grandfather, but I'm afraid it does not ring any bells. The navy had thousands of people in the 1900s and I am sorry that I did not encounter him subsequently. You can be proud of him, and it is first-class that his name will live on through you. To find out more about Albert, you could try the National Maritime Museum in Greenwich, the Royal Navy Museum in Portsmouth, or the National Records Office in Kew. They're all very helpful.

I'm not much good at giving marital advice, it's rather beyond my ken. These things are very personal and only those involved can make such decisions. You could have a confidential word with a marriage guidance counsellor, or perhaps the Citizens Advice Bureau could help.

Incidentally, though it's kind of you to say, I'm not in the least bit important, and doubt I ever was or ever will be. I am very flattered, however, that you should choose to take me into your confidence, and I am sorry that I cannot be of more help. I would like to wish you all the best in the future.

Lancing-Lancing
-

Dogs

Dear Admiral

Let me know what I owe you for the damage to the houseboat. We don't seem to have much luck with the Broads (unlike Ernie). First, we are dismasted under Potter Heigham Bridge (I still blame medieval architecture) and then we bring a sudden halt to Sodom and Gomorrah on the Costa Lotta houseboat. One couldn't make it up. It was a hell of a crash when we took out the bedroom window.

Little Ernie looked like Danny de Vito, short and startled in nothing but his vest. His friend got my flag up when I realised the full-Brazilian had reached Norfolk. She was amazingly composed, passing the gin round before we'd even got the bowsprit out of the mattress. It must have been a shock for them, it certainly wasn't the bang they expected. The race was superlative fun, but I might think twice before competing again, which should please Ernie.

George

-

Nest

George

Please don't worry about the money. Ernie's been in touch, and making so many confessions I feel like a priest. He's a nice chap and says I'm his new best friend. He's getting just a little pressing. C'est la vie.

Lancing-Lancing

-

The Houseboat Costa Lotta

Dear Admiral

I didn't mention I've had a few problems and I thought you ought to know that I'm still in therapy. I had a business which nearly went under, so trying to maintain my wife, who's very demanding where money is concerned, and my friend in the Costa Lotta, is getting quite costly.

I had a breakdown after becoming a gambler. I was putting money on horses to invest the winnings in my business (balls and bearings). I could walk to the racecourse from my house in Epsom. It was that close. But I went mad on an old nag called Couldn't Lose and then – guess what? – it lost. The business went from bad to worse, balls and bearings aren't what they were.

On top of everything else, Her Majesty in Epsom has got suspicious after she smelt scent on my Y-Fronts. It's called Algarve

Nights, and it's from Tesco (my friend on the Costa Lotta gets it cheap because she works there). She uses a lot of it. But Her Majesty said it stank like dead chrysanthemums. I told Her Majesty that it was only Big Man, my after-shave, but she didn't believe me, even when I said it was Big Man mixed with a late-night cocoa in Frankfurt, that I'd accidentally spilled down me while I was talking balls with Herr Bullentop (the Mr. Big of balls and bearings in the Rhine Valley).

She still wouldn't have any of it, and began shouting and going on saying it was all a pack of lies.

So, as you can see, life's getting a bit complicated. What do you think? I noticed on the internet that you'd got married. If *you* should ever play away from home you wouldn't need a houseboat, you could have a battleship in Malta or somewhere nice. Anyway, sorry to lumber you with my worries, just thought that as one of my best friends, you'd be interested.

Best wishes

Ernie

PS. Keep all this to yourself.

-

Ball, Shafts & Bearings Ltd

Unit 14a , behind Raj's Popadom Packs,

Slough Heritage Park.

Dear Admiral

Yes, it's me again, this time from my office (what's left of it; the bailiffs have been in). I just need somebody to talk to.

I am afraid things have gone belly up with Her Majesty in Epsom. She's knows about me and my friend on the Costa Lotta and all hell's broken loose. I don't know how she found out but she turned up in the Tesco at Stalham and set about my friend on cold meats. Things are coming to a head, as they say.

I'm thinking of taking my friend and disappearing to Wiseman's Bridge, near Saundersfoot. My friend's Norfolk but she's got a bit of Welsh in her. There are downsides to going Welsh: after coal and steel went down, ball-bearings aren't what they were in Wales. So rebuilding the business would be tricky. We also don't speak Welsh, and they can be funny that way. My friend says she'd like to run a B&B on a houseboat in Wales. It could be a lot of fun, but it'd be a bit cramped. There'd only be room for one guest at a time, and we wouldn't have much privacy, if you see what I mean.

I'll keep in touch, but I'll have to lie low for a while until things have cooled down.

Her Majesty told my friend that she's going to buy a big carving knife, or one of those Samurai swords, and that she'd turn her into enough gammon steaks to fill a freezer, and it's worried her.

Cheerio for now and thanks for all your help and advice.

Your friend

Ernie

-

The Nest

Dear Ernie

I am afraid I have been able to give you very little help. These are tumultuous developments and I wish you well in coping with them. You should think carefully before doing a runner. It is sometimes better to confront difficulties, as they have a nasty habit of coming back to haunt you. Try and talk to Relate, or some similar organization.

As for the rest of your note, I don't know what to say. Wales is very beautiful and I enjoy Welsh lamb, especially with mint sauce. I can see your friend's point of view, after all, nobody would want to be turned into gammon steaks. Don't rush matters, these things can resolve themselves if given sufficient time.

Lancing-Lancing

Honey Pot Villa

Furlong Way

Epsom

Dear Mr. Lunching

We haven't met but it's been reported to me that you and my husband and some trollop are involved in troilism in a plywood houseboat called the Costa Lotta on the Norfolk Broads.

There is no point in denying it because it's come from the horse's mouth, that of Ernie, my little toe-rag of a husband. I became suspicious when I was wringing out his smalls. I confronted him about his ball and shaft dealings, and got him in an arm-lock by the dog basket in the kitchen.

He was always saying he was going off to Frankfurt or Vilnius on ball business. But now I know the truth. He was tearing up the M11 to see his little scrubber, and to meet up with you and your filthy naval goings-on. He started yelling about bowsprits and having friends in high places and I thought it was all disgusting.

I didn't know what he was squealing about, but it's obviously some sort of perversion that you and he and that tart on cold meats get up to, sticking it right up through her bed.

Don't think I don't know all about you and your balloons and being on the TV. You and that dog are quite well-known and the newspapers will love this. But first you'll be hearing from Rabid & Pinching, my solicitors, who are getting the divorce papers ready.

When I'm through with Ernie Green he won't know his balls from his bearings, and if that little cow on cold meats thinks a bowsprit in her bed is hard she'll find it's nothing compared to what I'm going to give her.

What disappoints me is that if Ernie had taken me into his confidence we might have been able to work something out. You see, the thing is this. Over the years, I've secretly longed for a bit of troilism or quadism (is that four?) and this could be my chance.

I've seen your photo. You're not a bad looking chap and you scrub up quite well. Maybe there's still time for the four of us to work something out. I've included a photograph of myself. I'm younger than you and not in bad shape, and I don't mind putting up with an older bloke.

My 'phone number's here if you'd like to hear my purr. You can tell a lot from somebody's voice. Ernie says I'm too bossy and act like the Queen. He says I'm far too domineering. But with the right man I can be submissive, if that's what you like. Mind you, when I get my hands on that little madam, I'll be very strict. She'll pay for what she's been up to.

Well, what do you think? If this is of no interest I'll have to go back to Plan A and tell the newspapers and the lawyers . It would be a pity if it has to end on an unsatisfying note, when the four of us could have fun. I've never done it at sea, and you could instruct me in the ways of the navy, get the bowsprit out. I'm still not sure how you use it, or how big it is. But it sounds exciting and I'm a quick learner.

Here's hoping

Val Green

-

Nest

Dear Mrs. Green

Thank you for your letter which I found astonishing. Let me assure you I know little or nothing of your husband and his personal affairs. The only time I was in the Costa Lotta was with a companion trying to extricate my bowsprit from a scene of carnage in the bedroom. It's sizeable and had poked through the window and wedged itself in the mattress. As for your other suggestion, let me see if I can come up with something which will satisfy you.

Lancing-Lancing

Nest

George, dear boy

I enclose a copy of an amazing letter I have received from somebody called Val Green, the wife of Ernie, our mutual acquaintance. You will see from it that Ernie has been rumbled and that Val has discovered his floating love-nest.

If I'm not careful, I could be up the creek without the usual. What do you advise? As we used to say in the navy, foreign watering-holes can be dangerous, as Ernie is now beginning to find out. I have no desire to play a role in Val's fantasies and have talked the whole thing over with Sophie, who thinks it's hilarious and refuses to take it seriously. I'm not so sure. These people are deranged and need handling with finesse.

Sophie suggests we try and recruit Two-Fingers Maltby. He's always been an inveterate wick-dipper (old navy phrase) and could be my proxy. How we could lure him from Monaco, which is where he spends most of his time, to the a knocking-shop on the Norfolk Broads, I'm not sure. Our Val would have to lay out her wares in a very enticing way.

Lancing-Lancing
-

Honey Pot Villa

Furlong Way

Epsom

Darling Lance

I hope you don't mind me calling you that, now we're getting to know each other, sharing all our intimate little secrets. Lance puts me in mind of dashing soldiers in tight white breeches having sword fights, duelling over innocent young virgins, breasts heaving, hips thrusting.

I can't stop thinking about sailors and bowsprits and all those swinging things (hammocks! What did you think I meant? You naughty boy!) And the more I think about them, the more I warm to the idea. What's all this about your 'companion' on the houseboat. I didn't know there were four of you at it. Quadism! And with me that would Fiveism! Do you think he, or it could be a she for all I know, might be entertained by our plans for the future? I wouldn't mind, as far as I'm concerned, the more the merrier.

Now you're getting to know me, you'll be starting to realise I'm game for anything. I can't wait to hear back from you when you say you'll come up with something to satisfy me. You're so wicked! I keep reading your letter over and over and thinking about you in uniform, all that gold braid and the peak cap and stuff. I love uniforms. Will you wear sunglasses? I like those. They're sort of continental.

Val

-

Nest

Dear George

I enclose a copy of Val's latest missive. This is getting out of hand, it's gone from a trot to a gallop. My goose could be cooked if I can't find a solution. Cats are like this. We kept them in the bilges to keep the rats down, but they bred like mad and there were soon more cats than rats. When they're in the mood, there's no stopping them.

Lancing-Lancing

-

Dogs

Dear Admiral

Well, at least she thinks you're a good-looking boy, which is encouraging. Perhaps Two-Fingers *is* a possibility. But as you say, he's on the Riviera and favours bathing belles, preferably rich and young. Although, as Catharine says (she had a narrow squeak in a dinghy off Antibes when he was teaching her handling) he's been around a while, so maybe his charms are wearing a little thin. Any port in a storm, perhaps? We gave Fingers the brush-off about modelling in which he wanted you in uniform (what it is it about the admiral look?) so he might tell us to sling our hook.

There's always old knotty, Stag Hake, he's desperate, and as Buttocks says, he isn't particular as long as there's a pulse. Val sounds broad-minded, so perhaps she wouldn't mind being tied up with him.

Let me think about it. I'll come back to you. The easiest way out is for you to fulfil her needs. But Sophie would have an opinion, and extricating yourself from that would be harder than getting a bowsprit out of a mattress and through what was left of the Costa Lotta's window.

As ever

George

-

Dogs

Dear Admiral

I think I have a solution to Costa Lottagate. It's based on the idea of a toy-boy acting as your proxy, and I may have an alternative to Two Fingers. We could suggest to the panting Val an old acquaintance from the merchant marine. He was known as Robert the Donkey, feted in his circle as being a phenomenal performer with a physique to match.

In sailor towns around the world the Donkey's stamina was the stuff of legend. The last I heard, he had left his seafaring days behind and was working as a Tube train driver, as one does. I would think his prowess might still draw the needy.

If I can, ahem, track Robert the train driver down, we could arrange a tryst with Val which might include Ernie and his friend from cold meats. If things go well, it could even sate Val's craving for quadism (the mind boggles) which would get you off the hook.

George

-

Nest

George, dear boy

It's worth a go. I'm in a tight corner and this could be a way out. Good luck to both you and the Donkey.

Lancing-Lancing

-

Dogs

Admiral

We're getting things back on the rails. Robert the Donkey is a regular on the Circle Line. I found him through the League of Merchant Seamen. He was, shall we say, cock-a-hoop at the idea. He's older now, but assures me everything beneath the water-line is still tickety-boo, and that he often pops up to Norfolk for a spot of fishing. The idea of a regular overnight on a houseboat, with a full English, holds great appeal.

George.

-

Lancing-Lancing wrote to Val saying he had only recently married, that he now had a child, and, anyway, he wasn't as deft in the department in which she was interested as she might have imagined. Between shrieks of laughter, Sophie had helped him compose the letter. While Lancing-Lancing knew this would be disappointing to Val, and though complimented by her overtures, he had, however, an alternative suggestion.

He was able to offer her the services of Robert, a new and exciting man, one who boasted not one, but two uniforms. The first that of a Jolly Jack Tar, the second, that of a Circle Line tube driver. Lancing-Lancing made his suggestion on the understanding that if the plan proved satisfactory, Val would drop all her claims about him. He also urged her to patch things up with Ernie, and sought assurances that would she would not turn his friend into gammon steaks, and that the four of them, with Robert the driver, might live happily ever after on the Costa Lotta.

Val thought this was a splendid notion. She wrote back saying she agreed to all the terms, as long as Robert was up to the job, and that he'd wear one of his uniforms during bouts of Rest and Recuperation aboard the Costa Lotta.

She admitted that a divorce from Ernie would have been 'silly anyway, because he's got no money, Honey Pot Villa in Epsom is mortgaged to the hilt, the bottom's fallen out of balls and bearings, and I'd have ended up penniless while he was with Little Miss Fast Knickers off Tesco's cold meat counter.'

Lancing-Lancing wrote to Ernie, outlining the scheme, pointing out the many advantages.

Ernie wouldn't have to do a runner, he wouldn't have to endure a ruinous divorce, and Val had promised that she wouldn't set about his friend with a samurai sword. Lancing-Lancing said that the fun Ernie had been having with his friend could be doubled by the inclusion of Val and Robert the Donkey. Importantly, the plan would also allow Val to satisfy her deep and secret longings for Ernie, which he had failed to see because of his focus on balls and shafts.

From what had appeared a no-win situation, it could be a win-win for all parties. The only downside, Lancing-Lancing could see, was that the Costa Lotta would be well-used and crowded, and being of a flimsy construction, it would need regular maintenance with, among things, its bottom being scraped every year.

Honeypot Villa

Epsom

Dearest, darling Lance

Just a note to let you know that things are working out really well.
Robert pops up from the Underground, I call him Randy Robbie,
and we have a lovely time on the Costa Lotta.

You wouldn't believe the things we get up to, and Ernie and I are
closer than we've ever been. Seeing him in action with Charlene,
the girl off cold meats, has brought a new respect on my part. I
didn't know he'd got it in him.

Sometimes we all get mixed up with each other, it's a real
jumble, with Randy dressed as either a train driver or a seaman.
He's a marathon man, and unlike the Tube never stops. Sometimes
he even dresses up as a diver with a ping-pong ball on the end of
his snorkel.

The Costa Lotta bobs around a lot when we're all being friendly,
and the other night Randy cut his toe when he stuck it through the
wheel-house window. It didn't stop him, nothing does, but the sheets
were a bit bloody, as if I'd been doing it with a vampire. Charlene and
I have become close, the tricks she's taught me .. well, you wouldn't
believe. And she's learnt stuff off me, with me being more mature.

If ever you want to come over, with your bowsprit, and your
friend George, you'd be very welcome. We could have a full-dress
uniform party. There's another group we've run across, and they do
treacle parties in Thetford Forest.

Lots of love

Val

**

*Lancing–Lancing has never cared for tourism and what he sees as
the ruination of the environment by cyclists, councils, caravans and
people in red trousers.*

211

Dogs

Dear Admiral

Sailed at Crabster the other day on the north Norfolk coast. En route Catharine and I passed through Samphire Market. It was only midweek, but it was subsumed by cars, caravans and mobile homes called things like Tucson Apache.

It's a lovely place, with two greens and a stream. Yet there was no way you could see its beauty, buried beneath trippers and traffic. The golden goose of peace and quiet has been slaughtered, the very reason people were attracted in the first place. Do you remember when Norfolk was desolate and remote, next stop the Russian Steppes? Too much is now annexed by second-homers in red cords and four-wheel drives.

So we didn't stop at Samphire Market. I remember you had friends there and thought you'd be interested. My advice: make a detour.

George
-

Nest

Dear George

I was in a jam the other day behind three caravans and an Ohio Commander, a mobile home with a TV aerial and four bikes stuck on its rear. Charlie Wimbish (ex HMS *Fearsome*) wrote to me about the way Dunnin is being wrecked. Interminable road works with town-hall pedalista out to create a bike-nirvana. They're all real-ale drinkers in open-toed sandals and John Lennon caps last seen in 1965.

Roads are being dug up and made dangerously narrow for the installation of pedal ways, which are instantly obsolete as cyclists only ever use the pavement. They only seem to use roads if they want to jump lights. How come there's so much money for cyclists when the local hospital is dying through a lack of funds? It doesn't stop with bikes. The mayor is to hold a bonfire of traditions, burning his ceremonial robes and tricorn hat and smashing up his chain of office with a sledge-hammer. He's in his chair in the Mayor's Parlour in a pointy helmet and skin-tight lime-green Lycra.

Lancing-Lancing

-

The Old Pig Sty

Poundland Way

Dunnin-on-Thames

Dear Admiral Lancing-Lancing

Re: Sod Off

Your name has come to my attention as somebody bothered about councils sticking their digits into civic pies.

I run Sod Off (SO). It wants to stop councils squandering *our* money on pet schemes and generally arsing around trying to justify their existence. My committee and I would like you to join SO.

Typical of our work is a campaign to thwart plans to turn Dunnin into a cycle town. SO wants to tax cyclists. All other road users have to cough up, so why not the pedalista? Are they a protected species? Do they have God on their side? Their sense of entitlement is depressing. There are millions of them, so a tax would raise a fortune.

Dunnin council also has a thing about one-way systems. These guarantee circuitous journeys and turn straight-stretches into race-tracks. So it then imposes 20 mph speed limits. Dunnin has become Tortoise Town and something of a laughing stock: pray God you never need an ambulance or suffer a fire.

The council keeps turning roads into walking streets. This creates a ghost town, cold and windswept, with all life and vibrancy sucked out of it. The truth is that the council wants *all* traffic banned and it won't be happy until Dunnin is completely sealed up, open only to pedestrians and cyclists, with bikers in Lycra using walkers as skittles.

213

In Dunnin, too, there is a huge and abandoned office block, now vandalised and graffitied. Its ugliness blights the neighbourhood, but instead of doing something about it, the council still spends *our* money on feeding its highway habit. There was, at one time, a plan to destroy Dunnin's medieval market and turn it into a caravan park, but thanks to SO the plan was ditched.

Meanwhile, Dunnin Hospital, is on life-support for lack of funds. Sod Off wants more nurses, doctors and kidney machines than cycle ways. The apportionment of council money is barking.

I look forward to your response and hope you will join us.

Basil Trevitt, Chmn. Sod Off.

-

Nest

Dear Mr. Trevitt

Re: Doin' in Dunnin

While I agree with your sentiments, I will have to turn down your offer, Cornwall being too far from Dunnin for me to take an active role. Local councils botch everything and the less they intervene the better. I always imagined Dunnin, with the meandering Dud flowing through it, as a fine city, not a slow one.

In Cornwall, the latest craze is nude bike-ins with naked riders who wobble a lot.

There's to be a Tour de Pasty, an entirely bogus marketing ploy to boost tourism. Riders finish at Land's End where they take nude selfies and then dangle their bits at France. I wish you well in telling council busy-bodies to Sod Off. I have known more elegant imprecations, but it makes the point.

Lancing-Lancing.

-

Some weeks later, Basil Trevitt wrote again to Lancing–Lancing to say that Sod Off letters had been leaked to the Press by an embittered

214

Trevitt underling, a stop-at-nothing cyclist who wanted SO to be more pedal-friendly. Trevitt had told the underling to get on his bike, which he did, pedaling immediately to the offices of The Dunnin Weekly Observer.

The letters included Lancing–Lancing's reply to Trevitt's invitation to join Sod Off, and his disparaging remarks about the unstoppable rise and rise of Britain's pedalista. The leak resulted in Lancing–Lancing receiving a shoal of abusive letters, most of them anonymous, of which the following is an example:

Address: It don't matter where I live and it's none of your business, clever Dick.

To: Colonel bloody Lancing, or whatever you is

You don't live somewhere near us in Dunnin so keep your big conk out of it. Yer not in the army now. I been biking fifty years. I met my wife in the saddle. We spent day and night in it. What we want is less nobs in big cars and more in the saddle. Get out of yer tank and get on yer bike. Get some wind in yer brains and a saddle under yer bum. What yer want is a nice girl saddled up.
I love looking at nude bikers. I've got photos of my neighbours on a tandem. They're always riding.

Signed:

It don't matter who
-

Other letters and emails sent to Lancing–Lancing were too offensive to reprint. During this unfortunate episode he and Sophie and the baby woke early one Sunday morning to an alarming sight.

The Nest

Dear Mr. Trevitt

The leak of the Sod Off correspondence continues to cause me trouble.

The other day my wife and I were dismayed to find our home surrounded by a large number of caravans and mobile home people protesting about my comments. I went out and complained to Ron, the leader of the pack, who said he had travelled all the way down from Romford.

Ron said his caravan was a top of the range Sky Lark. He bought it by blowing his pension early. It was a toss up between the Sky Lark and a timeshare in Alicante. I told him that he ought to have chosen the latter. He couldn't understand why I wasn't taken by the Sky Lark's brown and cream paint job, which he felt blended in nicely with Cornish fields and hedgerows.

He said the Sky Lark cost a fortune, being deluxe, with steam-room, cocktail bar and hot tub. He thought its lines and paintwork matched the Parthenon. I told him the Parthenon wasn't painted and that he needed his head examined. I also asked him to move on, with the seventeen other caravans in the convoy.

At this, all the other caravanners stripped off and started taking naked selfies in front of their caravans, or 'vans,' as the aficionado call them.

Ron didn't know it but he was lucky that Albion didn't go for his Johnson. Things quietened down when a policeman arrived and told Ron and his confederates that they were causing a nuisance and would they please move on. Which they did, somewhat reluctantly. I gather that you too have been subject to unpleasantness.

Lancing-Lancing

-

The Old Piggery

Dunnin

Dear Admiral

Yes, a great deal of unpleasantness. My home was picketed by hordes of naked cyclists. The redundant office block I mentioned is said to be of the Stalinist school of architecture. It's now been granted Grade 1 Listed status after a campaign led by Callum McSky, the smug chap who presents *Dig This*, the TV allotment show. He's always in a straw boater and a striped blazer rowing a skiff on the moat at his 17th century manor house on the Hampshire Downs. I'm sure you can picture the chap. On TV he gives little homilies, as earnest as a vicar.

McSky once sought to List a block of flats in Hackney, describing its residents as 'a heavenly community blissful in their boulevards in the sky.' But the heavenly community tried to burn it down and said if it was so bloody good why didn't he live there? He said he'd love to, but somebody had to stay behind to look after the peacocks.

He'd List everything but would never live in them. Two hundred squatters now occupy the Stalinist block. If it was torn down they would be homeless. For pity's sake: where will all this end?

Basil Trevitt
-

It ended with Dunnin council converting the forsaken offices into a vast hostel for the homeless. Acres of graffiti exhort passers-by to rip off their clothes, to take up nude cycling, to smash capitalism and make love one to another.

It's under siege by tax-payers, by the Stalinist movement, worried its aesthetics are not being respected by its occupiers, and by Banksy followers, who say the graffiti is of such a poor standard it harms their hero's reputation as the new Matisse.

Pedalista are angry that plans to turn Dunnin into bike-heaven had to be curbed to raise money for the conversion of the block into a refuge, and to offer inmates such essentials as colonic irrigation, head kneading, Nepalese yoghurt making, ear candling, tattoo parlour, a Wash'n Go for Staffies, an STD clinic and a smoking lounge subsidised by the Santa Monica Charismatic Church of Hashish Theology.

A plan to dig out the basement as a secure room, in the event of an attack by increasingly restive tax-payers, had to be abandoned, after a protracted inquiry chaired by Sir Henry Glint QC, because of concerns that Dunnin is built on old salt-workings into which double-deckers and houses occasionally disappear.

Proceedings were further delayed by revelations that Glint was being paid three times more than the Prime Minister, that he had an uncle who had been the boss of a 17th century salt mine, for which Dunnin council and the pedalista Mayor demanded an apology, and whose Chambers were registered in Tonga for tax purposes.

**

Far from Dunnin and its pedalista problems, George Steel continued his journalistic forays, faithfully recording his peregrinations in his regular missives to Lancing-Lancing.

The Piri-Piri Hotel

Majorca

Dear Admiral

Out here doing a bit of scribbling for Keel International. It's not a bad rag, though it's brimming with literals after an abomination called Lol Sheer axed all the sub-editors. Sheer is one of those psychotic types, known to the reporters as Sneer or Osama. His official title is Executive Management Controller (no, me neither). The editor's a nervous wreck and the proprietor's an ill-tempered little man in an outsize trilby who looks very much like Truman Capote.

This is a hack's junket to Majorca organised by a hotel called The Piri-Piri. It's splitting the cost with Jet Off, the one that charges the obese and the handicapped double. I thought Piri-Piri was hot Portuguese chicken, and if you weren't in Albufeira or Faro you had it in Nando's. But, hey, what do I know?

The Piri-Piri is distinctly dodgy with iffy food (the chef's down with salmonella). It boasts the de rigeur five stars, of course. One member of the party hasn't been seen since the first night. He had the special of the day and was ambulanced away before the pudding.

218

It's near Deia, where Robert Graves is buried. All the usual free-loaders on the trip: Two-Fingers (with a giant blonde from Zagreb), Stag Hake (*so* grouchy), McButtocks (Fry's Chocolate Creams and a sack of gorgonzola crisps on a two-hour flight); and the American novelist, Harry 'Toots' Molloy, who wrote *Who Fracked Up Illinois*? about a clam-fisherman in Maine who didn't believe in birth control, and ended up living with nine wayward children in a tarpaulin shack in the Appalachians.

Toots is writing a piece for *Wide Open*, once the organ of the British Dental Federation, but it went downhill and was swallowed up by Ivan Stefanopolis, the New York filth peddler. Stefanopolis loved the name and turned it into a porn mag. He's got Presidential ambitions, so he wants *Wide Open* to carry more arty pieces aimed at a dirty-minded intellectual set, or as Toots says: 'It's always been read by dicks, but Stef wants clever ones.'

He's been commissioned to write an article on Majorca in the poetic-style of Graves, expressing in rhyme what Graves would think of Majorca and its night-life. Toots says: 'Journalistically it's a winner. Poetry and pics of junked up Euro-trash boogying the night away.'

Toots was rather taken with Maltby's companion, Busty, all the way from Zagreb, but it didn't take him long to fall out with McButtocks. McButtocks was enamoured with Toots's literary reputation (Hemingway: booze, birds & bullfights) and asked him to do a piece for *Boat Puffery*.

But when she told him the fee he sat at the bar and guffawed: 'Are you kiddin? Whadya run? A charity? I wouldn't write a grocery list for that.'

She was went off in a huff, while Toots, deep into a bottle of Southern Comfort, said he hadn't travelled all the way from the Bronx, to have some penny-pinching harridan insult his craft. He says she's even worse than his ex-wives.

George

Nest

George

Many years ago we paid a goodwill visit to Majorca when I was on HMS *Formidable*. I'm afraid my trombone recital quickly dispelled any goodwill. I've read *Big Tuna*, by Toots Molloy, and Sophie enjoyed his *Bad Nights on Staten*. He sounds an interesting chap.

Lancing-Lancing

-

The Amarillo Daily Candid

Hi Admiral

Heard some real nice things about you from George Steel a few weeks back. Some guy who's commissioned me wants a piece on how the Cornish navy had a role in the American war of Independence. He reckons there were good time gals on the early Brit warships. Kept your navy boys happy at sea. Wondering if I might drop by and see how you feel about Nelson having hookers on his boats. We could have a drink or two. Be a real pleasure and an honor to make your acquaintance.

Toots Molloy

Nest

Dear Mr. Molloy

I'd be delighted to meet you and help in any way that I can, though my knowledge about fallen ladies on Nelson's ships is somewhat lacking. That said, it would be a pleasure to meet you and to try and assist you in any way that you feel appropriate. Allow me to express my delight in your novel, *Big Tuna*, and my wife's great pleasure in *Bad Nights on Staten*. Please accept our warmest congratulations.

Lancing-Lancing

Nest
Dear George

After his initial visit here – when he was researching an article about Nelson's fondness for fallen angels – Toots Molloy has decided to stay on and now seems to have put down roots in Cornwall. He says he's in love with the place, and it's not just *amour geographic*. He's arm-in-arm with a young lady called Posie, who runs Ye Olde Gambolling Pisky Tea Shoppe, in Polperro, and he even talks of taking the plunge, for the fourth time. He says he's had enough of beating around the world and laying his head where he might.

He's working on a new book – an extended version of his article *Nelson's Trollops* – and has become a favourite with the locals, especially in the evenings, when he and Posie are to be found carousing with fishermen in The Lobster Pot.

He says he'll be travelling to Norfolk to research Nelson's birthplace, for his new book, an extended version of his article. He wondered if you and I would like to join him, as we know the area, and we might get in a spot of Broads sailing, which he would greatly enjoy.

I find him charming, bright and generous, and I'm pleased you made the introduction. Having said that, I think it could be a tiring excursion, as he seems to have a quite insatiable appetite for just about everything. He seems consumed by a Hemingway lust for life, which we find wonderfully infectious, if a mite exhausting. He is much smitten with my Jaguar, as Americans seem to be. They call them Jagwhaarrs.

I thought it would be a treat for him if I drove him to Norfolk in the Jaguar, via London, where I'll pick you up, before we motor east to Norfolk.

Lancing-Lancing

Dogs

Dear Admiral

Excellent idea. I've been asked to write a piece for *Uncharted Waters*, about wherries on the Broads, so this will be a good opportunity. Toots's article, *Nelson's Hookers*, caused a stir. *The Times* letters page was alive. Professor Ralph Gwork wrote that the article was an insult and that Toots should be flogged with a cat o'nine-tails. It led to a sharp riposte from the Be Kind to Cats charity, which was clearly confused.

The MP Marcus Blinofski (wife of the Home Secretary, she who dropped her trousers on the Net in an austerity protest) said it was a storm in a teacup as Nelson was gay and had a thing about Thomas Hardy, as evidenced by his last request. Toots will be a lively companion. You can overnight at the flat here on the Isle of Dogs and then we'll go to Norfolk. I think the trip from Cornwall to London will be enough for one day.

George

-

In London, on the first leg of their sojourn, Catharine prepared a magnificent supper. Close to midnight, with the others ready for bed, Toots wanted to sample London's night life. By the time they got back to the Isle of Dogs, from the West End, it was after 4am.

After the usual round of tourist traps in Covent Garden, Toots took them to the American Writers Club in Kensington (The Stab) where he introduced them to The Last Edition, a cocktail.

"I've worked in Fleet Street," he said. "Each paper kept to its own pub. The Mirror's was known as The Stab in the Back, Stab for short, and this place has plagiarised the name. I preferred the Mail pub, The White Swan, known as The Mucky Duck."

They had three Last Editions each, and in the taxi back to the Isle of Dogs, Toots said the cocktail was infamous for its delayed effect, like a time-bomb in Iraq, where he had driven an ambulance, helped at an orphanage, smuggled in medicines and smuggled out an elderly husband and wife who were now living happily in Wisconsin. He had chronicled his experiences in his book, A Bronx Boy in Bedlam. Lancing-Lancing, Steel and Catharine didn't hear any of this, being by then comatose in the cab.

They woke the next morning with splitting headaches.

'I must have Spanish blood in me,' Toots said, sipping a black coffee, having run four miles and back before the sun had risen over Canary Wharf Tower. 'I can never get going 'til after midnight'.

Dogs

Dear Admiral

Sorry I haven't been in touch for a while. I've been convalescing after the trip to Norfolk. With hindsight it was a mistake to encourage Toots to make his number with the Trafalgar Society. He said he had been nonplussed from the start when he walked in and found the attendees dressed up as sailors in Nelson's navy. That was a pretty broad hint that he'd dropped in on a nest of Nelson nutters.

I think they had laid a trap: invite Toots Molloy to give a talk in his capacity as an author, and then Kapow! make it clear that they were the world experts on Nelson and nobody else could possibly know anything about him, and certainly not a Yank from the Bronx, who wrote what they thought was a rubbish book.

We should have made a run for it before Toots began to expound on his not uncontroversial theory that as well as having an eye out for the ladies, so to speak, Nelson was also batting for the other side, that his second name was Cecil and that he (Toots) had dug up irrefutable proof of the great man's ambidextrous proclivities. It was those revelations which lit the touch paper. But we got out alive, and that's the main thing.

George

Nest

Dear George

I couldn't believe the damage. It looked as if a bomb had hit the village hall. The chap in the hooped jumper and the Nelson patch was seriously bananas. We should have known he was odd when he started wielding his cutlass. Things would have calmed down had he not flung the chair at Toots. I can't blame Toots for knocking him cold and, I must say, it was a very fine right-hook.

We weren't to know that members of the Pink Sailors Convention had infiltrated the room, disguised as Nelson lookalikes. I was once caught up in a brawl in Shanghai, but it had nothing on the way the Pink Mariners and the Nelson Trafalgar supporters set about each other.

As we were running for the Jag, I glanced round at the carnage. Windows smashed, broken bottles, Pinks and Trafalgar boys wrestling on the village green. As you say, we did well to get out unscathed.

Lancing-Lancing
-

Ye Olde Gambolling Pisky Tea Shoppe

Polperro

Dear Admiral

I want to apologise for what you Brits call a punch-up. I know you take Nelson seriously but that was something else.

When I was a kid in the Bronx, if you didn't fight the Jews you fought the Italians. If you didn't fight the Italians you fought the Blacks. If you weren't fighting the Blacks you fought the Greeks. And everybody fought the Irish. So I wasn't going to be phased by some pantomime sailor with a patch on his eye who's out to whack me with a chair.

On a happier note, I've written to George asking him and Catharine – with you and Sophie – to be guests when Posie and I get married. Would you to take us from the olde tea shoppe to the register office in the Jag? Posie would love that. Let's have a drink in the Lobster Pot. I won't inflict any Last Editions on you. After those you looked like you'd been hit by a Caribou in Alaska.

Toots

-

Toots and Posie were married and Lancing-Lancing took them to the register office in his Jaguar.

They live in a thatched cottage with roses round the door attached to the Ye Olde Gambolling Piskie Tea Shoppe, where Toots can sometimes be persuaded into giving readings from his works. He does it under pressure from Posie to boost takings out of season when business is slack.

His books, Nelson's Hookers, and the follow-up, Kiss me Sailor, have become best-sellers. His latest, a semi-factual memoir about a Brooklyn newspaperman running a Polperro tea shop, is being turned into a movie.

Picketing at the tea shop, and protests about his writing, led by the Nelson authority, Prof. Ralph Gwork, a regular letter-writer in The Times, fizzled out when Toots dug into Gwork's background and found that he had invented his curriculum vitae, and that he had been a scaffolder with a history of mental illness, rather than a professor of Georgian naval history at the Florida Swamps University of Maritime Affairs, which doesn't exist.

**

One of Lancing-Lancing's oldest friends is Commander Wentworth Craske, once a navy frogman, known as Crabs, not entirely for his underwater exploits. Bright, some say mad, he is exceedingly well-read and possessed of an extraordinary drive and manic energy. After leaving the navy he became a prolific inventor, a passion he shared with Lancing.-Lancing. He sometimes sent his prototypes to Lancing-Lancing to test.

The Whale House

Pickledidoo, Cumbria

How's the electric pram, Admiral?

Crabs

-

Nest

Dear Crabs

It unexpectedly took off at breakneck speed the other day with my baby son aboard and my wife clinging on for grim death. We live close to a cliff edge, so perhaps further development work is needed.

Lancing-Lancing

-

The Whale House

Dear Admiral

It must be to do with the accelerator and the twist grip on the handle.

The technology is simple enough if you think about electric bikes and electrically-assisted golf carts. But it's been a struggle. The batteries were so heavy that Norland nannies would have gone on strike. There was an obese woman in Salford who sued me because of her bad back, even though the judge ruled that her baby weighed a ton having been fed mainly on chips and tortilla crisps.

During the extensive testing programme, the pram coped manfully with the hills of Cumbria, close to my home, especially the double-version, twins being popular in my neck of the woods. Why twins are prevalent here I don't know. A doctor pal said there was nothing else to do in remote hamlets, so couples went at it hammer and tong for twice the normal length. I had no idea that going at it for double the customary time could result in twins, and it must be a crackpot theory because people with triplets would have died of exhaustion.

As a matter of fact, the doctor was struck off, not because of his twin-theories, but due to his goings-on with the vicar's wife behind the altar (Graham Greene also had a thing about that). Anyway, sorry, another literary diversion; my head is sometimes giddy with them.

The point that I was making is that the pram was beginning to prove itself a boon to Mums who would otherwise struggle while trying to get up hills.

However, I wanted really steep hills for some heavy-duty testing – extreme stuff – so I carted it off to Scotland to try it out among the heather and the mountains. I took the double-pram and loaded it with groceries, and a couple of dolls pumped full of plasticine to give them the equivalent weight of babies.

My assistant, Miss Dorothy Partridge, who has been with me a long time, switched to electric-drive and began pushing the pram up a rutted mountain track near Plockton, as if in imitation of a harassed crofter's wife walking back from the nearest Lidl, some twenty miles distant, to a simmering peat fire at her bothy, weighed down with twin bairns and an excessive amount of haggis.

I had dressed Miss Partridge in a kilt and tam o'shanter to give the experiment extra realism.

Suddenly, from out of the heavens, came an ear-piercing whistle and the pram, dolls and haggis were subject to the most terrible explosion, blasted to pieces by an enormous shell. Fortunately, Miss Partridge, though blackened and shocked, her tam o'shanter and kilt reduced to tatters, escaped relatively unharmed, having lived up to her name in a most surprising way, even though it wasn't the Glorious Twelth.

Moments later, a lunatic soldier by the name of General Axeblood, popped up out of the bracken, with a platoon of squaddies, each in camouflage with heather and gorse sticking out of their helmets, to inform me that we'd strayed on to Ministry of Defence land and that he had an unbreakable rule of shelling anything that moved.

There have been other incidents in trying to progress the perfect pram.

I experimented with a different type of propulsion using a dolly in a petrol-driven pram. But the doll turned black and oily and would have needed a gas mask, as would its mother. Now we seem to have a problem with the accelerator.

Yours is not the first complaint. Last week a woman and a baby were dragged through a shop window in Singapore. The accelerator had jammed, which sounds like your problem. There's an automatic cut-out but it's always been a bit dicky. These things happen and I'm confident I'll get there in the end, but I don't want any more casualties.

Is there any news on your very interesting creation, the remarkable Zip-Ahoy?

Keep your pecker up

Crabs

-

Nest

Dear Crabs

No, I have rather given up on Zip Ahoy. Its progress has not been helped by the cutback in smoking.

It's an astonishing coincidence that you have come across General Axeblood. I have had dealings with him and he can be a tricky customer. He has a thing about the ladies. Miss Partridge was lucky to get away with a torn tam o'shanter. Plockton must think that Vlad the Impaler is camped on their doorstep.

I'm working on something now that I thought would never appeal to me, being a surface sailor. But I read an enthralling book, *Sea Devils*, a history of pioneer submariners, and I'm now trying to develop a mini-submersible. It's still in the shed, in its early stages, but given your background it might be something which appeals to you. It'll be petrol driven on the surface, and use a battery when dived.

With your knowledge of batteries, underwater hazards and so on, you could bring a lot to the party. I see it as a midget underwater fun-machine, for taking myself, Sophie and the baby round the bay, or under it, though Sophie still has reservations.

Lancing-Lancing

-

Whale House

Dear Admiral

The midget sub sounds an exciting concept, and slightly nutty too, just the sort of thing I find beguiling. I've decided to take a break from runaway prams and, as one does, I've decided that I'm going to swim the coast of Britain, underwater (that's the novel bit). I want to raise a few bob for the widows of dead divers.

I'll swim beneath the water from Cumbria to Cornwall (while *Rising up for Breath*, of course; an early Blythe, as I'm sure you know) with flippers, mask, oxygen, the lot. When I reach your place we can get together and take a gander at your little submersible.

Up Periscope

Crabs

-

Crabs finally reached Cornwall, via an unexpected spell in Cardiff General Hospital, after an underwater contratemps with an oil tanker off Anglesey. On arrival at The Nest, clutching a small library of books, he was heavily bandaged but still bursting with enthusiasm.

Sophie said she had never met anybody like him, as bandaged as a Mummy but still exuding energy and excitement from every pore, not that any pores could be seen. He spent a couple of nights at the cottage before finding more permanent lodgings in the box room of the Ye Olde Gambolling Piskie Tea Shoppe, becoming firm friends with Toots Molloy and his new bride, Posie. The three of them spent literary evenings, which frequently turned argumentative and raucous, in The Lobster Pot.

After several weeks, Lancing–Lancing had made great strides with his underwater fun-machine. With some last-minute refinements suggested by Crabs, and with more help from a local garage mechanic, who everybody swore by and who was known as Moo, his father having been a cow man, and who was more used to working on tractors and milking machines than submersibles, the midget submarine was launched in Polperro harbour.

Dogs

Dear Admiral

Your new mini-submarine sounds enormous fun. I was most surprised by this venture, given that you once told me that life under water held little appeal. From what I gather, you have only tried it in the confines of the harbour. I would very much like to know what happens when you take it out to sea. Catharine and I beg you, *please*, be very careful.

George
-

Nest

Dear George

You and Catharine are most welcome to come for the sea trials. You can stay at the cottage and I'll take you both out for an underwater spin. You are quite right about submarining. It never held much attraction, but I underwent a conversion when I read its history. For better or worse, I'm hooked. Plummeting to the depths of the harbour was the easy bit, and to everybody's astonishment we came up again. We wore diving gear, just in case, and there's a sort of escape hatch. So there's not much to worry about, though we did, sadly, spring a little water. The open sea, as you suggest, will be an entirely different kettle of fish.

We've been helped by a chap called Moo. He's a dab hand with engines. The submarine is still a touch under-powered, being

230

driven by a Qualcast lawnmower engine. But Moo knows the location of a breakers yard where we might be able to acquire a car engine. If we could get a Jag motor we'd really rip along. All we need now is a torpedo to get rid of second-homers in red trousers floating around in their unspeakable gin-palaces.

Lancing-Lancing
-

Dogs

Dear Admiral

Catharine has forbidden me from joining you on your first ocean plunge. She says that you could be deranged, or heading that way, and that she couldn't afford to pay the mortgage on her own.

Secondly, a writing commission has come up in Fort Lauderdale, and there is a chance of a voyage in Bertha the Beast's dung-driven submarine, about which we have already corresponded. It will give me a fresh insight into life underwater for when I can, eventually, join you.

Thirdly, in truth, I am an abject coward.

Catharine says I must remind you that you are now married with a child. I know none of this will deter you, so all I can offer are my deepest condolences.

George
-

Some days later, and a dozen nautical miles from shore, Crabs and Lancing-Lancing made their first sea dive. It went well, and after a few minutes at no more than 100 feet, they surfaced to recharge the batteries. On the second dive they went deeper, and it was then that they found themselves in some difficulty, becoming entangled in an underwater obstruction. After a few anxious minutes they managed to free their little submarine and, once again, rose safely to the surface, plotting the precise location of the unknown object, before heading back to the less perilous waters of Polperro harbour.

The Nest

Dear George

Looking forward to seeing you and Catharine down this way. Don't worry at all about missing out on the maiden sea dive, which I have now undertaken with Crabs. He's a very good chap but he has this rather disconcerting habit of coming out with inappropriate literary quotes at crucial moments, and is also found of shouting out such things as 'Down we go!' and 'Hope you've made a will!' It's the sort of stuff which can affect one's concentration at the very moment that you most need it.

We got in a bit of a tangle with something underwater, but apart from that everything was hunky-dory. Crabs went back in his full diving paraphernalia to take a close look at the spot where we got caught up in something. He discovered that we had snagged the submarine on the hulk of an unplotted Spanish galleon. Most wrecks have been charted, or so it's thought, though how anybody can predict that with any real certainty is beyond me.

As you can imagine, it was rather exciting to make a new find. It'll be given official protection to dissuade leisure divers from going down and pilfering souvenirs. Any treasure subsequently brought to the surface by the proper authorities will go to tender – unless it's impossibly rare – and we've asked that the monies should used to help Britain's beleaguered fishing industry, what's left of it.

So, it seems that our first submarine foray has paid off surprisingly well, and we've lived to tell the tale. We'll take her for another run when you come and stay.

Lancing-Lancing

-

Subsequently, George and Catharine arrived at the Nest, and that evening spent a convivial hour or two in the Lobster Pot, renewing their friendship with Toots Molloy – who assured them that he wouldn't go down in a submarine for a million bucks, which he upped to two million when he learned that its chief engineer was called Moo.

The next morning George and the Admiral squeezed into the midget submarine and set off from Polperro harbour. After the discovery of the Spanish wreck, the submarine had been dry-docked and Moo, helped by Crabs, had installed a new and more powerful engine, salvaged from a scrap yard in Truro. It was not that of a Jaguar, to Lancing-Lancing's disappointment, but from a 1950s Leyland double-decker bus.

At sea, Lancing-Lancing closed the hatch in the top of the stubby conning tower, and prepared to give George his first dive in a submarine. Travelling just beneath the surface he raised the periscope, to show how the commander of a submariner can see the world above, without having to surface his craft.

As he pressed his eye to the steel tube he gave a sudden shout: " I can't believe this. It's that bugger Bogus Unearthed. He's going to try and cut us up again." As George hastily took his place at the tube, Lancing-Lancing made a crash dive, but not before a terrible grinding noise as the keel of a powerful speedboat scraped across the top of the conning tower. "He's barking," Lancing said, swiftly taking the submarine down another fifty feet. "I thought he was still in the nick."

After a few minutes, which seemed an eternity, he gingerly brought the submarine back to periscope depth, scanning the horizon to see if Bogus Unearthed was waiting to pounce.

But the periscope, which Lancing-Lancing had made by modifying an antique medical instrument given to him by a surgeon acquaintance, who collected such things (it had been used to check on problems affecting the small bowel) had become fogged with condensation. "We'll have to take a risk on and hope he's buggered off," Lancing-:Lancing said. "I can't see a damn thing through this. We've got to surface anyway .. the batteries are getting low."

To their relief, Bogus Unearthed had disappeared. "It was definitely him," Lancing-Lancing said. "He was grinning like a good 'un and waving his arms about like a windmill. He'd have done for us if we'd been a foot or two higher." Alarmed by the incident, they called it a day and headed with some speed back to the harbour.

It transpired that Bogus Unearthed had been sectioned, but let *out early after the eminent psychiatrist, Dr. Heinz Wolfendorff, of the respected Krakow Memorial Institute, had conducted intensive tests on gerbils, before concluding that Bogus-Unearthed no longer represented a threat to society and, further, that he had become a bed-blocker at the secure facility on Bodmin Moor, where he had been confined. Just in case, however, on his release he had been tagged, and Chief Inspector Magnus O'Shea, who had kept his usual beady eye on things, had little trouble in tracking him down to an abandoned tin-mine where he had set up camp.*

A raiding party on the abandoned mine, led by PC Butter, soon over-powered Bogus Unearthed. In his weeks on the run he had been reduced to little more than a crazy-eyed skeleton in rags, his hair matted and down to his waist. He had been living on nuts and bananas stolen from a distant Asda. PC Butter, at heart a gentle giant, took pity on him, and before taking him away to be incarcerated, fed him one of his special hot broths concocted to a highly secret menu. In no time at all Bogus Unearthed was a new man, becoming quite frenzied and leaping around like Ben Gunn.

Dogs

Dear Admiral

Well, that was scary. Of all the things that could go wrong, the one I never imagined was an attack by an inmate on the run from an asylum. I think your decision to stay with your sail boat, and to put submersibles behind you, is eminently sensible. It was caring of you to speak up, for a second time, on behalf of Bogus Unearthed, who clearly needs help. One can only pray that Herr Barkingdorff doesn't intervene. Donating the sub to Crabs and Moo was another sagacious move. Their underwater tours might prove a success, especially for those tourists of a more adventurous turn.

Is there any more antique medical paraphernalia which could be utilised in the manner of your bowel-scope? 'Bottoms up' might seem more appropriate than 'Up Periscope.' The needy NHS could sell off obsolete stuff, and the Paraguay Liberation Navy might be interested if you could develop a tube which doesn't fog up at crucial moments.

All in all, a most memorable sojourn. Incidentally, Catharine says she loves the little sub but is pleased she didn't hop aboard.

George

**

Lancing-Lancing was always unafraid of standing up for those who he felt had been wronged, and was especially quick to do so if such maltreatment involved members or former members of the navy.

Nest

To the Editor

The Western Daily Press

Dear Sir

The organisation 'Class Divide', which attacked the Tuddle Garden Centre, in Truro, on the dubious grounds that it sold plants to 'nobs in big houses,' according to Gary Sprigg, its leader, clearly had no idea that it was founded and run by Martin Tuddle, VC.

Martin was a boy sailor, awarded Britain's highest decoration, after he leaped in to a blazing sea to rescue shipmates, when his vessel was attacked in the closing stages of World War 11. Now elderly and infirm, he still suffers from the extensive burns he endured as a result of his bravery, and has spent the last twenty years confined to a wheelchair. His father was a shipyard worker in Birkenhead, who early in his life had been maimed in a dreadful welding accident. His mother was one of those forgotten souls who laboured day and night in a laundry to try and keep the family together.

The family lived in a back street hovel in which Martin, and his sister, had no idea where the next ha'penny would come from.

When Martin was invalided out of the navy he had saved a little money, and with a miserly amount of compensation, and a modest disability allowance, he was able to open the garden centre.

For many years he has only employed handicapped people and each year he donates half the profits of the business – which are miniscule – to The Wounded Sailors Fund. Nobody has had a harder background than Martin, nor contributed more to the wider society. Gary Sprigg and his cohorts need to apologise.

Lancing-Lancing.

-

Class Divide HQ

Hackney

To the editor of The Western Daily Press

Dear Sir,

'Class Divide' does not usually engage with newspapers, knowing they are the mouthpieces of global capitalism. However, in reply to the old war-horse who wrote to you, and who no doubt lives in a mansion, I would point out that Tuddle's Garden Centre was targeted because a) it makes its money out of a privileged coterie who live in posh houses with huge gardens, tennis-courts, swimming pools, Aga's, horses and Corgis and b) it's run by an ex-serviceman, who no doubt believes in flag, Queen, country, oil, nuclear, America, families, power-stations, cars, diesel, roads, fox-hunting, cheap socks from Bangladesh, carpets from India where child weavers go blind, bankers, hedge-fund managers, lawyers, reality TV, leather, meat, fish, trans-fats, whale-slaughter, badger-culls, putting cows on the roundabout and switching on the chickens, the *Telegraph*, *Times*, *The Daily Mail* and all the rest of the profit-driven Imperialist twaddle.

One grieves that Tuddle was injured, but it happens in war. The time has passed when the likes of Lancing-Lancing can order people around. What's he going to do? Challenge me to a duel?

Pistols at dawn on the poop deck?

Gary Sprigg.

-

Nest

To the editor of The Western Daily Press

Dear Sir

Mr. Sprigg's letter was stony-hearted and offensive. Had it not been for the likes of Martin Tuddle VC., Britain would have been under the heel of its enemies and Sprigg (had he been permitted to live, which would seem unlikely)) would not have been allowed to indulge in such remarks. A duel is not a bad idea. Pistols would be silly, but I'd be prepared to square up to him. What say you Sprigg?

Lancing-Lancing

-

Sprigg, 38, was a mature student at Sutton Coldfield University of Creative Light, reading post–Munchen-expressionism and the effects of polynurolene in carpets on badgers. Egged on by his army of Class Dividers, he accepted the challenge. Lancing-Lancing, for his part, went into training, jogging two miles a day along Dead Mans cliff, Albion panting and slobbering at his heels, trying to keep up.

George, Catharine, Sophie, and Toots Molloy, told him that he was being rash, and at his age, and with a prosthetic leg, implored him to call the whole thing off. But he remained implacable in his determination to show Sprigg and the Dividers what he was made of.

It was agreed that the two combatants would have a boxing match, to be conducted, not under Queensberry Rules, but historic Pisky Rules, which meant anything short of murder was allowed.

A boxing ring was erected on the edge of the harbour in Padstow, and a leading restauranteur said he would award the victor and four friends a free fish supper, an offer immediately rejected by Sprigg, on the grounds that he didn't eat fish as world stocks were being depleted, and that fishing as a hobby was cruel. It led to a further heated exchange of letters in the *Western Daily Press*, with Sprigg asking readers how they would like to suffer being yanked out of their natural environment by a hook in their throat.

Wally 'Barb Boy' Webb, one of Cornwall's most famous fishermen, whose fame had spread when he strangled with his bare hands a giant pike, which had pulled him off his fishing stool into the pike pond at Babbacombe Monastery, wrote that Sprigg was being silly, though in language so trenchant that the newspaper was obliged to deploy several lines of asterisks. After its publication, Sprigg said he now understood what the term 'coarse fisherman' really meant.

Some hours after the fight, Lancing-Lancing wrote to his wife.

Truro General Hospital

My dearest Sophie

I'm sorry I was a bit woozy when you popped in. I'm now out of the coma, obviously, and have been moved into The Queen of the Wad convalescence ward, so I'm making good progress and on the mend.

It's not easy to write with the strapping, and my good leg hoist up into the air. Apart from the break, the medics think it's nothing more than bruising.

I'm an old fool and, of course, you were right to warn me that I shouldn't engage in such antics. On the other hand, I have to say, managing to unfasten my gammy leg and being able to use it to knock him senseless, after he'd given me a bit of a pummelling and had me on the canvas, went down a treat with the crowd.

Spriggs fought like a mad thing, so well indeed that Toots was convinced he was on something. Spriggs is still in the Helford Passage Ward, not far away, and I thought I might send him a card and a box of smoked salmon as a get-well gift. It should raise his spirits, or do you think that would that be inappropriate?

This morning I had a visit from Barb Boy and his rods. He's quite a character. While showing a nurse how to cast and flick, he managed to hook the bandage off another patient's head, much to the patient's surprise. It led to a bit of kerfuffle, as you can imagine.

Hugely looking forward to our fish dinner in the Padstow restaurant, though we'd better keep it under our hats or it'll be picketed by the Dividers.

Ted

-

The Whale House

Pickledidoo

Cumbria

Dear Lancing-Lancing

Re: Your recent fracas.

I've been working (for years) on protective body armour designed to stun an assailant. It could be just the job if you find yourself in any further sticky situations. I've made great strides, though rather at the expense of the people testing it. They weren't too badly burned, but it's always a worry.

Anyway, you will have heard by now that the last time I was down your way, Moo and I ran into a spot of bother with the submarine. We had a little trouble with the revolutionary sonar and radar I'd invented, which was not quite as reliable as I had first imagined. The tourist who we'd squeezed aboard started screaming in terror and shouting 'We're going to die! We're going to die!'

Because of the dodgy radar we surfaced in an unexpected place and became tangled in the large net of the fishing trawler *Happy Days*. The skipper was surprisingly nonchalant, especially so given that we had torn a gaping hole in his net allowing most of his catch to scarper.

However, when I mentioned that you were the inventor of the submarine, he suddenly went crackers and ran back into the wheel-house, to reappear moments later brandishing a harpoon-gun. He was waving it about and telling us not to try and board him, and that he had had previous with you, when you tried to destroy his boat with your balloon. He thinks you've got it in for him. Anyway, after a few rather embarrassing minutes, we finally managed to free ourselves, got underway again, and that was that.

We feel, though, that we must offer some sort of modest fee by way of compensation, and wondered if you would care to join in? Apparently, he sustained heavy damage when the balloon swept across his vessel and that incident, together with our destruction of his net, has convinced him that he's the victim of some sort of terrible conspiracy.

His insurance company is playing silly B's, calling your sudden descent in the balloon, and the near-demolition of his wheel-house, an act of God, and is reluctant to cough up. He says the insurers will be incredulous when he tells them about a midget submarine costing him a thousand pounds worth of lost cod.

Your old pal Crabs.

PS. I'm developing a new high-powered pram with a ride-on seat. But we've had a slight set-back using a doll with a real mother at the controls. The pram took off at quite a lick and the test-Mum was thrown off as it careered round a bend. She's OK, a bit shaken up, but the doll took off like a projectile and the pram was a write-off. When I've made the necessary refinements, I'll send one to Sophie to test.

-

Nest

Dear Crabs

I will gladly contribute to the *Happy Days* fighting fund and enclose a cheque. However, with regard to your other suggestion, while not wishing to be in any way discouraging, Sophie says that she really enjoys the exercise that *pushing* the pram gives her, but thanks you very much for thinking of her.

Lancing-Lancing

**

**

The media interest in Lancing-Lancing's career continued to grow. He was bombarded with offers to write newspaper columns, present TV shows and conduct radio phone-ins.

TV Wad

Folkestone

Dear Admiral Lancing-Lancing

I present an animal programme on TV Wad and I was wondering if you would like to appear with Albion, your famous dog? After your many adventures together it would make an interesting item. TV Wad is transmitted in Hellesborne, a suburb of Bude, on a satellite channel, at 3pm on a Thursday afternoon, with repeats at 4am every Sunday morning.

We do not pay fees, but offer a £7.50 donation to the Over 70s Hellesborne Lindy Hop Club, members of which comprise a sizeable section of our growing audience. I look forward to meeting you.

Yours faithfully

Herbert Move, Executive Presenter, Giddy-Up!
-

TV Wad

Dear Admiral Lancing-Lancing

I understand that you and Albion had agreed to take part in Giddy-Up! if we were able to increase our donation to the old peoples' Lindy Hop Club. I am sorry to have to inform you, however, that Mr. Move has been arrested on charges of a delicate nature, which allegedly occurred when he was a young disc jockey, aka Baron Big, on a radio station, hosting the *Baron Herbie Makes It Big* show.

Pending inquiries, Mr. Move has been suspended from TV Wad and *Giddy Up!* has been taken off air.

It was very unfortunate that the police felt it necessary to arrest Mr. Move while he was on air presenting an edition of *Giddy Up!* a strategy which alarmed its audience, most of whom are elderly, and one of which, a lady with several cats and a large bowl of goldfish, went into a catatonic state before her relatives were able to reach her.

On a different, and rather happier matter, we are developing a new military history strand in which we will explore, among other subjects, the idea that cannibalism was once widespread among Cornish seaman. Or was this, perhaps, a slander invented by Spanish and French nincompoops who couldn't tell a pontoon from a pasty? If the show becomes a reality, I would like you to be its presenter. I do hope this idea appeals.

Yours faithfully

Earl Blazer, Executive Programme Controller, TV Wad.

-

TV Wad

Dear Admiral Lancing-Lancing

I am pleased to say that having spent several months investigating Mr. Move, the police have now dropped all charges and apologised for wrecking his life.

TV Wad, however, has decided to jettison *Giddy Up!* as the large contingent of pensioners who comprised its audience remain convinced that Mr. Move is a pervert, his alleged activities not only involving fans, but also Furry Boy, the show's much-loved Shetland pony.

Furry Boy was adopted as the programme pet after being found in a distressed state working as a pit pony in a tin mine, being operated illegally by a band of Albanians who, it is claimed, also ran a car-wash racket and chain-smoked Grade A budgie seed, better known as Trilski, in downtown Mousehole. Gang members had grown feathers and communicated in whistle-speak.

I will write again shortly about the military history strand, and I wish to reiterate my offer of making you the host of the series. You would bring a heady mix of brio and charm, and your knowledge of the sea and maritime affairs is, of course, a given.

Yours faithfully

Earl Blazer,

Exec. Programme Controller

-

Nest

Dear Mr. Blazer,

While complimented, I am afraid I have little expertise in television presenting or interviewing, having on occasion been an interviewee rather than the other way round.

For odd reasons, rather too complicated to go into, I do happen to be familiar with Grade A Trilski. Fortunately, I never indulged, so haven't sprung any feathers, suffered moult or taken up whistle-speak. Nor do I wear a bell or mirror through my nose.

As for your TV idea, which sounds first-class, are you really *quite* sure that you are thinking of the right person?

There are other naval (ish) types you might wish to consider, most of them moonlighting from full-time jobs in academe.

One such is Carlton Snaith, the Professor of Tides and Currents at the University of Uxbridge and Heathrow Terminal. Snaith sports a bow-tie, loud waistcoat, jungly mutton-chops and is never bereft of an umbrella. He boasts a string of rare qualifications and can be entertaining, being of a showbiz, rather than a factual bent.

There is also another chap: the hirsute Marxist professor Doug Soper (always wears black; he says it makes him look more piratical, and given the scale and density of his beard, he's not wrong). His specialist subjects are flogging and the slave trade.

As a 'celebrity' presenter he had his face 'blacked up', which caused widespread offence, before being thrown shackled and stripped into the hold of a collier (converted to look like a slave ship) while being beaten senseless and fed on bread fruit and contaminated water during a 'Hell Voyage,' as the programme billed it, from Brazil to Bristol.

The programme was over the top, with a surfeit of Soper in chains, but he certainly 'lived' the story, being subsequently hospitalised for emaciation, dehydration and salmonella.

Lancing-Lancing

-

TV Wad

Dear Admiral

I am afraid the names you mention, helpful and well intended as your suggestions are, do not quite fit the bill.

Carlton-Snaith is over-exposed. He currently presents a silly day-time strand about the dangers of polluted bath water; he did an impossibly garish makeover of a lighthouse, which led to litigation with Trinity House; and he fronted an arts programme in which he was roped to the mast of a yacht in a stormy sea while claiming this was how the painter William Mallord Turner went about his business (open to dispute). Carlton-Snaith also made, shall we say, a '*guest* appearance' in the Herbert Move scandal, which never was, but from which TV Wad is still trying to recover.

Doug Soper, the Marxist historian, was last heard of in Venezuela, helping to create a 'people's navy', in which officers were reduced to the lower ranks, and the lower ranks given officer status (you probably read about the Venezuelan warship which went into accidental reverse and destroyed several oil platforms, and the ship to air missile which took out the presidential palace).

Even if he was on the market, I don't think Soper would bring the necessary gravitas. You, on the other hand, have a superlative record and *real* maritime knowledge, while we at Wad have TV know-how.

I *know* we could make this new series an enormous (oceanic) success. I would like you to put your modesty aside, and join us in what will be a great and enjoyable adventure. I am going to 'phone you to see if I might call in at the cottage.

Earl Blazer

-

Nest

Dear Earl

After your visit to the Nest, and the impressively detailed presentation of your programme plans, I would be pleased to accept your invitation. I would like half my fee to be paid to the Fund for Distressed Sailors and Dependents. I will join you at the studios at the time and on the day you mentioned.

Lancing-Lancing

-

The Sea, a six-part series, was transmitted on TV Wad, and met with approval from its local audience. Earl Blazer showed the series to the network committee of ITV who said 'it had legs,' but needed 'tweaking.' Its members felt Albion was 'good value,' and that as a 'salty old sea-dog series,' it had possibilities, especially if Battersea Dogs Home, the Kennel Club and Winalot could be brought in as sponsors.

The network committee felt the series needed a new title, as The Sea sounded 'more label than title'. It was also of the opinion that the shows were 'too educational and perhaps needed a quiz-show element'. Keen for the programmes to have a canter on the national ITV network, Earl Blazer, well-versed in the byzantine politics of television scheduling, revamped the show, scrapping The Sea title and calling it The Admiral and his Dog.

He persuaded the committee that a quiz-show format would be inappropriate and that if the series could retain what he shrewdly called 'an accessible and personable authority' (a phrase the network committee found pleasing) it would be a useful strand to wheel out if

245

ever the government watchdog should feel that ITV was becoming too down market and money-driven.

The budget was stepped up, and filming took place around the world, so that ITV would be able to recoup its investment by selling the series to overseas broadcasters. The Admiral and his Dog became a successful and well thought of series, with Lancing-Lancing, and Albion slobbering and salivating at his heels, telling maritime stories across the globe.

After two series, however, Lancing-Lancing decided that he had had his fill of fame. He returned to his cottage determined to devote more time to Sophie, to his young son, George, to his books, his writing, his inventions and his beloved yacht, The Lily and George.

TV Wad, and Earl Blazer, were disappointed, but the Admiral told him that though he'd greatly enjoyed the experience, he'd had enough of beating around the world. During his years in the navy, globetrotting had been his life. He now wanted a more settled existence. The charity to which he devoted half his fees made him its honorary president. Of late, he and Sophie have spent hours in the summer house trying to catalogue a new batch of unpublished letters.

-

Nest

Dear George

I'm sitting in my study watching the snow falling on the sea. We're now in hibernation. With a pink gin, a generous chunk of Stilton and some warm company, life's not too bad in our little eyrie on the cliffs. Sometimes, with Sophie's encouragement, I even manage to get down to some serious tromboning.

If I close my eyes, I can remember those nights on the Bridge: a cold wind, duffel coat done up to the throat, steaming tea laced with a drop of Laphroaig, a steady swell, the chill on one's face, the throb of the engines, the tremble through the rail, that slight tang of oil and salt on the night air. They were good days, George, you must miss them too.

Comes a time when we're all in God's waiting room, about

to be summoned. Hey ho! Mustn't get too glum. We're greatly looking forward to seeing you and Catharine down here for Christmas. With the children and the grandchildren it'll be a full house. Toots is organizing a party, so bring the aspirins. We've still got a mountain of letters to sort through, and I'd appreciate your opinion. See you soon.

Yours aye

Lancing-Lancing

About the Author

John Swinfield has an MA in maritime history and is an ex-Fleet Street journalist, broadcaster and historian. A former Industrial Journalist of the Year, he was an on-screen reporter with Nationwide (BBC1) and The Money Programme (BBC2). For ITV/C4 he made the Enterprise series, an award-winning documentary strand where he travelled the globe, producing and directing myriad films about the rich and influential, such as David Rockefeller, Robert Maxwell, Richard Branson and Gloria Vanderbildt.

He has three Royal Television Society awards. He won the Sandford St. Martin Premier Award for his film Beggars in Paradise (ITV) shot in Peru, one of several documentaries he made about dispossessed peoples in the teeming slums of Latin America and south-east Asia. John Swinfield was also previously the executive producer of Arts & Features for Anglia Television and is a well-known public speaker.

His published works include two world histories *Airship: Design, Development & Disaster*; and the daring saga of early submariners, from Da Vinci's earliest imaginings to the underwater warriors of WW1, *Sea Devils: Pioneer Submariners*.